THE
Stratocaster
GUITAR
BOOK

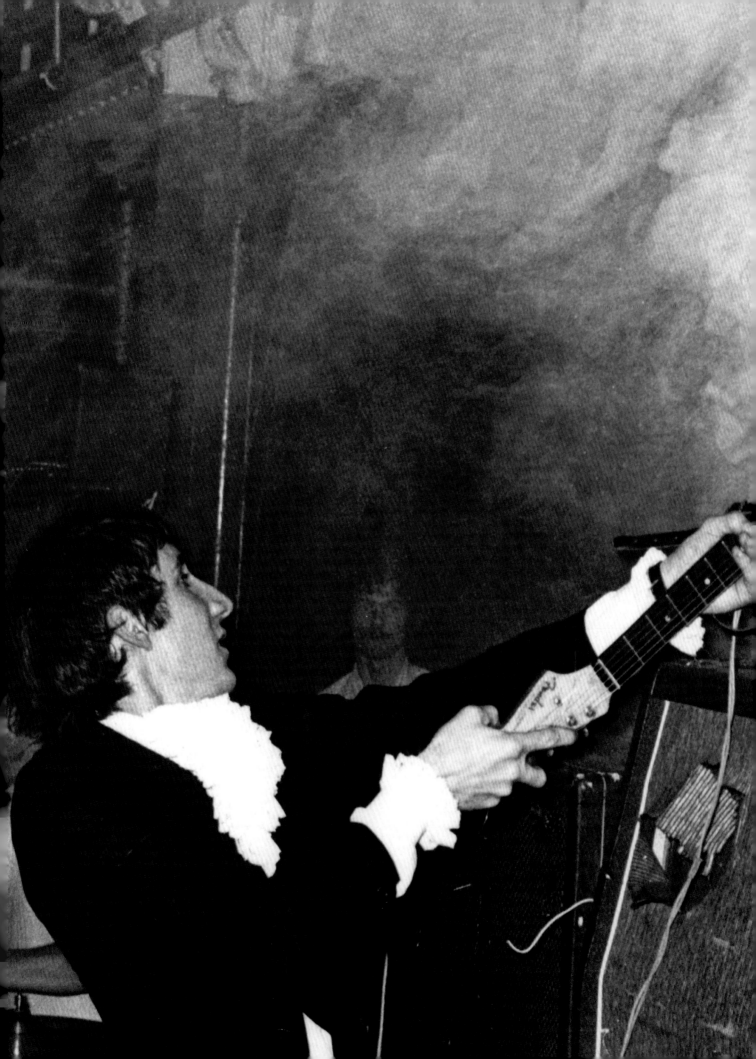

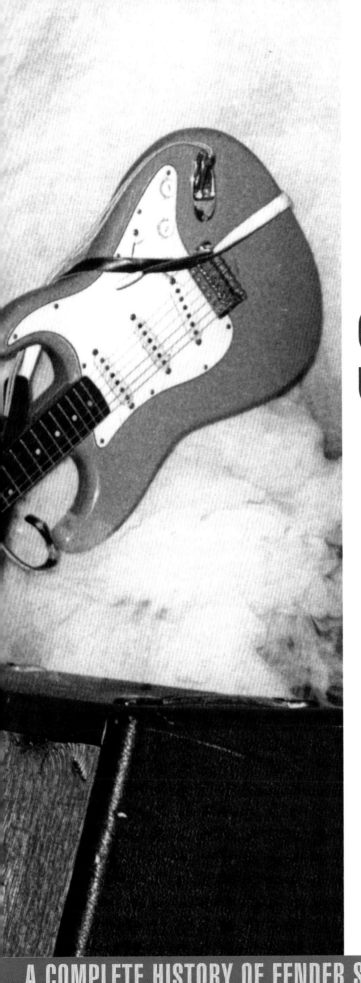

THE
Stratocaster
GUITAR
BOOK

A COMPLETE HISTORY OF FENDER STRATOCASTER GUITARS   TONY BACON

THE STRATOCASTER GUITAR BOOK
A Complete History Of Fender Stratocaster Guitars

by TONY BACON

A BACKBEAT BOOK
First edition 2010
Published by Backbeat Books
An Imprint of Hal Leonard Corporation
7777 West Bluemound Road,
Milwaukee, WI 53213
www.backbeatbooks.com

Devised and produced for Backbeat Books by
Outline Press Ltd
2A Union Court, 20-22 Union Road,
London SW4 6JP, England
www.jawbonepress.com

ISBN: 978-0-87930-996-1

DESIGN: Paul Cooper Design
EDITOR: Siobhan Pascoe

Origination and print by Regent Publishing Services Limited, China

10 11 12 13 14 5 4 3 2 1

CONTENTS

"The Esquire and Telecaster are pretty ugly guitars when it comes right down to it. We needed a fancier guitar. "

DON RANDALL
SALES BOSS, FENDER ELECTRIC INSTRUMENT CO

THE STRATOCASTER STORY

Sunday evening, and Jimi Hendrix waits backstage at the Monterey pop festival. He knows that Jimi the musician must step to one side tonight, that he has to upstage others on the bill by playing his role as the showman. He glances over at his two guitars. They symbolise the split. Both are Fender Stratocasters, but there the similarity ends. One is a black Strat he's been playing recently – a keeper. The other started life with a red body and is one of several Strats he's bought over the last few years. It's not a keeper. He's painted the body white and decorated it with vines and flowers and hearts, and tonight it will serve him a purpose beyond its function as a guitar.

Jimi goes on stage with his Experience and plays eight songs on the black Strat, then changes guitars. "I'm going to sacrifice something that I really love," he tells the audience before the last song of the set. "Today I think it's the right thing, all right, so I'm not losing my mind. This is this, for everybody here, man. This is the only way I can do it. So we're going to do the English and American combined anthem together, OK?"

He coaxes feedback from the painted Strat for a while, toying with the vibrato arm, then launches into 'Wild Thing'. He runs through his stage tricks – playing on his knees, behind his back, up against the speaker cabs – and finally lays the sacrificial Strat on the stage, squirts lighter fluid over it, kisses it goodbye, and strikes a match to set it on fire. Jimi watches the flames for a few seconds, then snatches up the guitar and smashes it against the stage. He throws the pieces to an adoring crowd. And then he walks off stage, knowing his black Strat is safe. The Stratocaster is dead. Long live the Stratocaster.

When Hendrix played that Monterey date in summer 1967, the Stratocaster was 13 years old. It was born in 1954, the product of a relatively new and certainly struggling California company that made guitars and amplifiers. The company's founder Leo Fender and his small team had already surprised the musical instrument world with the Telecaster, the first commercial solidbody electric guitar, and now they wanted something a little fancier to boost business. In the years and decades that followed, Fender's supreme Stratocaster model would turn into the most popular, the most copied, one of the most desired, and probably the most played electric guitar ever.

But the story starts with Leo. He was born Clarence Leonidas Fender, in 1909, in a barn near the borders of Anaheim and Fullerton in the Los Angeles area. The young Leo came to consider Fullerton as his home town. His parents, who built the barn first because they could not yet afford to build a house, had a modest farm growing vegetables and fruit, including the area's famous oranges. Leo's father had come to California from Illinois, and Leo's ancestors were American back to his great-great-great-great grandfather, who emigrated to the United States from Auerbach in Germany.

Leo's second wife spoke of a revealing episode from his early years. "When he was a little boy, his father told him that the only thing worthwhile in this whole world was what you accomplished at work, and that if you were not working you were lazy, which was a sin. So Leo judged himself and everyone else by that – and himself hardest of all."[1]

the stratocaster guitar book

Leo began work as an accountant, at first in the accounts section of the state highway department and then at a tyre distribution company, but his hobby was always electronics. In his twenties, he built amplifiers and PA systems for public events: sports gatherings, dances, and so on. He took a few piano lessons before trying the saxophone, but he was never serious, and he never learned to play the guitar.

When he lost his accounts job in the Depression, Leo took a bold step and opened his own radio and record store in Fullerton, around 1938. He called the new retail and repair shop Fender Radio Service, and it seemed a natural move for the ambitious and newly-married 30-year-old. He advertised his wares and services on his business card: "Electrical appliances, phonograph records, musical instruments & repairs, public address systems, sheet music."

His new store on South Spadra meant that Leo met many local musicians and characters in the music and electronics businesses. During the first few years he hooked up with several people who would prove important to his future success. First among these was a professional violinist and lap-steel guitarist, Clayton Orr Kauffman, known to all simply as Doc.

The story goes that some time around 1940, Doc brought an amplifier into Leo's shop for repair and the two got chatting. Doc had amplified his own guitars and made designs for an electric guitar and a vibrato system. By this time, Leo had started looking into the potential for electric guitars and was playing around with pickup designs. A crude solidbody guitar that Fender and Kauffman built in 1943 purely to test these early pickups – one design for which was patented in '44 – is today in the Roy Acuff Museum at Opryland, Nashville.

Doc went to work for an aircraft company during World War II, but the two incorrigible tinkerers still found time to get together and come up with a design for a record-changer good enough to net them $5,000. They used some of this money to bolster their shortlived company, K&F (for Kauffman & Fender), and began production of electric lap-steel guitars and small amplifiers in November 1945.

In the 20s, many people in America had taken up the little lap-steel guitar, often called the Hawaiian guitar, and the instrument was still tremendously popular. The steel had been the first type of guitar to go electric in the 30s. Several innovative companies, with Rickenbacker in the lead, experimented with electro-magnetic pickups, fixing them to guitars and feeding their signal out to small amplifiers. The attraction of the steel was that it was an easy-to-play instrument, and thus one suitable for beginners, but the electric version also proved appealing to professional musicians, especially in Hawaiian music and among country-and-western bands.

The musician would play the steel guitar on his lap or would step up to an instrument mounted on legs. The name came not from its construction – Fender's steels were all wooden – but from the metal bar that the player held in his left hand to stop the raised strings, which were generally tuned to an open chord. During the 30s and later the term

'Spanish' was used to identify the other (and then rather less popular) type of guitar, the one played upright against the body. Leo called this the standard guitar.

Doc Kauffman wrote later about the early days of K&F. "[Leo and I] would go down to the store, and at the rear was a metal building that housed the guitar department, and we would work till midnight." This description of a "guitar department" is certainly optimistic. Most people who saw the "metal building" have described it as a tin shack hastily and cheaply put up behind Leo's radio store. Doc said: "I used to assemble all our instruments and string them up and play a few steel licks, and Leo used to say he could tell how production was coming along by counting the tunes I was playing."[2]

Don Randall came next in Leo's line of important early partners. As we shall see, Randall would become a key contributor to the later success of the Fender company. For now, he was general manager of Radio & Television Equipment Co (known as Radio-Tel), based in Santa Ana, some 15 miles south of Fullerton. One of Randall's customers was the Fender Radio Service store.

Leo had not served in World War II because of a childhood illness that cost him his right eye. Randall, who spent three years in the army, recalled that Leo was able to expand his shop's trade in the war years. "During that period there weren't too many people about to do that kind of business," explained Randall. "When I got out of the service, I came back and started doing business with Leo again, selling parts and equipment."[3] Radio-Tel, owned by Francis Hall, became the exclusive distributor of K&F products early in 1946, with salesman Charlie Hayes heading the push to persuade dealers to stock these steels and amps.

It was around this time that Leo and Doc Kauffman decided to split. "It seems Doc was afraid to carry on with the business," Randall said. Leo was happy to work into the middle of the night at the tin shack making the K&F lap-steel guitars and amps, but Doc was not so keen to spend long hours locked away from the world. Leo said later: "It cost a lot of money to get into large-scale production, and the 30s depression was still fresh in Kauffman's mind, so he didn't want to get involved. He had a ranch or farm ... and he was afraid if we got over-extended on credit he might lose it. He thought he'd better pull out while he had a full skin, so in February of '46 he left it all with me."[4]

According to one colleague, Doc – who remained a lifelong friend to Leo – was asked later if he resented selling out, given the subsequent success of Fender. "And Doc said no, he was never sore – because Leo would have killed him before he got through with it anyway," referring to the long hours. "Doc liked to spend time with his family. He didn't like staying down the shack till 10 or 11 at night, seven days a week. Anyone that worked with Leo really had a hard time not over-working, because Leo expected you to be on call all hours."[5]

Leo and Doc parted. "His worry was right," Leo said later. "We had quite a few hard years ahead."[6] In 1946, Leo called his revised firm Fender Manufacturing, renaming it the Fender Electric Instrument Co in December 1947. He continued to make lap-steels and

the stratocaster guitar book

amps as he had with K&F, but gradually he developed new products. He expanded into larger premises on nearby Pomona Avenue in Fullerton, at the corner of Santa Fe Avenue, separate from the radio store. The new property was described by one observer as "two plain steel buildings, not very handsome". Another Fender associate remembered that the Pomona buildings did not have their own toilets. Consequently, Fender workers had to cross the nearby railroad tracks to use the rest-rooms in the Santa Fe station. Eventually one rather elderly employee couldn't make the treacherous trans-railroad journey, and the next day Leo had no choice but to hire a portable toilet.

Dale Hyatt was another important new member of the gradually growing Fender team. He joined the company in January 1946 and would later become a crucial member of the Fender sales force. One of his early tasks, in late 1947 or early 1948, was to take over the radio store business, because Leo was busy getting things started at Pomona Avenue. However, business was slow, and Fender had to rely on a loan from Radio-Tel's Francis Hall to keep going.

Leo was an introverted, hard-working man, enjoying long hours and selfless application to the task in hand. He was happiest when by himself, drawing up designs for new projects. He thought that if there was a product on the market already, he could make it better and cheaper – and make a profit in the process. Despite spectacular later successes, during these early years the new Fender company came perilously close to failing. It was Leo's sheer determination combined with his skill and luck in surrounding himself with clever, dedicated people that helped pull through these difficult times.

Now that the war was over, there was a general feeling that a fresh start was possible, and one of the processes that many American businessmen began to exploit was mass production. Leo's particular application of this technique to guitar manufacturing was to be his master-stroke, but at first he still needed outside expertise in the mass-production of parts. And so another piece of the jigsaw came into place.

Karl Olmsted and his partner Lymon Race left the services in 1947 and decided to start a much-needed tool-and-die company in Fullerton, making specialist tools and dies that their customers could use to stamp out metal parts on punch presses. "We were looking for work," Olmsted said, "and Leo had reached the point where he needed dies to be made for production work. They'd been making parts by hand, cutting out the metal any way they could. But he was getting to the point where they wanted to make several of each thing." Race & Olmsted continued to make Fender's tooling and most metal parts for the next 30 years and more. "As it progressed, so we progressed to more complicated, sophisticated, high-production tooling," said Olmsted.[7]

Next to join Fender's company was George Fullerton, who became what one colleague described as "Leo's faithful workhorse". The two had met at one of the outdoor events for which Leo supplied a PA system, and the young George – "I was going to school," said Fullerton, "playing music, repairing radios, and delivering furniture" – started to help Leo with the PA events. Gradually, George's radio repair turned to fixing amps and lap-steels, and he began working at Pomona Avenue in February 1948. "It was only a small place then," he remembered, "only two or three people, a couple of girls."[8]

The business was not only small but still precarious. Lack of cash-flow was a regular problem at Fender back then. One employee reported that there were times when it was hard to cash Fender cheques locally – especially if Leo's wife, Esther, was late in receiving her wages from the phone company. An early ad for the new Fender company's wares in 1947 featured just three lap-steel models and a couple of amplifiers. Fender stressed the plus-points of the guitars in the ad copy: "Exclusive new patented pickup unit [which provides] greater brilliance and presence. Equal volume output from all strings without compensating adjustments."

Leo and Don Randall were two highly motivated men with very different ways of working. "Leo sometimes was very resistant to change: you had to prove everything to him," said Dale Hyatt. "Nothing wrong with that; you just had to do it. Randall, of course, was much the same way: he was also rather stubborn in his realm of thinking. It's been said that they fought like cats and dogs, but I don't believe that's true at all. They couldn't fight – because they just didn't talk to each other, period. But I think one was as good as the other – and they were good for each other. I don't say that Leo Fender was the greatest thing that ever happened to Don Randall or vice versa. No, I think they were the greatest thing that happened to each other."[9]

Leo was certainly single-minded. He would have been happy if he could just continue to slave away in his workshop, sketching out pickup designs or fiddling with a new piece of machinery. As far as he was concerned, the fewer people who got in the way of all this, the better. And, generally speaking, Leo was – according to Leo – the only one able to get such things done.

One of his colleagues said: "Leo might come in one morning and, buddy, he had something in his mind that he wanted to try. The place is burning down? Let it burn down. He wanted to do what he was on. And he wasn't one to give any compliments. You could tell Leo something and you'd give him an idea. You could tell he was looking straight at you and thinking. Wouldn't say a thing; wouldn't agree that you'd even told him anything. Then later on your idea would show up on something."[10]

Randall wanted good products at a competitive price that would rock the market, and he often had to shake things up at the factory to get results. Leo, meanwhile, would be changing a particular wiring set-up for the umpteenth time. He was constantly trying to perfect this guitar or that amp. "Leo was a strange man in a way," Randall said. "He had a fetish for machinery. Nothing was done economically, necessarily. If you could do it on a big machine, well, let's buy the big machine and use it – when you might have been able to buy the part the machine made a lot cheaper from a supplier."[11]

Karl Olmsted agreed. "Leo would say that he'd like a certain part, and we'd take it back to our workshop," Olmsted recalled. "Then I'd say, Leo, we'd have to hand-make every one of these, there's no way you can mass-produce it, it's going to be slow and expensive.

the stratocaster guitar book

He'd say well, what can you come up with that's cheap and that'll make me happy? Almost every job was that way."[12]

Fender's electric lap-steels began to enjoy local and increasingly wider success, on the West Coast and in the Southwest, and further eastwards. The local Fullerton paper reported in November 1949 that the Fender firm was "well known throughout the country" and yet "almost anonymous" in its home town.[13] Then Leo began to think about producing an electric 'Spanish' guitar, in other words one of standard shape and playing-style rather than his existing lap models. He had converted a few regular acoustic guitars to electric for individual customers but wanted to go further.

Guitar-makers and musicians really didn't understand or appreciate the potential for electric guitars, which were still in their infancy. Since the 30s, Rickenbacker, National, Gibson, and Epiphone had made regular 'Spanish' archtop hollowbody acoustic guitars with f-holes and built-in electric pickups and associated controls. Aside from a handful of notable exceptions, however, guitarists had made little impact on the music with these new instruments.

Rickenbacker was located in Los Angeles, not far from Fender, and had been the first with an electro-magnetic pickup – the type used since on virtually every electric guitar. Gibson set the style for the best hollowbody electrics, launching, for example, the accomplished ES-175 in 1949. And while demand was rising from dance-band guitarists, who found themselves increasingly unable to compete with the volume of the rest of the band, these early electric-acoustic guitars were more or less experimental, only partially successful from a technical standpoint, and still to become a commercial sensation.

A number of guitar-makers, musicians, and amateur inventors in America wondered about the possibility of a solidbody instrument. Leo himself had already made one: the pickup testbed that he'd built with Doc Kauffman in the early 40s. The attraction of a solidbody guitar to players was that it would cut the annoying feedback that amplified hollowbody guitars often produced. At the same time, a solid instrument would reduce the body's interference with the guitar's tone and so more accurately reproduce and sustain the sound of the strings.

Rickenbacker had introduced a relatively solid Bakelite-body electric guitar in 1935 – the type that Doc Kauffman had played – but the guitar, offered in lap and Spanish forms, was small and awkward. Around 1940, in New York City, guitarist Les Paul built what he called his 'log', a testbed electric that he cobbled together from a number of instruments and centred on a solid through-neck block of pine. A little later, Les concocted a couple of similar instruments for regular playing, which he called his clunkers.

In Downey, California, about 15 miles to the west of Fender's operation in Fullerton, Paul Bigsby had a small workshop where he spent time fixing motorcycles and, later, making some fine pedal-steel guitars and vibrato units. He also ventured into making solidbody electric guitars and mandolins. He hand-built a small number of distinctive instruments, with fewer than 25 guitars known to have survived at the time of writing. He started in 1948 with the historic Merle Travis guitar, a solidbody that had through-neck construction (like the testbed guitars that Les Paul and Leo had made) and a headstock with the tuners all on one side, similar to the type seen on Martin and other German-influenced acoustic guitars of the early 19th century.

No one knows for sure who first thought of a Fender Spanish-style electric, although salesman Charlie Hayes may have suggested it to Leo. If he did, then it was easily the most important contribution he made to the company's prosperity, far beyond all the amps and instruments he sold and the dozens of dealers he enrolled and encouraged.

At first, in 1950, Fender called its new model the Esquire, then the Broadcaster, and finally, the following year, after a complaint from Gretsch about prior use of that name, the Telecaster. "Telecaster" was on the headstocks of the two-pickup model by April 1951, and Fender's new $189.50 solidbody electric had a permanent name. The single-pickup Esquire was available by then, too, priced at $40 less than the Tele. The new Fenders did not prove an instant success, and other guitar-makers could not at first see the point of a solidbody electric. "Our new guitar was called everything from a canoe paddle to the snow shovel," Randall said with a sigh. "There was a lot of derision."[14]

In California, Fender pressed ahead on its own course, oblivious to the sneers from the guitar establishment in the Midwest and the East. Some of the most important aspects of the design of the company's new solidbody were adapted from its existing lap-steel instruments. The wonderful bridge pickup – arguably the key component of the sound of the Telecaster and Esquire – was based on the unit already fitted to the Fender Champion steel, launched in 1949. The pickup was slanted to emphasise treble tones – just as Gibson had done with the pickup on its ES-300 model, introduced in 1940. The Fender bridge pickup would come to be recognised as one of the company's finest achievements, with a tone all its own that would attract generations of players to the Telecaster and the Esquire.

Leo based the solid construction of the new guitar on the way he made his solid-wood steels. He wanted to maintain the advantages of these relatively easy-to-make guitars. There was absolutely no point, as far as he was concerned, to even consider the relatively complex methods used by contemporary electric guitar makers like Gibson and Epiphone. Their workers had to deal with multiple parts and spend a great deal of time and skilled effort to construct the hollowbody instruments. It's often been said that Fender's workshop was more like a furniture factory than an instrument factory. Leo's head was ruled by simple expediency and straightforward practicality, and so, therefore, was the Fender shop.

We know that Doc Kauffman had a Rickenbacker semi-solidbody guitar. The inquisitive Leo must have studied the design of his friend's instrument in detail, and he couldn't have failed to notice that the Rick had a detachable neck. He realised this made sense for easy repair and service – returns of some early Fender products told him how important this was – and a detachable neck must have appealed to his love of simple, economic methods of working. National and Dobro, too, made their guitars with detachable necks, but along with Rickenbacker they were in the minority. Most mainstream makers employed the more time-consuming glued-on neck that, again, needed the attention of skilled workers.

Leo was well aware that he could manufacture a solidbody electric guitar practically and cheaply. He knew that such an instrument would make sense to musicians and offer them musical advantages. He explained later: "I guess you would say the objectives were durability, performance, and tone." He looked again at his existing steels when he considered the kind of tone that he had in mind for his new guitars. He said: "We wanted a standard guitar that had a little bit more of the sound of the steel guitar."[15] A Fender catalogue of the time highlighted the attractions of the new-fangled construction. "Because the body is solid, there is no acoustic cavity to resonate and cause feedback as in all other box type Spanish guitars. The guitar can be played at extreme volume without the danger of feedback."

Hollowbody electric guitars of the time generally delivered a warm, woody tone, reflecting the construction of the instrument and the position of the pickup near the neck. Jazz guitarists loved that sound. Leo had something quite different in mind. Not for Fender the fat Gibson and Epiphone jazz voice. His lap-steels had a cleaner, sustained tone, and that's what he wanted for his new solidbody guitars, something like a cross between a clear acoustic guitar and a cutting electric lap-steel. Leo explained later: "I wanted to get the sound you hear when you hold the head of an acoustic guitar against your ear and pluck a string."[16]

Business began to pick up as news of the Telecaster and Esquire spread and as Randall's five Radio-Tel salesmen – Charlie Hayes, Don Patton, Dave Driver, Mike Cole, and Art Bates – began to persuade store owners to stock the company's new solidbody instruments. Fender launched another important instrument in 1951, the Precision Bass – the first commercially successful solidbody electric bass guitar. (This was the exception to Randall naming the instruments; 'Precision' was Leo's idea.) The Precision Bass was typical of Fender's early products: it had an elegant simplicity and was designed for easy piece-together construction.

Leo always opted for function over looks. "I had so many years of experience with work on radios and electronic gear," he said, "and my main interest was in the utility aspects of an item – that was the main thing. Appearance came next. That gets turned around sometimes."[17] His second wife, Phyllis, who would live with him for the last 11 years of his life, said: "Leo would sit in his room for hours playing with his cameras, and then he'd go outside and take pictures of trash cans. I'd say honey, why are you taking pictures of these? 'Oh, I was just trying out these lenses and filters.' So why not take a picture of a tree? 'They were just something to photograph,' he'd tell me. 'They were near the back door and I didn't have to go far.' Convenient, you know?"[18]

Early in 1953, Fender's existing sales set-up with Radio-Tel was re-organised into a new Fender Sales distribution company, operational by June. Based like Radio-Tel in Santa Ana, Fender Sales had four business partners: Leo, Don Randall, Francis Hall, and Charlie Hayes (the latter three coming from Radio-Tel). This was in fact the start of a power shift away from Hall.

Hayes, who had been Radio-Tel's first salesman, was killed in a road accident in 1955. Dale Hyatt took over his sales patch – Fender's radio store had closed in 1951. Late in '53, Hall had effectively sealed his own fate by buying the Rickenbacker company and becoming a competitor. So in 1955, Fender Sales changed into a partnership between Leo and Randall, although it was Randall who actually ran this pivotal part of the Fender business. As Dale Hyatt said, "You can make the finest guitar in the world, but if you don't sell the first one you're not going to get the chance to make another."[19]

Despite Fender's exciting new developments with the solidbody guitar and bass, during the early 50s the company's main business remained in amplifiers and electric steel guitars. They were vitally important to the reorganised Fender operation, and the lines were rapidly expanded. The sales side of Fender was now under the control of Don Randall and his team, but another important addition came in 1953 when steel guitarist Freddie Tavares joined the California guitar maker, mainly to help Leo design new products. Tavares was best known for his swooping steel intro over the titles of the *Looney Tunes* cartoons, but he played on more than 500 recording sessions, with everyone from Doris Day to Elvis Presley.

Tavares was a native Hawaiian, and as a young musician he bought a Rickenbacker electric steel guitar to play for his gig with a local professional dance band, Harry Owens' Royal Hawaiians. He moved to California in 1942, soon becoming a busy session player for movies, records, radio, and TV and also playing in local country bands. He'd since moved to a Magnatone steel. It was Spade Cooley's steel player Noel Boggs who introduced Tavares to Leo Fender.

Freddie's son Terry recalled his father as a passionate perfectionist. Terry was just ten when Freddie went to work for Leo in 1953. "He was playing steel guitar at the time with Wade Ray & His Ozark Mountain Boys at a big club in south Los Angeles called Cowtown," said Terry. "One time, dad's friend Noel Boggs came in with Leo Fender, and after the show Noel introduced Leo to dad. Leo asked dad who made his steel guitar and amp. Dad said he did – and then proceeded to tell Leo what was wrong with his amps. Leo whipped out a screwdriver, opened dad's amp, and examined the circuits. Soon after that, he offered dad a job at his small factory shop next to the post office in Fullerton. Dad had an agreement with Leo that whenever he got a record session or movie-studio call he could leave his work at Fender and attend to it. He was very busy designing guitars and amps and with studio work."[20]

Freddie himself explained the working methods at the Fullerton workshop. "When it was just Leo and I, we did what we pleased," said Tavares. "In other words, Leo did what he pleased, and I was just his assistant."[21] A colleague described Tavares, who died in 1990, as "one of the best musicians I have ever known, and just as good at engineering. A very talented man".[22]

In June 1953, Fender acquired a three-and-a-half-acre plot at South Raymond Avenue and Valencia Drive in Fullerton and put up three new buildings. Fullerton's City Council was on a programme of rapid and significant industrial development. "Prior to 1950," reported the *Los Angeles Times*, "Fullerton was a citrus area with its industries primarily devoted to citrus products and food processing." The paper quoted a Fullerton official who talked of the changes being made in the new decade. "Everyone liked the peaceful area geared to country living," he said. "But some began to realise that industry was needed to balance the economy as more and more people came in. Now there's almost 100 percent support for it."[23]

The new Fender buildings in the heart of Fullerton's development area showed that the company was keen to expand its line of products. As well as the two electric guitars, the Telecaster and Esquire, Fender had a line of seven amplifiers (Bandmaster, Bassman, Champ, Deluxe, Princeton, Super, Twin Amp), five electric steel guitars (Custom, Deluxe, Dual, Stringmaster, Student), and the Precision Bass. But the firm wanted to produce more. *The Music Trades* magazine reported that with the new property Fender "hoped that production will be upped by almost 100 percent in the next few months".[24] First, however, the somewhat haphazard production methods had to be organised more efficiently.

This job fell into the very capable hands of another newcomer, Forrest White. He had worked as an industrial engineer at an aircraft firm in Akron, Ohio, but during a business trip to Los Angeles in 1944 he'd fallen in love with the area and resolved to move there. White had built several guitars in his spare time, including an early solidbody electric ("way before Leo did," he claimed later).

White's opportunity to move out west came in 1951 when he was hired by a Los Angeles company. He'd already met Leo a few times, and one day in spring 1954 they had lunch. Leo asked White if he'd be interested in helping him sort out some "management problems" at Fender. White remembered their conversation. "Freddie Tavares had told Leo that the company was ready to go down the drain. It was that bad. Leo had no credit whatsoever and had to pay cash buying any material and so on. Some of the employees' cheques were bouncing. Freddie had said that Leo didn't have anyone in the plant who could do what needed to be done. So it just so happened that my timing was right."[25]

Karl Olmsted of Race & Olmsted, Fender's tool-and-die maker, recalled how close Fender came to going broke at the time. "He tried to buy us with stock, to get out of paying our bills, and like idiots we didn't take the bait," said Olmsted later, in hindsight. "But, actually, I'm not sorry, because I'm not sure that I could have worked for Leo day in, day out. At least we had the advantage of occasionally being able to say, 'Leo, this is all we can take,' and stepping back. As good as the relationship was, once in a while you had to do that – and I couldn't if they'd taken us over. We just gave him credit and credit and credit, practically to the point where we couldn't make our payroll and bills and everything else. If this guitar craze hadn't taken off, he wouldn't have made it. So genius has to have some luck – and he had both."[26]

Meanwhile, Leo took an intrigued Forrest White to look at Fender's set-up at the new South Raymond buildings. "And it was a mess," White recalled. "There was no planning whatsoever, because Leo was not an engineer; he was an accountant. Things had just been set down any place. Man, everything was just so mixed up, you can't believe it. There was no planning whatsoever, because, in all fairness to him, he didn't have any experience in things like that."

White agreed to come in and work for Leo, beginning in May 1954. "But I said it depends on one thing. If I can have a free hand to do what I know has to be done, fine. Otherwise I'm not interested. He gave me that free hand. When I stepped in, from that point on I ran the company. He stayed in design, but I ran it."

White resolved a troubling production problem at the Fender factory by devising an incentive scheme that was tied to quality control. Assemblers on the production line were not allowed to accept a product from the previous stage unless they were happy that it was perfect – effectively making each assembler an inspector. "The reason for that," White explained, "was that if something had to be re-worked, it was on their own time. If someone loused up, then hey – once they accepted it, it's their problem. But as long as they turned out good production that passed, they made good money, darned good money."[27]

Now Leo had able men – Forrest White and Don Randall – poised at the head of the production and sales halves of the Fender company. He had a new factory and a small but growing reputation. And he had the start of a fresh generation of guitars – the solidbody Telecaster, Esquire, and Precision Bass – with Freddie Tavares on board and ready to help him design new ones.

Leo being Leo, he was not content to stay still. Soon, he and the team were working on a new guitar – the one that would be released during 1954 as the Stratocaster. George Fullerton remembered that planning for it had begun before the move to South Raymond in summer '53, and others recalled Leo and Freddie Tavares making early sketches of the instrument. Tavares said that when he joined Fender in early '53 he did odd jobs and then helped Leo "lay out the Stratocaster" on the drawing board.

"I remember that we had a piece of paper with lines drawn on it: six lines for the strings and two crosslines for the nut and the bridge," said Tavares. "Then we drew a body on it, erasing here and there until we got the shape we liked." With Leo in charge, said Tavares, there were advantages, not least Leo's insistence that they press ahead and get things sorted out. "Leo would say, 'That's the shape I like,' or, 'Let's put in three pickups – two is good, but three will kill 'em.' And it would get done."[28]

Leo seems to have viewed the Telecaster and the Stratocaster not as individual instruments but as a sort of single work in progress, a developmental whole. He actually thought that the new, improved model would necessarily replace the Telecaster. Don Randall was typically unsentimental in his recollection of the birth. "You know, the Esquire and Telecaster are pretty ugly guitars when it comes right down to it. In the days of Gibsons and others with bound necks and purfling, they were plain vanilla. But we thought they were beautiful because we were making money with them. The Stratocaster was brought about just as a necessary adjunct to the guitars we had, the Esquire and the Telecaster," said Randall. "We needed a fancier guitar, an upgrade guitar."[29]

This pressure from the sales arm of Fender makes sense now when you look back at what was going on at the time. We've already seen how at first other makers mocked Fender's unique solidbody guitars. But soon Gibson had joined in with its Les Paul, Gretsch with its Duo Jet, Kay with its K-125 model. Harmony had a cheap new electric solidbody model, too, and called it the Stratotone – a name that someone at Fender probably noticed. Competition was building.

Leo and Freddie, meanwhile, were listening hard to players' comments about the "plain vanilla" Tele and Esquire. This was a regular part of the working day at Fender, and a task that often went on into the night. Leo consulted many local musicians, trying out prototypes with them, putting testbed instruments in their hands, and constantly asking their opinions on this pickup arrangement or that control scheme. He remembered: "About 25 percent of every day was spent with visiting musicians, trying to figure out what would suit their needs best."[30] One guinea pig said that often he'd turn around on stage at a local gig to see Leo "oblivious of musicians, audience, club management, and disruption generally," busily changing amp controls or suggesting guitar settings – and usually in mid-song.[31]

Don Randall recalled the unglamorous process. "A guitar would start out, and we'd put it in the hands of a player. We'd tell him to play it and let us know what he liked and didn't like about it. So the guy would say this knob ought to be here, and this one there, this switch ought to be so-and-so, things of that nature. Finally, after three or four guinea pigs had looked at it, we'd come up with a composite of these various ideas, and it would pretty well satisfy most of the players. That's the way the guitars happened: they were an offshoot or an improvement or a change of the ones that had gone before, either a body change, or appearance, more pickups, a switching arrangement – just an outgrowth of whatever went before. So it wasn't a matter of inventing or anything like that; it was just development."[32]

The Stratocaster model that Fender began to produce in 1954 was a beautiful and impressive object. As with any solidbody electric guitar, it consisted of three principal systems that must co-exist to form, ideally, a successfully integrated whole. Those three systems are the woodwork, the electronics, and the hardware. The woodwork is the body and neck, and also includes the finish. The electronics is the pickups, wiring, and controls, and the hardware is all the other essential bits and pieces fitted to the instrument.

The original Stratocaster had an ash body, usually two, sometimes three pieces glued together, edge to edge, to make a solid whole. Its radically sleek look was based on the outline of the company's earlier Precision Bass. It had two cutaways at the neck and a sculpted shape. Some of Fender's guinea pigs complained that the hard edges on the

Telecaster's body were uncomfortable, prompting Leo and his team to think about a partly-shaped body with gentle contours. Among the dissenting voices was Rex Gallion. "He was a big man who complained that his guitar used to cut into his body a lot," said George Fullerton. "He worked the Las Vegas, Reno, and Lake Tahoe circuit, but occasionally he was in the Los Angeles area. He always tried to spend time at the factory, talking about new ideas and improving some things."[33]

Western swing guitarist Bill Carson moved to California in 1951 and soon sought out Leo Fender. He had tried a Broadcaster, loved its feel, and wanted one. Leo gave him a Telecaster and amp, but Carson didn't have enough to buy them outright, so he agreed to pay $18 a month and become a guinea pig. He gradually came to the conclusion that he wanted something more than his Telecaster. In later years, with the benefit of hindsight, he described his early-50s dream guitar as follows: "Six bridges that would adjust vertically and horizontally; four pickups; the guitar should fit like a good shirt, with body contours, and stay balanced at all times, have a Bigsby-style headstock, and a vibrato that would not only come back to exact string pitch after use but that would sharp or flat half a tone at least and hold the chord." Not far from what became the Stratocaster, in other words. "And according to Leo," said Carson, "that was tough to do."

Carson recalled seeing some trial Strat bodies at Fender in the early stages of the new model's development. "I went to the shop one morning, and Leo and George Fullerton had roughed up four bodies with different contours and body reliefs on each one. I picked out one that was closer to my idea, and then a few days later Leo had a very ugly but very playable guitar. But it came out to be a pretty usable instrument on the bandstand. It was still in a very raw form when I was using it in the clubs, and I would use sandpaper and sand down the contours sometimes during the job on the bandstand. One bandleader I worked for almost fired me one time for sanding that guitar on the job. It was ugly, sure, but it played in tune and performed like nothing else that was available. I didn't care one way or another, really, as I had what I wanted: I had a good playable guitar that was doing me well for session and club work."[34]

What Fender called the Strat's new Original Contour Body was subtly shaped for comfort, with rounded edges, a scoop on the rear to ease contact with the player's ribcage, and a gentle sloping-away on the front where the right arm falls. Beyond comfort was practicality, and the body had various cavities routed into it: on the front for the pickups, wiring, controls, bridge, and jack; on the back for some of the vibrato mechanism. The main front rout was covered by the pickguard, the rear rout with another plastic plate, fixed to the body with six screws. That rear plate had six holes through which the strings went, and on those earliest Strats it had a serial number stamped into the top.

The original Stratocaster's one-piece maple neck followed Fender's regular assembly method: it was fixed to the body with four screws through a metal plate on the rear. The 21 metal frets were laid directly into tight slots in the face of the maple neck. The fingerboard radius was about seven inches, which meant a relatively rounded feel. A strengthening metal truss-rod sat in a channel in the rear of the neck and was permanently covered with a walnut strip, later nicknamed a skunk stripe. The rod could be adjusted to correct neck relief using the screw located at the body end of the neck.

In the face of the fingerboard were small circular black plastic position markers, known as dot markers because of their shape, inlaid in front of the third, fifth, seventh, ninth, twelfth, fifteenth, seventeenth, nineteenth, and twenty-first frets, with the twelfth-fret octave position marked by a pair of dots. Corresponding to these positions, on the top side of the neck as viewed by the player, were nine more tinier position dots, again with a double-dot marking the twelfth-fret position. At the top of the fingerboard was the nut, made of white bone, which stopped and spaced the strings there. The scale length was twenty-five and a half inches, the same as for the Telecaster.

The headstock on the Strat was a new and striking design. Or was it new? Considering it alongside the through-neck electric guitar that Paul Bigsby had made for the famous picker Merle Travis in nearby Downey in 1948, it's hard to ignore the similarities and impossible to deny some influence from the earlier instrument. Perhaps Bigsby and Fender were equally influenced by the headstock shape of 19th-century acoustic guitars by Martin and others, which in turn derived from a German design? Leo himself said he saw a touring Croatian group with instruments (probably tamburitsas) with the same kind of head design, and he said he'd spotted an ancient African instrument in a New York museum with a similar head. It must have seemed safer to credit these distant people than a potentially litigious alive-and-well Orange County resident. Years later, Don Randall was clear about the lineage when he recalled how the Strat's headstock was changed from the Telecaster design. "It was a little more graceful," said Randall, "a little more lute-ish, a little more Paul Bigsby-ish."[35]

On the Strat's headstock were six in-line Kluson tuners, each with a closed metal back and an oval metal button on a thin metal shaft. There was a circular string retainer screwed to the headstock face, designed to keep the high E and B strings in place, and two decals fixed to the headstock face: one with a black-outline gold spaghetti-like "Fender" logo, a black "Stratocaster", and a black "With Synchronized Tremolo"; the other a smaller black one that read "Original Contour Body".

Fender gave the new Strat body a Sunburst finish. Gibson and other guitar-makers had regularly used sunbursts since at least the 20s, but this was the first time Fender had used such a finish on a production model. The existing Telecaster and Esquire models had a plain yellow-ish 'Blond' finish. A sunburst finish is supposed to conjure up the real thing, and workers at the Fender shop applied two coloured nitro-cellulose lacquers to the front and back of the ash body: a yellow lacquer for the bright centre and then a black lacquer to create the shaded tones for the gradually darkening edges.

Fender fitted various items to that Sunburst-finish ash body and the lacquered maple neck. There were two metal strap buttons, one screwed to the base of the body and the other to the top body horn. A single-layer pickguard of white plastic was fixed to the body

Leo Fender set up his small manufacturing operation in the late 40s in Fullerton, California. At first, his firm made only small amplifiers and lap-steel guitars, like the **1958 Champ** model (above). In 1950, Fender produced its ground-breaking solidbody electric guitar, at first called the Broadcaster, which paved the way for some remarkable achievements.

the stratocaster guitar book

■ Fender's amplifiers provided the backbone of the company's products and would prove as important to its success as the solidbody guitars and basses. The model shown is a **1953 Deluxe** (right), finished in Fender's distinctive tweed covering and with the 'wide panel' cabinet design that was introduced in the early 50s.

■ An important early addition to the Fender lines was the first commercial solidbody electric bass guitar. Pictured is a **1951 Precision Bass** (centre), from the first year of production. It followed the earlier Broadcaster six-string guitar and was further evidence that Fender intended to create a full line of modern solidbody guitars that would appeal to all kinds of musicians.

■ Fender's early Broadcaster was renamed the Telecaster in 1951, and it quickly established itself as a fine instrument. The **1953 Telecaster** pictured (left) is typical of the earliest style of the model. A **1952 ad** (above) shows how steels and amps continued to dominate the Fender catalogue, despite the intriguing newcomers.

with eight screws. The pickguard had almost all the electrical components and wiring fitted to it – another clever piece of manufacturing stealth. On the face of the guard were the tops of the three single-coil pickups, the three control knobs, and a three-way selector switch. Underneath, and thus hidden from view, was the circuitry: three potentiometers or pots (the two tone pots each with an added capacitor); the body of the selector-switch mechanism; and various soldered hook-up wires to connect everything. A thin metallic sheet was fitted under this circuitry, to the underside of the pickguard, with the intention of providing some shielding to reduce electrical hum.

The three identical pickups each had a white plastic cover, inside which was a bobbin wound with 42-gauge enamel wire, wax-dipped for solidity, around six cylindrical Alnico magnets or polepieces. Each cover had six holes to reveal the tops of the polepieces, which were staggered in height to compensate for string volume. The cover was fixed to the body with two sprung screws, and the bridge pickup was angled, like the one on the earlier Telecaster, providing extra top-end.

Each of the three white plastic control knobs was attached to the top of one of the shafts of the three pots. As the guitarist looked down to play his instrument, the knob nearest the bridge was for master volume, marked "Volume" on top, and below that were the two tone knobs, each marked "Tone" on top, the nearest one for neck-pickup tone and the bottom one for middle-pickup tone. All three knobs were marked with the numerals 1 to 10 around the flared skirt at the base.

The three-way selector switch had a metal lever with a white plastic tip and was held in place with two screws. The three positions provided each of the three pickups individually: nearest the player for the neck pickup; in the centre for the centre pickup; and in the lowest spot for the rear pickup. Soon, players discovered in-between positions for alternative tones. The one remaining part of the electronics, the output jack, was located separately, next to the pickguard, angled and recessed in a stylish metal plate fixed to the body with two screws.

Bill Carson remembered that it was George Fullerton who suggested this practical new idea. "George said, well, we've wrecked so many Telecaster jacks by guys stepping on the cord, why don't we put a front-mounted jack on it, so that if you step on the cord it won't wreck that jack? So the front-mounted jack was George's idea, and a good one."[36] Fender's tool-and-die maker, Karl Olmsted, had the job of turning the new jack design into reality. "It was quite a project, getting something to make Leo happy," said Olmsted. "Something that just used to stick in the side ... he didn't want that. He wanted something that would let the plug come out at the angle he wanted, and something that could practically be drawn without breaking."[37]

The Stratocaster featured a newly-designed built-in vibrato unit, which Fender called the Synchronized Tremolo. It provided the player with pitch-bending for single-line work and shimmering chordal effects. Randall said it was "Leo's pride and joy".[38] But it gave the Fender team plenty of headaches during its development. In fact, the first version was entirely scrapped. George Fullerton: "When the first one came off the line I grabbed it, but it was terrible – it sounded terrible, tinny, and wouldn't sustain sound. So I rushed down to the lab, where it was all set up for production, and I said, 'Leo, we've got to stop this.' Well, that whole thing was thrown out, all the parts, all the tooling, many, many thousands of dollars worth." Leo put the damage at $5,000. "It had to be redesigned," said Fullerton, "not only to sustain notes but to give a solid sound."[39]

The result of all this work produced a good second version, the world's first self-contained vibrato unit, and Leo eventually applied for a patent at the end of August 1954. It consisted of an adjustable bridge, a tailpiece, and a vibrato system – all in one. Not a simple mechanism for the time, but a reasonably effective one. It followed the Fender principle of taking an existing product (in this case the Bigsby vibrato) and improving it. Leo knew that the weakness of existing vibratos was the way they moved strings back and forth over a fixed bridge, which often put the guitar out of tune. His idea was to make the entire unit move together as one unified system.

The bridge's metal baseplate was fixed to the top of the body by six screws (in front of the saddles) on which it pivoted. The arm, with a white plastic tip, screwed into the baseplate. The bridge came with a metal cover, usually quickly discarded or used as an ashtray, which explains its nickname. Protruding downward from the baseplate and hidden from view was a long 'inertia block' or 'sustain block' that went through a hole in the body to the cavity at the rear. The strings travelled through the base of the bridge and into the block, and were anchored at its base, visible in that rear cavity. The tension of the strings was balanced by up to five springs fixed to the block in the cavity. Adjusting the number of springs and their fixing point allowed the player to fine-tune the feel and efficiency of the vibrato system. It was an ingenious device.

The new Strat vibrato's six bent-steel bridge-pieces, or saddles, were adjustable for height and length, which meant that the feel of the strings could be personalised and the guitar brought more closely in tune with itself. Bill Carson later claimed he was important in bringing the idea of separate saddles to Fender's attention, and at least one salesman had told Randall that the Tele's three saddles was a serious limitation. "I was having trouble with the Telecaster," said Carson, "because I was playing several hours each weekend on record sessions and in clubs, and the intonation for recording was a real problem. The Tele has three sets of two strings each going over a common bridge, so you just cannot intonate it. You couldn't then and you can't now.

"I sawed each of my Tele's three bridges in two and made me six bridges, and I pretty clumsily propped up each half section with a striker-strip section from a bookmatch packet – I had that little sandpaper grit on there and it helped to hold it in place. That way I could intonate the instrument and play in tune. A lot of the recordings in those days were with big-band arrangements where the guitar player would probably be playing a part with a reed or brass section, and if you couldn't play in tune, the producer wouldn't call you back for other record dates. So you'd lose money if you couldn't do that."[40]

■ After Fender's introduction of the Telecaster, other makers began to produce competing models in the new solidbody electric style, such as Gibson with its Les Paul (**1954 Goldtop**, above) and Gretsch with its Jet series (**1956 Duo Jet**, opposite).

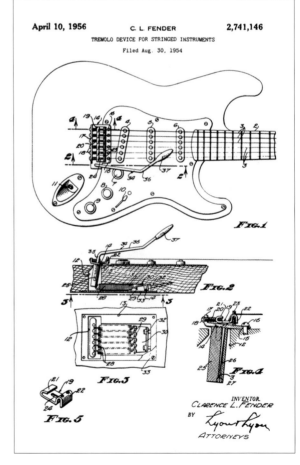

the stratocaster guitar book

■ During 1953, Fender began work on a new model designed to expand its lines and trounce the competition. An important part of the process was to find out what guitarists wanted. A **group of local musicians** (opposite) snapped by Leo Fender in late 1953 includes a 'guinea pig' guitarist (far right) with a prototype of the guitar that became the Stratocaster. Fender's Freddie Tavares is on-stage, too (far left). Musician **Rex Gallion** (below) tries another early Strat, this time at the Fender factory, in the early months of 1954. The vibrato system of the Stratocaster caused many developmental problems, with the **patent** (centre) finally filed in the summer of 1954.

Fender's Stratocaster wasn't the first to attempt a six-way bridge with string-length adjustment: Gretsch's Melita had appeared around 1952 and Gibson's Tune-o-Matic soon after that. But the Strat's bridge offered adjustment of the height as well as the length of each string. All in all, the new vibrato bridge was a master-stroke, a brilliant example of Leo's ability to think through an idea and, with the help of his team and guinea pigs, to make it work mechanically and musically.

The Fender Stratocaster was a stunner. It looked and played like no other guitar around – and in some ways seemed to owe more to contemporary automobile design than traditional guitar forms, especially in the flowing, sensual curves of that beautifully proportioned and timeless body. As an object, it was the embodiment of tailfin-flash 50s American design. Imagine the impact this gorgeous object had at the time! Even the shape of the pickguard complemented the body lines perfectly, and the overall impression was of a guitar where all the components suited one another with impeccable style and grace.

The Stratocaster was first and foremost a mass-produced guitar. Fender was not particularly interested in craft and workmanship, as were other older and more traditional American makers such as Gibson and Martin. The focus, as with the Telecaster before, was on a guitar that could be produced on an assembly line. Perhaps not a line with the level of sophistication seen at one of Henry Ford's factories, but one that at least aspired to the same general principles.

Mass production was a big part of American capitalism. A product is successful if it is made in large quantities: the manufacturer has to make more of something to ensure that it costs less to produce, meaning that he makes more profit. Probably no one at Fender in the early days thought too much about all this: it was simply what you did if you had a manufacturing business. Joe Perry of Aerosmith, when asked much later about his view of the importance of Fender, said: "The Stratocaster symbolises so much of what America is, because of its design and that it was able to be mass-produced."[41]

It's doubtful that anyone at Fender back in the 50s would have described themselves as a designer. Maybe Leo was the closest, but if anything he was more of an engineer. One measure of a good design is to look at the object and see if anything can be taken away. Looking at the Stratocaster, everything seems to be there for a purpose. It's a good design. "My feeling about a perfect design is that it has to be functional," said Eric Clapton, decades later, "and with the Strat, its functionality really steers it. That's what makes the design so beautiful. It's superbly thought out."[42]

Fender made proper samples of its new model early in 1954. Following the first ads and press for the guitar in April and May – introducing "one of the most revolutionary of the amplified string instruments" – some sporadic production began around May, June, and July. Randall said in a letter to dealers that he expected shipments to begin on May 15. Forrest White recalled later that the first proper production run came in October, for 100 Stratocasters, filling an order from Fender Sales dated October 13. Once again, Randall named the new model, and he said later that his inspiration had been the dawning space

the stratocaster guitar book

age and the lure of the stratosphere. As a keen pilot, he'd probably noticed that Boeing's jet bomber, the B-47, was called a Stratojet, and it was around this time that Pontiac launched its sleek Strato-Streak model automobile. And Randall, who regularly attended instrument trade shows, had almost certainly seen Harmony's new-for-1953 Stratotone electric guitar.

Randall set the list price of the new guitar at $249.50 (or $229.50 without vibrato) plus $39.50 for a case. The Stratocaster sat on Fender's 1954 pricelist above the $199.50 Precision Bass, the $189.50 Telecaster, and the $149.50 Esquire. Comparable competitors included Gibson's Les Paul Goldtop, listed that year at $225, while over at Gretsch the Duo Jet and Silver Jet each listed at $230. That $249.50 for a launch-year Strat had the same buying power then as about $2,000 of today's money.

A fold-out leaflet that Fender issued in 1954 described the company's aims for the new instrument. "This three-pickup Stratocaster represents an entirely new approach in basic guitar design. For tone, appearance, and versatility, the Stratocaster has been engineered to give the player every possible advantage. This is the guitar that brings the player live, true tremolo action at the flick of a wrist. The three pickups, a special tone control circuit, a new surface mounted plug receptacle all mean faster action, better, clearer music. The Stratocaster can be played 'straight' or while using the revolutionary Tremolo action lever. The Stratocaster also features advances in design never before available in the field. The instrument is actually 'comfort contoured' to fit the artist's body … designed to be part of the player! Available in either Tremolo or regular models."

It's no surprise the Strat is still thriving around 60 years since its birth at the Fender company's functional buildings in Fullerton, California. On its 40th anniversary in 1994, an official Fender estimate put Stratocaster sales so far at between a million and a million-and-a-half guitars. By now it must have climbed nearer to three million. But still we can only play one at a time.

In the beginning, however, during the mid 50s, the Stratocaster wasn't a world-beater. Only later in rock'n'roll would it find its true home. Fender historian Richard Smith discovered that during 1954 and '55 Fender sold 720 Strats, compared to 1,027 Teles and Esquires. Salesman Dale Hyatt: "Let me tell you, the dealers didn't just grab the Stratocaster, they didn't take 'em away from you. The vibrato system was something that was very difficult for most of them to get used to. They said, 'It'll never work. Who needs it? You can bend the neck to do this kind of thing.' But it caught on, nevertheless," laughed Hyatt. "It forced the musician to create a brand new wave of sound, a different style of playing."[43]

Forrest White explained later that the manufacturing process for electric guitars was simple and effective at Fender in the 50s. The workers received ash or alder for bodies in 18 or 20-feet lengths. They would cut and glue them together to make a block of wood the size of a guitar body. "Then we had what we called router plates made out of quarter-inch steel in the shape of the guitar body, usually two different plates," said White. "You'd

■ This **1954 Stratocaster** (main guitar) has a neck date of May, placing it in the earliest months of production. The new model was a remarkable addition to Fender's catalogue and a boon to the musicians who were drawn to the guitar in its early existence. One such was **Bill Carson** (right), another of the 'guinea pigs' who helped the Fender team develop the design of the new instrument, with its three pickups, pitch-bending vibrato system, comfort-contoured sunburst-finish body, sleek design, and cool playability. The attributes were summed up in Fender's **1954 leaflet** (below), alongside the existing Tele, Esquire, and P-Bass. The Stratocaster, said Fender's copy-writer, "represents an entirely new approach in basic guitar design".

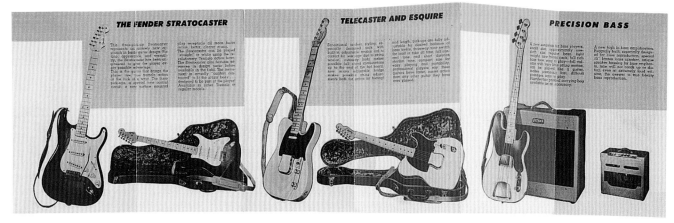

the spectacular PONTIAC STRATO STREAK

■ **Leo Fender** pictured (below) in 1954 standing proudly by a new punch-press for the factory. He loved machines and always wanted the latest gadget. That same year saw the launch of the Stratocaster, and elsewhere in the factory his slowly growing team of managers and workers would be pulling the first models from the line to ship to dealers and on to musicians. Automobiles had a marked influence on the production, marketing, and even naming of Fender instruments: this car ad (above right) shows a **1954 Pontiac Strato-Streak**.

■ The elegance of Fender's Strat was matched by the launch-year **catalogue cover** (above), a spot-lit angular amalgam featuring a stylised guitar and bold amplifier.

attach one to the bottom with a couple of screws, and you could drill on that side, where the neck plate and everything went. On the other side went the plate where the pickups and everything ran. So you always had a minimum of two plates, sometimes three, depending on how sophisticated the instrument was – some might have more cut-outs and so on. You'd screw those on, trace around them, band-saw the body roughly to shape, then take off the excess on the router, and on it would go for sanding."

For shaping the necks, which Fender called ovalling, White said the factory had a couple of sanders that would swing the neck back and forth. "And then there was a mandrel that had the holes cut out for the frets. Leo designed almost all of the tooling himself. It was very simple, but it was a case of having to walk before you ran. We didn't have any computerised routers and so on like they have now, where they can cut out half-a-dozen necks at a time. It was one at a time back then, and everything was simple. Crude, really, but it got the job done."[44]

There were more crude machines throughout Fender's factories. The workers used some to wind pickups – ramshackle affairs with wheels and pulleys – while another area housed a few ad hoc finish-spray booths alongside a wall of racks for drying the freshly sprayed bodies. There were punch presses for making metal parts and benches at which workers did final assembly. For Stratocasters, one worker would solder the electronics together, and another would screw the pickguard assembly and jack housing, then the bridge, to the body. Finally, new Strats would be strung up and tested through a handy amp lifted from the line.

Among collectors, some of the people who worked on Fender's shop floor in the 50s have become almost as well known as Leo, Forrest, Don, Freddie, George, and the rest. This renown has developed thanks to the approval system, where the worker would often sign parts of the guitar as it went through production. One well known signature is the pencilled TG or TAD that indicates Tadeo Gomez.

Gomez started at Fender in the late 40s and soon worked with guitar necks. Like many of the factory people that Fender employed, Gomez was born in Mexico. He moved to the USA when he was in his teens, finally settling in La Habra, a mile or two north of Fullerton. His son Ben Gomez said: "I remember my father taking me to work at Fender's. There used to be quite a few from La Habra that worked [there]. Women worked there doing soldering and the electrical wiring. Some other [men] made the body; dad would be outside sanding and shaping the necks. Sometimes he carved a little to get it just right. He had taught himself woodworking. Nothing was too hard for him to learn."[45] Gomez left Fender in the late 50s to work at Disneyland, but he returned in the mid 60s. He died in 1986.

For now, Fender continued to sell its established lines. Steel guitars were virtually unchanged, but Fender had fresh ideas for the ever-popular amplifiers. There was a new effect that Fender again chose to call tremolo, just as it had with the vibrato unit on the Stratocaster, but this time it meant a regular, rhythmic fluctuation in volume, an effect already heard on some home organs. The amp that introduced this to the Fender line was the Tremolux of 1955. A year later, the one-pickup Musicmaster and two-pickup Duo-Sonic appeared, a pair of cheaper new solidbody guitars alongside the Strat, Tele, and Esquire. The two new models were described as "three-quarter size" and thus "ideal for students and adults with small hands".

One apparently attractive feature of the new Duo-Sonic and Musicmaster – and a few early Stratocasters – was what Fender called gold-finished pickguards. They were made from a gold-coloured anodised aluminium. The metal provided excellent electrical shielding, meaning less extraneous noise. However, the electrolytic anodised 'skin' would soon wear through to the aluminium below as the player strummed and picked, leaving unsightly grey patches. The anodised guards did not last much beyond the 50s, although they would be revived on some later reissues.

Karl Olmsted, Fender's tool-and-die maker, explained the process. "You made a die and stamped your pickguard out, then you'd send it out to the plater, an aluminium anodising company. They'd buff the edges, polish it, and then anodise it whatever colour you wanted it: plain or satin or yellow, the different colours of anodising. The anodising process also gives it a hard skin, a little harder than the regular aluminium, which scratches so easily. So even if you were going to leave it the plain aluminium colour, you'd have it anodised – anodising stopped the corrosion process for some time."[46]

By now there were over 50 people working at Fender, and the factory was humming with constant activity. Work would sometimes spill out into the alleyways, a distinct advantage of the California climate. But Leo was almost always inside, and often he would burn the midnight oil. Soon, his firm's problem was not how to sell the guitars, but how to make enough of them to meet the apparently ever-increasing demand. As blues, rhythm & blues, and rock'n'roll grew in popularity, Fender's place in music history would become assured. "After rock'n'roll started," said Fender salesman Dale Hyatt, "of course all the dealers who had been so hesitant began teaching the electric Spanish guitar."[47]

While most of its business was aimed at the bigger market of would-be guitarists and jobbing musicians, Fender must have been pleased by the number of Stratocasters turning up in the hands of successful stars of the new music. Johnny Meeks played his Strat in a rockabilly picking-and-chords style on some lively Gene Vincent cuts, such as 'Lotta Lovin'', a Number 13 hit in summer 1957, and Meeks made effective use of the vibrato in his concise solos. It was around this time that Fender gave Vincent's band a cache of guitars, basses, and amps – "a lease or whatever, for the publicity"[48] said bassist Bobby Jones – including an impressive matching set of Blond-finish Stratocasters.

Ike Turner is best known now for his work as a duo with Tina Turner from 1960, but before that he enjoyed a career with his own R&B band and as a session pianist and guitarist. He bought his first Strat in Memphis soon after Fender launched the instrument and plays it on singles such as 'The World Is Yours' / 'Suffocate', two cuts from 1955 by Johnny Wright With Ike Turner's Orchestra. Turner offers some pleasing vibrato action on

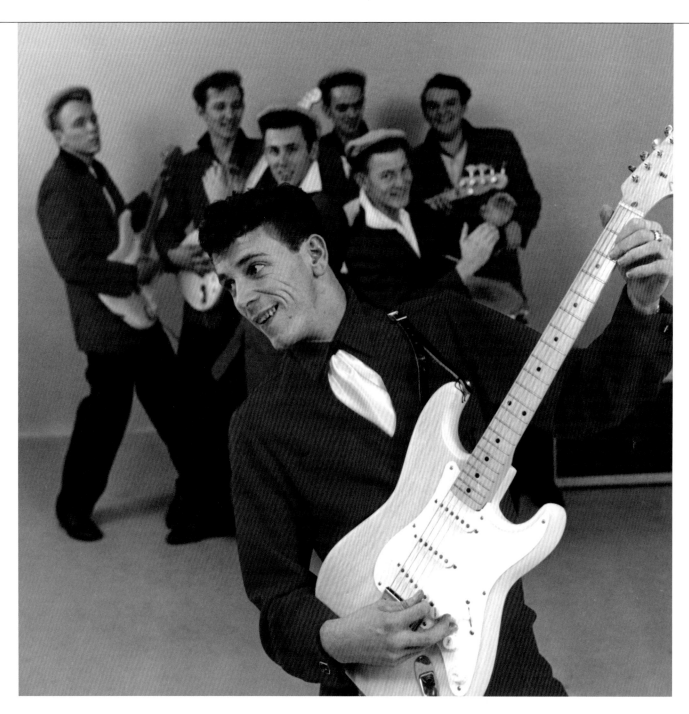

■ Fender's fortunes improved in the 50s, with an expanding **factory** at South Raymond in Fullerton (pictured, left, in 1957), birthplace of the Strat. In 1954, Fender sales boss **Don Randall** took time out to present a non-standard dark-coloured Strat to a dealer visiting the factory (opposite, centre). Fender's ads were more confident, too, like the **cool cat** featured opposite.

the stratocaster guitar book

■ Guitarists were lining up to play the Stratocaster in the 50s: sales were rising and guitar music was even higher. Around 1957, **Gene Vincent** and a roomful of Blue Caps (opposite) are celebrating after Fender provided a set of blond-finish guitars, including three Strats and a Precision. **Ike Turner** (top left, centre) is pictured in 1956 playing a Strat with his Kings Of Rhythm band, while **Johnny Guitar Watson** (above right) picks yet another beautiful 50s Strat in an early promo shot. This **1954 Stratocaster** (above) in non-standard finish, and now owned by David Gilmour, has serial number 0001. Evidence indicates that it was not the very first Strat made, but perhaps a special one-off.

the A-side's solo and an assured rhythmic role on the flip. The Strat also enjoyed a welcome dose of mainstream publicity in 1955 when a 19-year-old guitarist by the name of Buddy Merrill began playing his new Fender on the weekly ABC Lawrence Welk TV show. Welk was a bandleader who played a sort of anodyne MOR noise known as champagne music. The show's safe musical atmosphere may have provided a bonus for Fender sales, however, as watching parents, beguiled by Welk's inoffensive aura, perhaps felt more inclined now to go ahead and indulge a guitar-demanding child.

The decade's most influential televisual appearance for the Stratocaster came on December 1 1957 when Buddy Holly & The Crickets appeared on CBS's *Ed Sullivan Show*. Holly had hit Number 1 back in August with 'That'll Be The Day', and now he was on national TV to promote his new single, 'Peggy Sue'. Musicians watching would have been unsurprised by the hardware that Holly's bandmates displayed: a four-drum set for Jerry Allison; an upright bass for Joe B. Mauldin; and an electric archtop, probably a Gibson ES-225, for Niki Sullivan.

Holly, however, had something quite different on show, right at the front of the TV picture. Guitarists would have ignored the mic hung on a cord around Holly's neck, just below his bow-tie, and instead concentrated on the gleaming new Fender Stratocaster that Holly strummed: with a capo at the fifth fret through 'That'll Be The Day', and then capo-less for 'Peggy Sue'. Niki Sullivan would soon quit the band, and his guitar wasn't even audible, but through the murk of 50s TV audio, Holly's Strat was clearly there, clanging away. For once, however, it wasn't only about the sound. Most of the guitarists watching the show probably wondered what on earth was that strange-looking instrument Holly was playing. They'd find out soon enough.

Buddy had asked his brother Larry for a loan of $1,000 to buy new instruments for the group, just before they went to Nashville in the early weeks of 1956 for their first recording session, with Decca. Larry wondered if it was such a good idea. "And [Buddy] said, 'No, I know what I'm doing, I'm going to be a star now, and everything I do has got to be the best, and my guitar has got to be the best.' And I gave him the money," Larry recalled. "I didn't doubt that he'd be able to pay it back eventually, when he got big. That was when he bought that Fender Stratocaster, the one he used on all his records and in his concerts."[49] Holly in fact had at least one more Stratocaster; his original, the one he bought with Larry's loan, was stolen in 1958 and replaced with another similar model.

Sonny Curtis played lead on some of Holly's early recordings, but he left The Crickets in 1956. "When I left the group – to go on the road with Slim Whitman – Buddy started playing that really powerful rhythmic lead style," Curtis remembered. "He had to – he was the only guitarist. I think that was a style waiting to happen."[50] No one would claim Holly was a great technician as a guitar player, but that wasn't the point. Almost everyone of a certain age claims him as a great influence. What he developed on his Fender Stratocaster in the wake of Curtis's departure was a practical chord-based style, and, where necessary, Holly would shift that into almost-lead playing. The best results still sound fresh and inspired, and place Holly as a significant and early pop guitar stylist. 'Peggy Sue', a perfect pop single, was recorded in summer 1957 and beamed to the nation on that shiny Stratocaster a few months later. Fender's salesmen must have had an especially good Christmas that year.

Back at Fender HQ, the Strat was undergoing a series of small changes to the specs of the original 1954 model. From about 1956, bodies were more likely to be alder, although ash was still sometimes used for any Blond-finish guitars. The neck profile became more pointed – later the shape would become known as the 'v' neck – for a couple of years from 1955, and from that year the holes in the vibrato backplate were made oval rather than round to help thread strings into place. In 1956, the round string-guide on the headstock was changed to a 'butterfly' shape, and two years later the Sunburst shifted from two colours to a more striking three-tone effect, adding red to the yellow and black.

Most of the work on Fender's early publicity and ads fell to Don Randall. But it was clear that help was needed to give the brand a strong push among musicians and dealers. Advertising in America was becoming a more sophisticated affair, and smart agencies were increasingly adept at convincing companies to spend more on slick ads to provide a uniform identity for a set of products.

In 1957, Fender hired Bob Perine from the Perine-Jacoby agency of Newport Beach, California. He continued to shape the look of Fender publicity until 1969. Perine, a keen amateur guitarist, transformed Fender's image and created some of the most stylish and memorable guitar ads and catalogues ever printed. Some collectors today seem to value prime 'Fender paper' of the 50s and 60s almost as highly as the instruments themselves.

One of Perine's early tasks was to devise and shoot a series of press ads based on a brilliantly simple idea. He would present a Fender product in an unlikely setting, set off with the tag line "You won't part with yours either". In other words, your Fender guitar or amp is so important to you, you'll take it anywhere, too, just like the mad fool in this ad. The "won't part" ads began to appear in 1957, and one of the first showed a cool gent sitting in his tiny Isetta bubble-car, Strat and amp on the passenger seat, while the perfectly-50s-attired girlfriend stands unwanted on the pavement. Another from late '57 has a jet pilot about to climb into his cockpit – with Strat strapped to his back, of course.

Many ads followed in the "won't part" series, along with a few variant taglines, such as "Wherever you go you'll find Fender". Guitars were seen perched on army tanks, erect at the drive-in cinema, in mid-air around a skydiver's neck, strapped to a surfer ... in fact, pretty much anywhere. Perine and his team must have had a lot of fun.

The Fender catalogues, too, became beautiful objects under Perine's direction. The 1958/59 catalogue was Fender's first with a full-colour front-and-back cover, which opened out to display a luscious panorama of prime gear, including Sunburst Strats with and without trem and a red Strat with gold-plated hardware, all eyed up by a couple of cool crewcut gents. The booklet was a model of clear, simple design. No matter that the picture of the (black-and-white) Strat inside was of the obsolete-from-'59 maple-neck type:

■ Television provided a boost for Strat fame in the 50s, notably at the end of 1957 when **Buddy Holly** (above) went on to the CBS Ed Sullivan show and picked a prominent Strat. The guitar also featured on Holly and the Crickets' **1957 album cover** (below). Elsewhere, a young **Buddy Merrill** (left) was seen regularly on ABC's Lawrence Welk show with another lovely Strat.

■ **Leo Fender**, photographed in 1957 (below), must have been proud of the effect the Strat was having on Fender sales and its status among guitar players. It's not hard to imagine why, confronted with what many guitarists and collectors consider the epitome of the genre: a mint **1956 Stratocaster** (left). Bob Perine's new **ads** were a perfect complement, too, as a clever series portrayed guitars in ever more unlikely settings (above).

the stratocaster guitar book

you couldn't help but want everything, no matter about the details. And one fact in particular, tucked alongside a snap of a Blond Strat, might have caught your eye: "The Stratocaster is available in Custom Colors or Blond finish at an additional 5% cost," it said.

That line first appeared in the previous catalogue, dated 1957/58, and announced that all Fenders were now officially available in Custom Colors beyond the regular finishes. This would explain that red Stratocaster proudly displayed on the cover of the 58/59 catalogue. Most Fenders of the 50s had come in a standard finish only: Sunburst for Strats; Blond for Teles. Nonetheless a few guitars, specially made at the factory effectively as one-offs, were finished in solid colours. The rare surviving examples indicate that this practice was under way by 1954, but few players back then seemed interested in slinging on a coloured guitar, and Fender's main production remained in regular-finish instruments.

Fender also announced early in 1957 a Strat in see-through Blond finish and with gold-plated hardware. Randall said the gold plating was his idea. "The White Falcon had come out from Gretsch, and we couldn't be outdone. It wasn't a very good move, actually. It was very hard to keep the gold to stay on. We found ourselves having to apologise and do it over."[51] George Fullerton also recalled the difficulties such luxury caused. "Whatever was on your hands – sweat, dirt, acid, alcohol – had a tendency to eat through the gold-plating pretty fast. Wasn't long before it looked bad. So we didn't feel that was a good advertisement for the musician or the company or anybody else, and we resisted somewhat making gold-finish instruments."[52]

That gold-hardware Blond Strat was in effect Fender's first official Custom Color guitar – although the term has always been more popularly applied since to solid-colour varieties. This specific Blond-and-gold scheme on a Strat later became known as the Mary Kaye style, thanks to the Hawaiian-born singer and guitarist who appeared with a mid-50s Blond-body/gold-hardware Strat in a series of photos that ran in various Fender print material after first appearing in the firm's 1956/57 catalogue.

Kaye had met Fender's Don Randall through another guitarist, Steve Gibson, who, like Kaye and her trio, played the Las Vegas all-night casino lounge scene. "Around 1954, Don brought me a Fender guitar – not the Strat – to play onstage," Kaye recalled later. "Though I refused to play it, Don started bringing me Fender amps to use with my D'Angelicos. In '55, Fender delivered the Blond Strat to me, prior to the Trio going onstage at the Frontier Hotel, for the famous publicity shot, taken backstage." The guitar was returned to Fender later that evening, Kaye reported.

"Six months later, Billy, our manager, set up an arrangement with Fender to let me use the Blond Stratocaster in a Columbia movie," Kaye continued, "and again it was returned to Fender. ... Billy was upset that the guitar was returned to Fender after Leo Fender had promised it to me. We were too busy with the Trio's career to ever look back and correct the mistake."[53] That movie was *Cha-Cha-Cha Boom!*, released in late 1956, and in three featured performances Kaye plays what has since become a very famous Strat ... a guitar that, in fact, she never possessed for longer than a few hours at a time.

Fender's production of special-colour guitars was certainly casual in the 50s. The informality shifted to a rather more commercial footing for the first time in the company's sales literature of 1956 when "player's choice" coloured guitars were noted as an option, at five percent extra cost. In the following year, as we've seen, these Du Pont paint finishes were described in Fender's catalogue as Custom Colors, a name that has stuck ever since, and in the pricelist as "custom Du Pont Duco finishes", still at five percent on top of regular prices.

Fender eventually came up with a defined list of the officially available Custom Colors, and in the early 60s, when more Custom Color Fenders were being made, the company issued a series of three colour charts to publicise and help selection of the various shades. The original, in 1961, featured Black, Burgundy Mist Metallic, Dakota Red, Daphne Blue, Fiesta Red, Foam Green, Inca Silver Metallic, Lake Placid Blue Metallic, Olympic White, Shell Pink, Sherwood Green Metallic, Shoreline Gold Metallic, Sonic Blue, and Surf Green. The second, in 1963, lost Shell Pink and gained Candy Apple Red Metallic. The third, in 1965, lost Burgundy Mist Metallic, Daphne Blue, Inca Silver Metallic, Sherwood Green Metallic, Shoreline Gold Metallic, and Surf Green, and gained – all Metallics – Blue Ice, Charcoal Frost, Firemist Gold, Firemist Silver, Ocean Turquoise, and Teal Green.

The automobile industry had a profound effect on American guitar manufacturers in the 50s, not least in this ability to enhance the look of an already stylish object with a rich, sparkling paint job. In fact, it was the Gretsch company in New York City that was the first guitar-maker to adopt car paints as standard colours for guitar models. Gretsch created new-look electric instruments such as the 'Cadillac Green' Country Club and the 'Jaguar Tan' Streamliner, both in 1954.

Du Pont was the biggest supplier of paint to the car factories, most notably to the vast General Motors operation. Fender used paints from Du Pont's Duco nitro-cellulose lines, such as Fiesta Red or Foam Green, as well as the more colour-retentive Lucite acrylics like Lake Placid Blue Metallic or Burgundy Mist Metallic. As Custom Color researcher Clay Harrell has established, the names that Fender gave to the colours mostly came from the original car makers' terms: Fiesta Red, for example, was first used by Ford in 1956 for a Thunderbird colour, while Lake Placid Blue originally appeared on a 1958 Cadillac Brougham. Candy Apple Red, however, was a Fender original and not a car colour.

George Fullerton remembered going out to a local paint store around 1957, buying a Fiesta Red mix, and then going back to the factory and applying it to a Stratocaster body. He insisted that this experiment was what started Fender's defined Custom Color line. "That first one became Fiesta Red," said Fullerton. "The Du Pont company made that colour and you could buy it right across the counter. That should have been a patent, that colour, but who knows at the time you do a thing? Meanwhile, the sales office and Don Randall laughed at it, said who in hell wants a coloured guitar, specially a red one."[54] Don Randall had a different recollection of the genesis of the colour options. "Gretsch had their Country Club, which was green, the White Falcon, which was white, and there were

■ The instrument pictured here is the actual **1956 Stratocaster** (main guitar) that Mary Kaye played in the now-famous photograph that first appeared (top left) in Fender's 1956/57 catalogue. The particular look – blond finish, gold-plated hardware – is now known as "a Mary Kaye". Kaye played the Las Vegas lounge scene, and she clearly appealed to Fender's publicity-conscious team. In fact, she never owned the Strat, which was tracked down years later. Back at the **Fender factory**, the assembly workers grew in numbers as production increased, and 50s catalogues featured them at work, including jobs such as the placement of fingerboard dot-markers (top right) and final checking and tuning (right).

the stratocaster guitar book

■ Fenders in solid colours began to appear in the 50s, and this **1958 Stratocaster** (above) in gold is a wonderful example, set off by optional gold-plated hardware. The first sign of what Fender called Custom Colors appeared in late-50s pricelists, and the **1958/59 catalogue** cover (left) featured a gorgeous red Strat. Meanwhile, players like **Buddy Guy** (above) cared little for finishes and simply played the thing.

others. So it was just my idea to diversify and get another product on the market. They didn't sell as well as the traditional Sunburst and Blond colours."[55]

Whatever the origins of Fender's Custom Colors, decades later the guitars bearing these original Fiesta Reds, Sonic Blues, Burgundy Mists, and the like have proved very desirable among collectors, many of whom rate a Custom Color Fender, especially an early one, as a prime catch. The colours didn't add much to the price, originally. In 1958, for example, a Custom Color would add just $13.72 extra on top of a regular $274.50 Stratocaster. In today's collector market, the price differential between an original regular Sunburst Strat and one finished in a genuine Custom Color is certainly greater – despite the prevalence of very convincing re-finished guitars. These have become so accurate that even alleged experts can be fooled into declaring a fake finish as original.

Back at Fender in the 50s, more changes were underway. Four new factory buildings and a warehouse were added to the South Raymond site in 1958, and by the following year the number of employees topped 100 for the first time. Some further small cosmetic and production adjustments were made to the company's electric guitars. The Jazzmaster was a new top-of-the-line solid electric for 1958, and one of its unusual features (for Fender, at least) was a separate rosewood fingerboard on the regular maple neck. Some players like the smooth, slippery style of maple; others prefer the more textured feel of rosewood.

During 1959, the rosewood fingerboard was adopted for all Fender models, including Stratocasters. Also, the position dots changed colour, from the original black to a lighter colour, and these are now known as clay dots. The rosewood board replaced Fender's previous construction where frets were slid directly into the solid maple neck. At first, the new rosewood fingerboard had a flat base to match the top of the maple, and this became known as a slab board.

In 1962, Fender changed the rosewood to a thinner board with a curved base; the following year, the board was made thinner still (known as a 'laminate'). Some players insist that the thinner style helps get closer to the earlier all-maple-neck tone as it allows the tang or base of the fret to contact the maple below the rosewood. Full maple remained as an option on the Strat and some other models at various times following the introduction of rosewood.

Also in 1959, Fender changed the original one-piece pickguard to a new three-layer version, fixed to the body with eleven rather the earlier type's eight screws. The outer layers of the new guard were white, with a central black layer, and the black plastic often leeched into the white to give the surface a grey or, most noticeably, green tinge. As a result, these new pickguards are now sometimes known as green guards, and as such they add a pleasing period vibe to some instruments. Fender also used plastic tortoiseshell-finish pickguards on some guitars in the 60s.

Meanwhile, blues guitarists were discovering the charms of the Stratocaster. Buddy Guy bought one when he relocated to Chicago in 1957, after his Les Paul Goldtop was stolen. His career took off when he began recording for Chess, and he played many sessions for that label and others. "First of all, I liked what I heard in the Strat," said Guy. He added a practical note: "I found out that if I dropped it or it fell, it stayed in one piece, and that made me love it more than anything else."[56] His first Chess single, cut in 1960, was a classic, 'The First Time I Met The Blues', with Guy's glassy-toned Strat cutting through so perfectly that it must have caused a good few bluesmen and would-be bluesmen to seek out one of these West Coast solidbody wonders for themselves.

Guitar-based pop groups were multiplying at a rate that must have satisfied Fender Sales, too, with instrumental combos especially popular. Dick Dale headed one faction, with some calling him the king of the surf guitar. Left-hander Dale and his distinctive gold-sparkle Strat poured out surging, staccato lines, borrowing scales from his East European heritage, all played on heavy-gauge strings and set adrift in a sea of reverb. His big hit was 'Let's Go Trippin'' in 1961, but his best shot was a follow-up from '62, 'Miserlou'. Surf music wouldn't last much beyond the British invasion a few years later. The most successful US instro group was The Ventures, who hit Number 2 with 'Walk – Don't Run' in 1960. At first they played Fender – Don Wilson on a Stratocaster, Bob Bogle with a Jazzmaster – but a few years later they moved to Mosrite guitars.

Fender was well placed to feed the growing rock revolution and naturally happy to ensure that players had a good supply of affordable guitars available in large numbers. In a relatively short period, the brilliantly inventive quartet of Stratocaster, Telecaster, Precision Bass, and the new Jazz Bass combined to establish in the minds of musicians and guitar-makers the idea of the solidbody electric guitar as a viable modern instrument. What is remarkable is that in these circumstances Fender got so much right, and nearly always the first time. In short, the company had become remarkably successful.

Exporting became important to that success. Don Randall began the process in 1960 when he visited the leading European trade show at Frankfurt, Germany. "Our products were known over there because of the GIs playing our guitars," he recalled, "and they were very much prized. So we started doing business in Europe."[57] Britain became an especially important market because of the worldwide success of its pop groups. Up to the start of the 60s it had been virtually impossible for musicians in the UK to buy Fenders, because from 1951 to 1959 there was a ban by the British government on importing some American merchandise, including guitars.

British singer Cliff Richard and his guitarists Hank Marvin and Bruce Welch loved American records, and they particularly liked those that featured ace picker James Burton. They were pretty sure that Burton played a Fender. They wrote to Fender in California for a brochure and drooled over the 58/59 catalogue they received, especially that luscious red Strat with gold-plated hardware and maple neck that was pictured on the front. They guessed that Burton himself must surely play this most luxurious Fender, and the generous Cliff ordered one for his group. Only later did they discover that Burton was, in fact, a confirmed Telecaster man. So Hank Marvin found himself early in 1959 playing a red Stratocaster with gold-plated hardware. It was one of the first Strats in the UK, and

■ **The Shadows** (below) hold a prized new possession in 1959: one of the first Strats in the UK, where the importing of US instruments had been banned for most of the decade. The group's lead guitarist, bespectacled Hank Marvin, played the guitar proudly on many of their hits. His **1959 Stratocaster** is pictured (above) in its current refinished state. Fender worked hard to promote the Custom Color option for Strats and other models, issuing its first **colour chart** (right) in 1961. As the 60s progressed, the company continued Bob Perine's stylish and attention-grabbing ad series that placed guitars in arresting situations. The **1966 ad** featured here (below right) has the standard line for the series: "You Won't Part With Yours Either."

the stratocaster guitar book

■ During 1959, Fender changed the look of the Strat, with a rosewood fingerboard, three-layer pickguard, and three-colour sunburst – all seen on this **1959 Stratocaster** (above). In the early 60s, Strats found good homes with US guitarists, including lefty surf king **Dick Dale** (top) and **The Ventures'** Don Wilson (right).

■ Another example of a Custom Color to die for: this fine **1961 Stratocaster** is finished in Burgundy Mist Metallic, one of the DuPont paint colours that Fender offered as an option on the Strat. It put five percent on the retail price, adding up to $303.97. A bargain.

certainly the most visible. There were earlier, unofficial arrivals, not least through stewards on the US–UK liner fleet who would happily visit Manny's store in New York City and bring back a prime six-string for Brits with the contacts and the cash. But it was Hank and The Shadows who displayed this rare American prize to thousands of adoring fans as Cliff and the quartet began their rise to fame.

Marvin recalled later that he used it for the first time for the sessions for the *Cliff Sings* album, recorded at Abbey Road in London in September 1959 and released that November.[58] The Strat is certainly evident, and Marvin gives his new guitar's vibrato an interesting workout on 'Mean Woman Blues'. The Shadows alone scored a string of instrumental Number One hits in Britain between 1960 and '63 – 'Apache', 'Kon-Tiki', 'Wonderful Land', 'Dance On', 'Foot Tapper' – and Marvin's clean, spare Stratocaster lines are at the heart of almost all of them.

"The tremolo arm was something that was pretty new," Marvin remembered later. "So I developed a technique very quickly where I was holding the tremolo in the palm of my hand while I was picking notes at every opportunity. Just after I got the Strat, I was exposed to an Italian echo box, and you could get that lovely rock'n'roll echo sound. So it was all taking shape now: the Strat; the echo box; my Vox AC-30; wobbling the tremolo arm. It was all beginning to happen. The particular sound I developed, more by accident than anything else, started to become very recognisable, to the point where people were talking about a Shadows sound."[59]

Another European source of twangy Fender-like instrumental sounds were the soundtracks by Italian composer Ennio Morricone for the so-called spaghetti westerns of director Sergio Leone, beginning with *A Fistful Of Dollars* in 1964 and culminating with the atmospheric theme for *The Good, The Bad, And The Ugly* two years later. It's unclear exactly who played what on these recordings, but guitarists Bruno Battisti D'Amario and Alessandro Alessandroni were Morricone session regulars, and Alessandroni in particular probably used a Strat.

In Britain, the year after the import ban was lifted in 1959, Jennings became the first official distributor of Fender gear, joined by Selmer in 1962. A Jennings catalogue from 1961 pitches the UK list price of the Stratocaster at £147/17s/6d (£147.88; about $400 at the time), and three years later it had crept up to £160/13s/0d (£160.65; nearer $450). By summer 1965, both Selmer and Jennings had been replaced as the British Fender distributor by Arbiter, which continued for many years as the brand's UK agent.

"Fender was the biggest musical instrument exporter in the United States," said Randall. "In fact I think we exported more US-made musical products than all the other companies combined. We had it to ourselves for maybe three or four years."[60] Western Europe was the firm's biggest export market, but Fender also did well in Scandinavia, South Africa, Rhodesia (now Zimbabwe), Japan, Australia, and Canada.

Fender boasted what seemed to be an ever-extending line of products. By the summer of '62, the pricelist included an array of products. A regular Sunburst Stratocaster with

the stratocaster guitar book

vibrato listed at $289.50 ($30 less for a 'hardtail' with no trem), with a Blond or Custom Color finish at $303.97, and the same with gold-plated hardware at $349.50. In addition to the Strat there were eight more electric guitars (Duo-Sonic, Esquire, Esquire Custom, Jaguar, Jazzmaster, Musicmaster, Telecaster, and Telecaster Custom) and three electric basses (Precision Bass, Jazz Bass, and VI). There were 13 amplifiers (Bandmaster, Bassman, Champ, Concert, Deluxe, Princeton, Pro Amp, Showman, Super, Tremolux, Twin Amp, Vibrasonic, and Vibrolux). Completing the line-up were five steel guitars (Champ, Deluxe, Dual, Stringmaster, and Studio Deluxe) and two pedal-steel guitars (models 400 and 1000).

The Jaguar was Fender's new top-of-the-line electric, its shorter 24-inch-scale neck a come-on to Gibson players. It shared the novel offset-waist body shape that the Jazzmaster had introduced and an even more detailed control layout than that model. The Jaguar was offered from the start in four different neck widths. One was a size narrower and two were wider than normal, and they were coded A, B, C or D, from narrowest to widest, with 'normal' B the most common. These neck options, with the same codes, were offered from 1962 on the Stratocaster (and also on the Jazzmaster).

Many buildings had been added to cope with increased manufacturing demands, and by 1964 Fender employed around 600 people (500 in manufacturing) spread over 29 buildings. Forrest White said his guitar production staff were making 1,500 instruments a week at the end of 1964, compared to the 40 a week when he joined the company ten years earlier. As well as electric guitars and amplifiers, Fender's early-60s pricelists offered acoustic guitars, effects units, a host of related accessories, and Fender-Rhodes electric pianos, which were added to the line in 1963.

Don Randall remembered writing a million dollars' worth of sales during his first year in the 50s, but in the mid 60s that rose to some ten million dollars' worth, translating to about forty million dollars' worth of retail sales. By now, the beat boom, triggered by The Beatles and the so-called British Invasion of pop groups, was taking the United States by storm. Electric guitars were at their peak of popularity and Fender was among the biggest and most successful producers.

Suddenly, however, in January 1965, the Fender companies were sold to the mighty Columbia Broadcasting System Inc, better known as CBS. *The Music Trades* magazine reported in somewhat shocked tones: "The purchase price of $13 million is by far the highest ever offered in the history of the [musical instrument] industry for any single manufacturer. ... The acquisition, a sterling proof of the music industry's growth potential, marks the first time that one of the nation's largest corporations has entered our field. With sales volume in excess of half a billion dollars annually, CBS currently does more business than the entire [US musical instrument] industry does at retail. Actual purchase of Fender was made by the Columbia Records Distribution Division of CBS, whose outstanding recent feats have included the production of *My Fair Lady*."[61]

Economic analysts were advising big corporations to diversify and acquire companies from a variety of different businesses. They presumably also advised the corporations that all they had to do was finance and expand the new acquisitions, and rich pickings would follow. Columbia Records boss Goddard Lieberson said of Fender: "This is a fast growing business tied into the expanding leisure-time market. We expect this industry to grow by 23 percent in the next two years."[62]

Leo Fender was by all accounts a hypochondriac, and the sale of Fender was prompted by his acute worries about his health, principally the staph infection in his sinuses that had troubled him since the mid 50s. Also, he was nervous about financing expansion. He recalled later: "I thought I was going to have to retire. I had been suffering for years with a virus infection of the sinuses and it made my life a misery. I felt that I wasn't going to be in the health to carry on."[63]

Don Randall said: "Leo was a faddist: he'd get on these health kicks. One time, he heard that carrot juice was the thing, the panacea, so he and his friend Ronnie Beers got these big commercial juicers and they went and bought carrots by the sackload. And all of a sudden they started turning red. That cured him of that. Then his next kick, he'd come and say hey, try this, this is the best thing for you – you can't believe how good it makes you feel. You had to have a tablespoonful of cider vinegar in a glass of hot water. I said, oh, Leo … ."[64]

Randall handled the sale of Fender to CBS. He said that Leo had earlier offered him the company for a million-and-a-half dollars, but he didn't feel he was ready for that kind of career move and so suggested to Leo that he might see what he could get from an outside buyer. Leo agreed, and Randall's first tentative discussions took place early in 1964 with the Baldwin Piano & Organ Co of Ohio. Randall also contacted an investment banker, who at first suggested that Fender go public, which neither Leo nor Randall wished to pursue. The bankers then came up with CBS as a potential purchaser.

"Now we had two companies up there," Randall remembered, "but Baldwin's attitude to purchasing turned out to be totally unsatisfactory for our purposes. So finally we got down to the nitty gritty with Columbia, and I made about a half-dozen trips back and forth to New York: jam sessions with attorneys and financial people.

"The guys at CBS came in with a really low price at first, but eventually we came to a fairly agreeable price, and I called Leo and said how does that suit you? He said, 'Oh Don, I can't believe it, are you trying to pull my leg?' And I said no – does that sound like a satisfactory deal we can close on? 'Well anything you say, Don, that's fine, you just go ahead and do it,' he said. And so the rest is history: we went on and sold it to CBS after a lot of investigation. They did a big study on us – people came in to justify the sale and the price paid – and we consummated the deal. Leo wouldn't even go back to New York for the signing, for the pay-off, or anything. 'You get the money and you bring it out to me,' he said."[65]

In the year following the Fender acquisition, CBS published a survey that estimated the number of guitar players in the USA at nine million and placed total American retail sales of guitars during 1965 at $185 million, up from $24 million in 1958. CBS was clearly

the stratocaster guitar book

enthusiastic about the potential for music, and the corporation went on to buy more instrument companies, including brands such as Rogers (drums), Steinway (pianos), and Leslie (organ loudspeaker cabinets).

Over the years, the sale of Fender to CBS provoked much retrospective dismay among guitar players and collectors, some of whom consider so-called 'pre-CBS' instruments – in other words those made prior to the beginning of 1965 – as superior to those made after that date. This is a meaningless generalisation. But there can be little doubt that, over a period of time after the sale, CBS did introduce a series of changes to the production methods of Fender guitars, and a number of these changes were detrimental to the quality of some instruments.

According to insiders, the problem with CBS at this time was that it seemed to believe that all it had to do was simply pour a great deal of money into Fender. And certainly Fender's sales did increase and profits did go up. Randall recalled income almost doubling in the first year that CBS owned Fender. Profit became paramount, said Forrest White, who remained as manager of electric guitar and amplifier production. "CBS had a vice president for everything. I think they had a vice president for cleaning the toilets. You name it: whatever it was, it had a vice president."[66]

Here was a significant clash of cultures. The new CBS men, often trained engineers with college degrees, believed in high-volume production. Fender's old guard were long-serving craft workers without formal qualifications. A job ad in the *Los Angeles Times* in March 1966 summed up the changes. It was for a Systems Analyst to oversee a computer feasibility study at Fender, for a "management information system" covering "sales order processing, material control, manufacturing systems, and accounting systems". It's not hard to imagine the rumours that this probably set in motion among the old team. They want to run the place with computers! Whatever next?

Among many of the old-guard Fender men who talked later about the experience, opinion about the effect of the CBS takeover on Fender's guitars was divided. George Fullerton said that management was first alerted to criticisms when complaints started to filter back from the dealers through the sales reps. "They'd say the guitars don't play like they used to, they aren't adjusted like they used to be," Fullerton remembered.[67]

Salesman Dale Hyatt reckoned that the quality stayed relatively stable until around 1968, and then quality-control declined. "It got to the point where I did not enjoy going to any store anywhere, because every time I walked in I found myself defending some poor piece of workmanship. They got very sloppy with the finish, with far too many bad spots. They created their own competition, letting the door wide open for everybody else, including the Japanese."[68]

Under the new owner, Randall became vice president and general manager of Fender Musical Instruments and Fender Sales (both soon part of the new CBS Musical Instruments Division). He thought the supposition that quality deteriorated when CBS took over was a fallacy. "I will say this for CBS: they were just as interested in quality as we were," said

Randall. "They spared no amount of time or effort to ensure the quality was there. There's always this suspicion when a big company takes over that they're going to make a lousy product and sell it for a higher price, and that's not true here. But the other problems that existed were multiple."[69]

CBS retained Leo Fender's services as "special consultant in research and development". The corporation's confidential pre-sale report into the Fender operation had concluded that Leo, unlike Randall, was not a necessity to running the business, and that while "a competent chief engineer" could easily keep products moving forward in the contemporary marketplace, it would be "highly desirable, at least for a period of four or five years, to maintain the active interest and creativity of Mr Fender".[70] In other words, CBS didn't want Leo taking his ideas elsewhere, but didn't particularly want him getting in the way of the newly efficient Fender business machine. So he was set up away from the Fender buildings, allowed to tinker as much as he liked – with very little effect on the product. A 1965 CBS brochure showing the key personnel at Fender listed Leo way down in 18th place among the 28 management posts.

A couple of years after the sale to CBS, Leo changed doctors and was given a massive dose of antibiotics that cured his sinus complaint. He completed a few projects for CBS but left when his five-year contract expired in 1970. He went on to make instruments for the Music Man company (originally set up in 1972 although not named Music Man until 1974) and his later G&L operation, where the Nighthawk model was more or less a Stratocaster with a different name.

Leo was not the first of the old guard to leave CBS. Forrest White departed in 1967, because, he said, "I wouldn't build some products – the solid state amps – that I thought were unworthy of Leo's name."[71] He went on to work with Leo at Music Man, as well as for CMI, which owned Gibson, and Rickenbacker. White died in November 1994. Don Randall resigned from CBS in April 1969, disenchanted with corporate life, and formed Randall Electric Instruments, which he sold in 1987. He died in December 2008. George Fullerton left CBS in 1970, worked at Ernie Ball for a while, and with Leo formed the G&L company in 1979, although Fullerton sold his interest in 1986. (G&L at first stood for "George & Leo", later "Guitars by Leo".) Fullerton died in July 2009. Dale Hyatt resigned from CBS in 1972. Hyatt, too, became part of the G&L set-up, which was sold to BBE Sound Inc after Leo Fender's death in March 1991 at the age of 82.

One of Fender's first CBS-era pricelists, dated April 1965, revealed a burgeoning line of products. A regular Sunburst Stratocaster with trem had a list price of $289.50; a trem-less version was $259.50, a Custom Color version $303.97, and Custom Color plus gold-plated hardware $349.97. There were seven more electric guitar models: Duo-Sonic, Electric XII, Jaguar, Jazzmaster, Musicmaster, Mustang, and Telecaster. The other lines included three bass guitars (Jazz, Precision, VI), six flat-top acoustics (Classic, Concert, King, Malibu, Newporter, Palomino) and 15 amplifiers (Bandmaster, Bassman, Champ, Deluxe, Deluxe Reverb, Dual Showman, Princeton, Princeton Reverb, Pro Reverb, Showman, Super Reverb,

Tremolux, Twin Reverb, Vibro Champ, Vibrolux Reverb), as well as various Fender-Rhodes keyboards, steel and pedal steel guitars, a solidbody electric mandolin, and reverb and echo units.

The arrival of the CBS era began to affect the Stratocaster. Back around 1960, Fender had started to use a modernised 'chunky' Fender logo in company literature. The first electric model to brandish the new design on its headstock was the new-for-'62 Jaguar. During the following years, Fender gradually applied it to all guitars, although it didn't arrive on the Stratocaster until 1964. This new logo, drawn up by adman Bob Perine, is known now among collectors as the 'transition' logo, because it leads from the original thin 'spaghetti' logo to a bolder black version, sometimes known as the CBS logo, introduced around 1968. In 1965, Fender began to stamp the modernised 'F' of the new logo on to guitar neck-plates and, shortly after, on to new-design tuners.

An especially evident design change that has come to distinguish Strats made after CBS's acquisition of Fender affected the headstock. In 1965, the Stratocaster gained a broader headstock to match that of the Jazzmaster and Jaguar. Also that year, Fender added binding to the edge of the fingerboards of the Jaguar and Jazzmaster and, in 1966, added block-shaped fingerboard inlays rather than the previous dot markers, but fortunately these revisions did not happen to the Strat (although a rare few got the binding). The three-layer pickguards were replaced with single-layer white plastic in '65.

During 1966, CBS completed the construction of a new Fender factory (planned before its purchase of the company) at a cost of $1.3 million. It was situated next to Fender's existing buildings on the South Raymond site. Clearly the new owners were getting ready for a profound push on production. But in the late 60s at Fender there were unusual signs of weakness. The company tried and failed with some solid-state amplifiers, quietly dropped most of its relatively new hollowbody electric models, and knocked together some ugly 'new' solidbody models designed to soak up unused parts.

Alongside the amps, speakers, effects, pianos, organs, steel guitars, banjos, acoustics, and all the rest on Fender's bursting 1968 pricelist were nine basic solidbody electrics in addition to the Strat: the Bronco, Duo-Sonic, Electric XII, Esquire, Jaguar, Jazzmaster, Musicmaster, Mustang, and Telecaster. By now a Sunburst Strat with vibrato listed at $314.50 ($50 less for the hardtail), and with Blond or Custom Color finish the price went up to $330. But aside from costs and prices, CBS had little cause for concern when it came to demand for their products. Pop music was, of course, flourishing in the 60s, and Stratocasters were everywhere.

An apparently casual Bob Dylan performance at the Newport folk festival in July 1965 turned into an event that ever since has been labelled as the moment when folk music went electric. Dylan's guitarist for the show, Michael Bloomfield, played a Telecaster, but for Dylan himself it had to be a black Stratocaster, a potent symbol of modern electric music. Some conservative folkies in the audience may not have been convinced, but Dylan and the music never looked back.

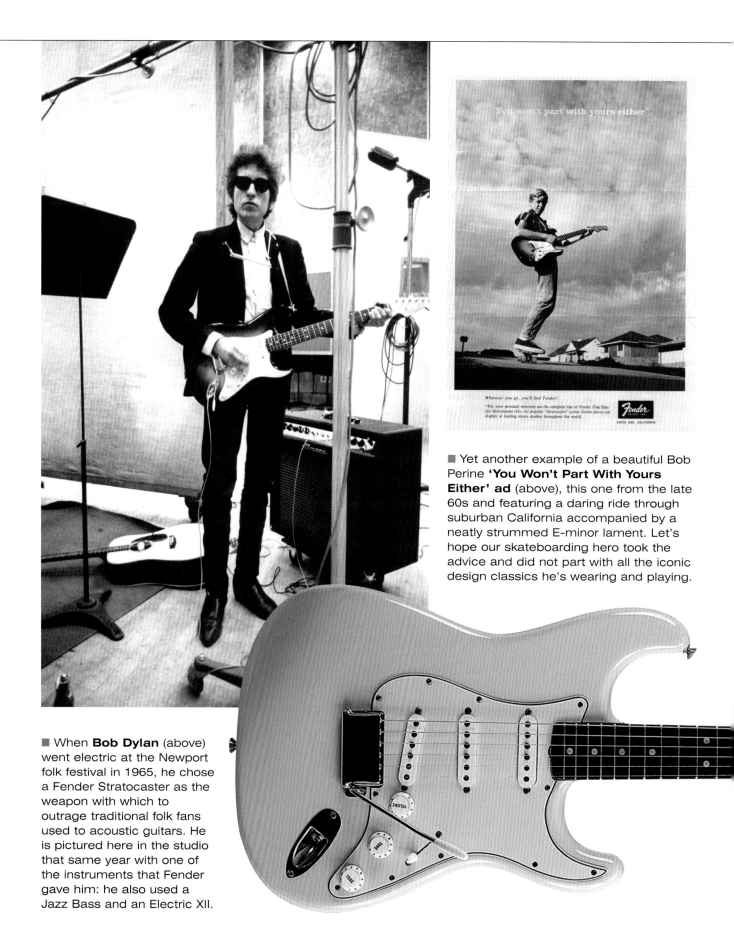

You won't part with yours either

*For your personal selection see the complete line of Fender Fine Electric Instruments (like the popular "Stratocaster" guitar shown above) on display at leading music dealers throughout the world.

Wherever you go, you'll find Fender!

Fender

SALES, INC.

SANTA ANA, CALIFORNIA

■ Yet another example of a beautiful Bob Perine **'You Won't Part With Yours Either' ad** (above), this one from the late 60s and featuring a daring ride through suburban California accompanied by a neatly strummed E-minor lament. Let's hope our skateboarding hero took the advice and did not part with all the iconic design classics he's wearing and playing.

■ When **Bob Dylan** (above) went electric at the Newport folk festival in 1965, he chose a Fender Stratocaster as the weapon with which to outrage traditional folk fans used to acoustic guitars. He is pictured here in the studio that same year with one of the instruments that Fender gave him: he also used a Jazz Bass and an Electric XII.

54

■ This group of 60s Strats has a lot going for it. The **1964 Stratocaster** (main guitar, below) is finished in Sonic Blue and is similar to the pair that John Lennon and George Harrison acquired around the start of 1965. This **1962 Stratocaster** (right) is in Foam Green and has gold-plated hardware. **CBS** (letter-head, bottom) bought Fender in 1965, and this **1965 Stratocaster** (far right) in Black shows the change to a bigger headstock made that year. The **1966 Stratocaster** (top) shows one of the more vibrant sunbursts of the period.

The Beatles dominated pop music in the mid 60s. Fans lucky enough to see them live knew George Harrison and John Lennon primarily as players of Gretsch and Rickenbacker guitars. But in the mid 60s the two each acquired a Stratocaster, both finished in Sonic Blue, for studio use. They probably acquired the pair of Strats around the time of the group's Christmas shows in London in December 1964 and January '65 – at least one photograph survives of Lennon playing his on-stage during the 20-night residency. The group was in an acquisitive mood, and Paul McCartney bought an Epiphone Casino electric and Texan acoustic at the same time. It's nice to imagine roadie Mal Evans, dressed perhaps as Santa Claus, returning from a store with all four guitars in a big sack.

John used his Strat almost immediately, for 'Ticket To Ride', recorded in January. He and George can be heard with their newly-acquired Fenders on various other recordings made after that, for example dueting during the solo in 'Nowhere Man' – from the group's album *Rubber Soul* recorded later in 1965 – complete with its distinctive signature 'ping' harmonic, as much the song's hook as anything else on the track.

In 1967, Harrison took some paint and nail varnish and transformed his Strat into a personalised psychedelic artwork. That summer, his newly daubed Fender would be just about visible – in glorious black-and-white – as the group performed 'All You Need Is Love' for the *Our World* global satellite broadcast. For guitar-savvy viewers, his psych Strat was more colourfully displayed in the 'I Am The Walrus' sequence from their TV film shown that Christmas, *Magical Mystery Tour*.

As the close of the 60s loomed, Strats took a much bigger boost when an inspired musician by the name of Jimi Hendrix applied the model's sensuous curves and glorious tones to his live cavorting and studio experiments. Fender salesman Dale Hyatt said: "When guys like that came along, we couldn't build enough of them. As a matter of fact, I think Jimi Hendrix caused more Stratocasters to be sold than all the Fender salesmen put together."[72]

Hendrix got his first Strat in 1966 – he'd already tried a couple of Duo-Sonics and a Jazzmaster or two – and almost instantly made it his own. He may have been influenced in the choice by one of his heroes, Curtis Mayfield, who played a Strat. In the first few years of his career, Hendrix generally played new rosewood-board models, mainly in Sunburst, Black, or Olympic White finish. In the final period of his life, between 1968 and 1970, he mainly played two Strats, both new '68 maple-board models, one in Black and the other Olympic White. "The Stratocaster is the best all-around guitar for the stuff we're doing," Hendrix said in summer 1967. "You can get the very bright trebles and the deep bass sound."[73]

When Hendrix started out, he usually tuned his guitars to regular concert pitch, but increasingly he came to favour tuning down his Strats by a half-step and sometimes a whole-step. This would mean less strain on his voice, since he would be singing in a slightly lower register, but also the lower-pitched strings would be slightly slacker, making it easier for him to bend them. Hendrix liked the neck pickup's full tone, but occasionally used other settings, too, including the 'hollow' tones found between the Strat's official three selector positions.

All Hendrix's Stratocasters were regular guitars that he would flip over and re-string to accommodate his left-handedness. Guitarists debate endlessly on how much difference this made to his sound – the reversed nut, the angled bridge pickup accentuating different strings than intended, the vibrato handled differently – but with the high volume levels at which Hendrix played, and his natural dexterity and playing skill, any differences were probably minimal. Less open to debate is that Hendrix made more players aware of the Strat's tonal and musical possibilities than any other individual before or since. One of many great recordings that captures Hendrix and Strat in full flight is his live-in-the-studio performance of 'Come On (Pt. 1)' from the 1968 album *Electric Ladyland*.

As we all know, Hendrix died shockingly young in 1970. A stone monument stands to him at Greenwood Memorial Park in Renton, Washington, and it has an appropriate motto upon it: "Forever in our hearts." Alongside that and his dates of birth and death is the depiction of an electric guitar. It is unmistakeably and proudly a Fender Stratocaster. That mesmerising combination – Jimi and his Strat – still haunts guitarists to this day.

One of Eric Clapton's early inspirations was Buddy Holly, and the first album Clapton bought was Holly's *Chirping Crickets* – the one with Buddy holding a Stratocaster on the front. As an impressionable 12-year-old, Clapton saw Holly in 1958 on the British TV show *Sunday Night At The London Palladium*. "I thought I'd died and gone to heaven," Clapton wrote later in his autobiography. "That was when I saw my first Fender guitar. It was like seeing an instrument from outer space, and I said to myself: 'That's the future – that's what I want.' Suddenly, I realised I was in a village that was never going to change, yet there on TV was something out of the future. And I wanted to go there."[74]

Clapton began that future as a young professional musician with The Yardbirds and a Fender – a red Telecaster owned by the group – but he soon changed allegiance to Gibson guitars, which he used to great effect through the 60s with John Mayall and with Cream. A significant purchase came in May 1967, however, when he went to the Sound City store in central London and for a pretty steep £150 (about $350 at the time) bought a secondhand 1956 Stratocaster, which later became known as Brownie. Perhaps he'd asked the store to keep an eye out for an original Strat just like Buddy Holly's, with sunburst body and maple neck?

Steve Winwood was another inspiration. The two had been friends since the mid 60s when Winwood was with Spencer Davis and Clapton with John Mayall, and although Winwood is best known as an organist and singer, he's a fine guitarist, too, and often in The Spencer Davis Group he would play an early white maple-neck Strat, which he seems to have acquired around 1965. "Steve Winwood had kind of got me interested in [Stratocasters]," Clapton said later, "because he was playing a blond-necked Strat. It sounded great. Then I thought, 'Well, yeah, Buddy Guy used to play one,' and I remembered a great picture of Johnny Guitar Watson playing one."[75]

58   the stratocaster guitar book

■ Beatle **George Harrison** (opposite) is pictured in the studio in 1967 with the **1961 Stratocaster** (main guitar), originally in Sonic Blue, that he hand-painted that year to create Rocky, a glowing psychedelic art object. He used it on many studio recordings and is seen with it in the Magical Mystery Tour film. **Jimi Hendrix** (right), the most famous Stratocaster-player ever, tunes one of his Strats in 1967 with the help of roadie Gerry Stickells. The **1968 Stratocaster** (below) in Olympic White was sold at auction in 1990 as the guitar that Hendrix played at the Woodstock festival in 1969.

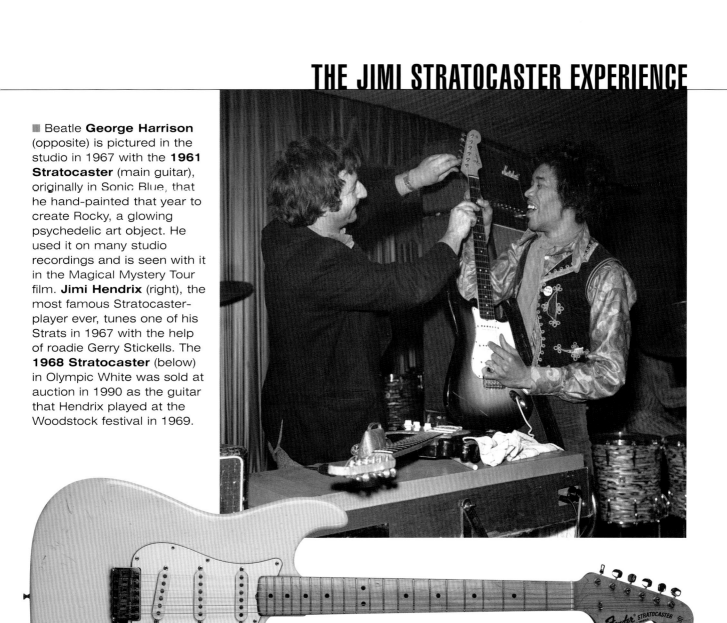

■ Meanwhile, among the psychedelia, the regular sunburst Strat of the 60s looked like this **1964 Stratocaster** (below), adding from 1965 a deeper headstock, like the one on Jimi's Woodstock Strat above. Fender continued to produce fine-looking promo material, as the example from inside the **1965/66 catalogue** (opposite) demonstrates. Alongside the Jazzmasters are three luscious Strats, still with small headstocks and finished in sunburst, Sonic Blue, and Burgundy Mist Metallic.

Clapton bought that Brownie Strat in London just days before Cream travelled to New York City to record their *Disraeli Gears* album, and he may have used it to record 'Tales Of Brave Ulysses', which features Strat-like tones and aggressive wah-wah in what almost amounts to a homage to the Strat king of the day, Jimi Hendrix. Clapton certainly used his new Fender at least once on stage for that song: an observer at a Scottish gig in August 1967 wrote: "'Tales Of Brave Ulysses' was next on the agenda, Clapton swapping his weirdly-painted Gibson SG Special for a conventional-coloured Fender Strat to produce unbelievable backing sounds behind Jack Bruce's vocal."[76]

Aside from those sporadic uses of Brownie, Clapton began playing it regularly when he toured with Delaney & Bonnie, starting in late 1969, as well as for the recording of his first solo album, *Eric Clapton*, in January 1970, for *The London Howlin' Wolf Sessions* in May, and for the *Layla* album, recorded later in 1970. For Clapton, his new/old Strat reflected and, in a way, symbolised his change of musical pace. Out with the frenzied, lengthy Gibson jamming of live Cream; in with a generally more relaxed, contemplative Fender outlook. He was in no doubt that he'd acquired a great instrument. "I use an old Stratocaster I've acquired which is really, really good," he said in an interview in 1970, "a great sound."[77]

Years later, in 1999, Clapton sold Brownie at a Christie's auction, where Microsoft co-founder Paul Allen bought it for his Experience Music Project museum. It benefited Clapton's Crossroads charity to the tune of $497,500 (plus buyer's premium), establishing a record sum for a guitar – a price Clapton himself described as "astonishing".[78]

In November 1970, during a visit to Nashville with Derek & The Dominos to record *The Johnny Cash Show* for ABC TV, Clapton bought some more Strats. He recalled buying them for $100 each at the Sho-Bud store, although he may have acquired some at the city's GTR store. Of the six or so guitars, Clapton gave three to friends (George Harrison, Pete Townshend, and Steve Winwood) and used various parts from each of the remaining guitars to assemble one fine Stratocaster. This wasn't a new idea: he'd also botched together an odd Tele-Strat hybrid while in Cream and Blind Faith, at first adding to the Custom Telecaster body a contemporary rosewood Strat neck with 'big' headstock, and later (as seen at Blind Faith's famous Hyde Park concert in June 1969) the neck from Brownie. Clapton was simply exploiting the bolt-together nature of Fender guitars.

Reports suggest that Clapton put together three of the Fenders he'd acquired in Nashville in 1970 in order to create the Strat that would become known as Blackie, combining a '57 neck, a refinished black '56 body, two 50s pickups, and a circa 1970 pickup. "[I took] pickups from one, [pickguard] from another, and the neck from another," Clapton explained. "The reason I chose that neck is because it's got quite an extreme V. It's the most extreme V on a maple neck that I've found. It's a beautiful neck. It has a lovely feel," he said. "Brownie was a much more industrial guitar. This one is really refined; it's like the racer."[79]

Clapton used Blackie as his main live and studio electric until 1985. Eventually, he again sold the worn-out guitar at auction, this time in 2004. Guitar Center, the US music-store chain, bought it at Christie's in New York City for a further record-breaking price, a breathtaking $959,000 (plus buyer's premium), again benefiting Clapton's Crossroads drug-rehab charity. Not a bad return on $300 or so.

Some players and collectors believe that the 70s are the poorest years of Fender's production history, although others who got their first instruments then are likely to have fonder memories. There's little doubt that quality control slipped and more low-standard Fenders were made during this decade than any other. But some fine Fender guitars were produced in the 70s as well. It's just that there were more average guitars made than good guitars, and often it seems as if the good ones were produced in spite rather than because of the company's policies and activities.

Starting in 1971, two changes were made to the Strat. The adjustment point for the truss-rod was moved from the body-end of the neck to the headstock, and Fender placed a new bullet-shaped adjuster there. A neck-tilt mechanism was also added, adjustable at the neck-plate, to make it easier to alter neck pitch or angle, and the neck-to-body joining screws (usually called bolts) were reduced from four to three. These were reasonable changes in themselves, but other problems due to increased production and sloppy quality-control coloured the reputation of 70s Strats for a time. "The neck sockets were being cut way over size," said salesman Dale Hyatt. "They blamed the new three-bolt neck, but it wasn't that – you could have put six bolts in it, and it still would have moved."[80]

Also around 1971, Fender changed the way the Strat vibrato was manufactured, casting the base plate and inertia block as one piece and using cast saddles to replace the original stamped bent-steel ones. The single string-tree on the headstock was replaced with two, and a few years later the pickup polepieces were made a uniform height rather than staggered as before. Again, some players did not view these changes as advantageous to tone or playability.

Also at this time, the company began to use its new high-gloss 'thick skin' finish, achieved by spraying more than a dozen coats of polyester on to the unfortunate instrument, and today its plastic appearance is a giveaway sign of a 70s Fender.

Fender applied humbucking pickups to some of its Telecaster models in the 70s, but never to a Strat – not officially, at least. One of the humbucker'd Teles was the Telecaster Deluxe, launched in 1973, which seemed like a cross between the big-headstock neck of the contemporary Stratocaster (some examples even came with Strat-style vibratos), the body of a Telecaster, and the pickups and controls of a Gibson electric.

Blues-rock was alive and well, and one of its finest exponents was Rory Gallagher, the international blues hero from Ireland. His battered '61 Strat was his trademark guitar, bought by Gallagher in Cork for £100 in 1963. The original sunburst body was down to bare wood almost everywhere, the pickups were all replacements, the controls were revised to provide simply a master volume and tone, and the much-refretted fingerboard responded perfectly to Gallagher's nimble fingers, in his band Taste and then solo from 1971. *Deuce* from that year is among his best all-round albums.

■ **Eric Clapton** bought his first
Strat in 1967 and began using it
regularly with Delaney & Bonnie
two years later. It marked a
change from the Gibsons he'd
favoured until then and matched
a musical shift for Clapton. He's
pictured with that Strat, which
became known as Brownie, on
his **1970 solo debut** (below).

the stratocaster guitar book

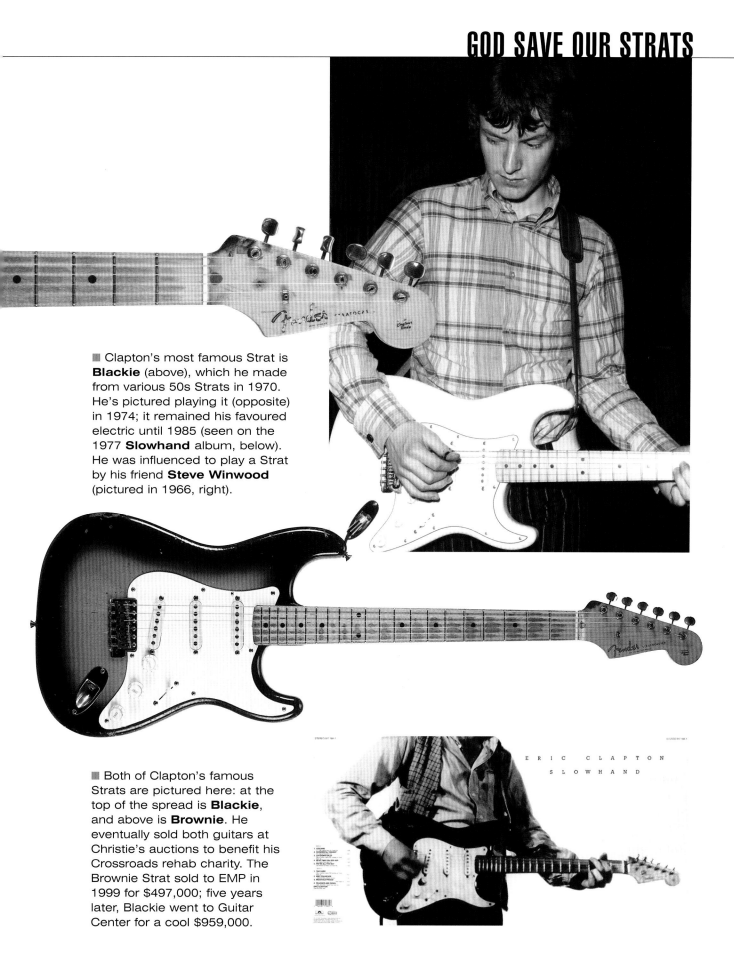

■ Clapton's most famous Strat is **Blackie** (above), which he made from various 50s Strats in 1970. He's pictured playing it (opposite) in 1974; it remained his favoured electric until 1985 (seen on the 1977 **Slowhand** album, below). He was influenced to play a Strat by his friend **Steve Winwood** (pictured in 1966, right).

■ Both of Clapton's famous Strats are pictured here: at the top of the spread is **Blackie**, and above is **Brownie**. He eventually sold both guitars at Christie's auctions to benefit his Crossroads rehab charity. The Brownie Strat sold to EMP in 1999 for $497,000; five years later, Blackie went to Guitar Center for a cool $959,000.

ERIC CLAPTON
SLOWHAND

the stratocaster guitar book

Gallagher once explained how his Strat started life in good condition. "But it's got so battered now, it's got a kind of tattoo quality about it. There's now a theory that the less paint or varnish on a guitar, acoustic or electric, the better: the wood breathes more. But it's all psychological. I just like the sound of it," he said. "It's also a good luck thing: it was stolen one time, and it came back. It's kind of a lucky charm. The guitar is a part of me. B.B. King might have several Lucilles, but I've only got the one Strat. I don't even call it a woman's name. It's what it is. I still play it every day; I just love playing it."[81] Gallagher continued to promote the blues with a passion until his untimely death in 1995.

Other notable Strat players in the 70s included Nils Lofgren, who would join Bruce Springsteen's band in later years. The ex-Neil Young sideman released his first solo album in 1975, and it showcased his talents as a composer and a thoughtful, creative guitarist. Lowell George in Little Feat was another gifted songwriter and fine guitar stylist. He was a master at drawing carefully constructed lines from his Strat, adopting a beautifully sustained and compressed sound, and his slide work in particular was the envy of many fellow players. George suffered a wastefully early death, in 1979.

Robbie Robertson used a Telecaster for much of his early work in The Band but shifted to Strats in 1975, and his controlled minimalism and distinctive voice on the instrument has been a joy to behold. Tom Petty often used a Stratocaster live and in the studio for his popular work with The Heartbreakers, alongside a Tele and a Rickenbacker 12-string, while George Harrison played a white Strat at the Concert For Bangladesh, a pair of benefit performances he staged in 1971 to help refugees. His Stratocaster was seen in the film of the event and heard on the bestselling triple-LP boxed set that both appeared the following year.

Jeff Beck had been a confirmed Gibson Les Paul player since moving on from the Tele and Esquire he'd played in The Yardbirds. However, quite a few years before that, one of his first proper electrics had been a rosewood-neck Strat, back in 1961, as he found his way in his earliest bands. "It was a 1960 sunburst, which I painted pink, or lavender," recalled Beck. "I remember it split in two: this big split appeared along the back of it, because I'd whacked something with it. But I wanted a car and had to sell it. So, as I travelled on the train to sell it, I touched up the split with my girlfriend's nail varnish. It matched perfectly! Fantastic story, eh? And they never spotted it."[82]

He bought his first Gibson Les Paul in early 1966, but in his post-Yardbirds band, The Jeff Beck Group, he also started to play Strats, around 1968. "I'd played a Les Paul for a while and never really played anything else," Beck recalled. "But I think it was when we did the *Beck-Ola* album that I got fed up with the sound of it. In the studio, the Les Paul didn't sound a lot different to the John Mayall's Bluesbreakers. Lovely sound, but every track ends up sounding very similar. The Strat seemed to respond more to my aggressive playing than the Les Paul. The Les Paul just sounds dreadful if you start hitting it."[83]

Beck continued to use a '54 Strat, together with a Les Paul, for the revised Jeff Beck Group that followed, and then he moved on to a new-looking big-headstock rosewood-neck Strat, which he used in that group and, from late 1972, with his new band, Beck Bogert & Appice. His third Strat, probably a '56 model, came along in time for his jazz-rock *Blow By Blow* album, recorded with producer George Martin toward the end of 1974.

"I was still divvying about between Strat and Les Paul," said Beck. "The Les Paul is more attuned for jazz-rock, and it was partly because of George that I used it: his ears were having a bit of trouble handling the raucous screaming that I was doing. George would flinch and start walking around and making tea and things. He likes good mellow sounds. So I thought well, there's no point in making the guy suffer. I may as well play melodically. And then maybe I'll come back one night and scrub over it with the Strat. Eventually, when I started to do 'Freeway Jam' and stuff like that and needed to go crazy, I decided the Strat was more my tool, you know?"[84]

Beck reflected on the timeless qualities of the Stratocaster. "You don't get kids saying: 'What's that old guitar; ain't you got a new one?' It still looks futuristic, and it's still an unbeatable shape, as is the Tele. I don't think you can improve on those two guitars, the all-time great rock guitars." In fact, said Beck, he would blame the Stratocaster for his early conversion to the power of rock. "The reason I left school was because of that guitar. I mean, that is brain damage when you're a kid of 14 and you see something like that. It's just a piece of equipment that you dream about touching, never mind owning. The first day I stood in Lew Davis's, or one of those other London shops, I just went into a trance, and I got the wrong bus home, just dreaming about it. You know? It just blew my brains apart, and it's never been any different since. It's taken me all round the world and given me everything I've got – just that Strat, really. So it is a particular favourite of mine."[85]

Beck has been a Strat evangelist ever since, using a number of further examples over the years. As one of the greatest rock guitarists ever, his continuing allegiance must have helped Fender sell countless instruments over the years. His signature model first made a showing in the Fender line in 1991.

Back in the 70s, and there was plenty more Strat action, with many noteworthy names looming from a lively musical decade. Deep Purple's Ritchie Blackmore was a stylist with a taste for classical-leaning melodic invention in a heavy setting; Robin Trower drew on Hendrix and created his own thick tone and weaving sound; Curtis Mayfield played clean Strat lines on his perfect soul records; Ernie Isley spun his flowing, Hendrix-flavoured leads through classic Isley Brothers funk; and Phil Manzanera showcased a new direction for modern Strat sounds with Roxy Music.

Fender executive Dave Gupton announced that 1972 was a record year for the company, with unit production and dollar sales figures both higher than ever before. He was in little doubt that 1973 would yield still higher figures and that the trend would continue upward. A major expansion program was on at the Fullerton plant to boost output further, completed in summer 1974 and providing Fender with a new total of 289,600 square feet of production, warehouse, and shipping space. This is precisely why CBS purchased Fender back in 1965. But the increase in the number of instruments

The world's favorite flying machine

■ Fender's promo department decided to make an update on the classic 'You Won't Part With Yours' Either ad series, and came up with a modern take that stressed favouritism. This almost Disney-like **1973 ad** (above) is the Stratocaster entry.

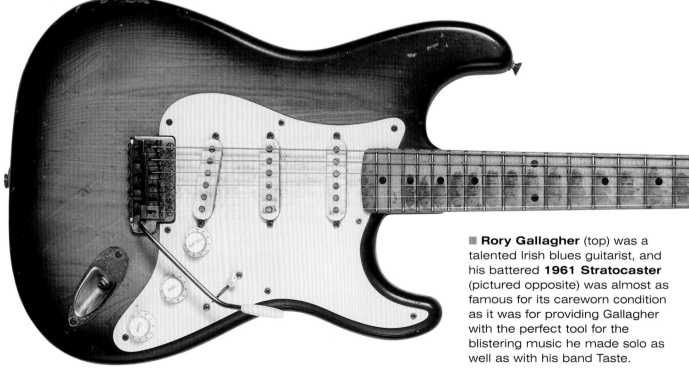

■ **Rory Gallagher** (top) was a talented Irish blues guitarist, and his battered **1961 Stratocaster** (pictured opposite) was almost as famous for its careworn condition as it was for providing Gallagher with the perfect tool for the blistering music he made solo as well as with his band Taste.

■ **Jeff Beck** (above) moved from Gibson Les Pauls to Stratocasters around 1968. He's used a number of different Strats since, including this **1954 Stratocaster** (main guitar, left), which he acquired from Steve Marriott in the late 70s. Earlier in the decade he briefly used the relatively new blond model seen in the 1972 concert shot above.

the stratocaster guitar book

leaving the factory inevitably affected quality. A feeling was beginning to set in that Fenders were not made like they used to be. Some top musicians regularly played old guitars, now described as 'vintage' instruments, adding to the growing impression that numbers might be more important to the contemporary Fender company than quality. A number of guitarists were becoming convinced that older instruments were somehow more playable and sounded better than new guitars.

Eric Clapton was one of the first musicians who was reported in print offering advice on the matter. In 1967, just around the time that he bought Brownie, a '56 Stratocaster, he told a journalist: "When you're starting, always buy a secondhand guitar, because it will be 'broken in' and easier to play, apart from the fact that the older the guitar the better it seems to have been made."[86] This is in essence the vintage guitar argument, in one of its earliest airings, and in one sentence.

A further early sign of this new old-is-best idea came in a piece published in the *Washington Post* at the end of 1972. Reporter Tom Zito spotted a trend where some local musicians were out hunting for early Fenders. "Available for a mere $150 in 1952," wrote Zito, more or less accurately, "this humble electric guitar has already increased in value some 500 percent. ... Proof, in the buy-it-on-time, wear-it-out, and throw-it-away world of rock, that enduring value does indeed exist."

Zito contacted Leo Fender and told him that some guitarists now considered vintage Fenders in a similar light to the hallowed and immensely valuable Stradivarius violins of 17th-century Italy. Apparently the 65-year-old Leo paused, as well he might. Then he said: "Well, I'm sure a lot of musicians feel just like that about 'em. Now I'll give you an example. In 1929 I bought a Model 12 Remington. I mean, I could really hit a target with that old rifle. One time I got a jack rabbit at better than 300 yards. You see, some pieces of machinery just suit people."

The reporter then turned to Freddie Tavares at Fender, who told him that the continuing demand for Fender guitars, old and new, was down to the sound. "Now how do you describe that? I'll tell you. It's the kind of sound that says, 'Listen, you bugger, I'm talkin', so shut up!'"[87]

The search for old guitars and the notion that they were mysteriously and inherently better grew steadily during the 70s. Stephen Stills summed up the attitude to vintage axes in a 1975 interview, when he said: "Nothing new has been built since the 60s that's worth a damn."[88] Norman's Rare Guitars, established in California during the middle of the decade, was one of the new dealers specialising in the vintage requirements of rock players. Proprietor Norman Harris was in no doubt why so many guitarists were taking up older instruments – like those he offered for sale. "You simply cannot compare what I have to offer with what the big companies are mass producing today," he boasted.[89] The first published attempt to sort out the various old Strats and their dates of manufacture came in Tom Wheeler's *The Guitar Book* in 1974 and later more specifically in André Duchossoir's *The Fender Stratocaster* (first published 1988).

Freddie Tavares's son Terry recalled how one person's junk can become another's collectable. "I can remember dad bringing home trunk-loads of rejected necks and bodies which the saws and routers had nicked, and we burned them in the fireplace. Little did we know that if we had just saved them for 45 years they'd be worth millions today as ding'd-up mid-50s Strats and Teles."[90]

Meanwhile, over at Fender HQ in Fullerton, California, CBS management was cutting back on the existing Fender product lines and offering hardly any new models. The last Esquires and Duo-Sonics of the period were made in 1969. The Jaguar disappeared around 1975, and by 1980 the Bronco, Jazzmaster, Musicmaster, and Thinline Tele would all be phased out of production.

The humbucker-equipped Telecaster Deluxe and Custom models had both gone by 1981, the same time that the Mustang went. Most were later reissued, but back in the day it made for a bare catalogue. The original acoustic flat-tops had all gone by 1971, and ten years later the steels and pedal steels would disappear, with only amplifiers (some 14 models) offering anything like Fender's early coverage of the market.

The December 1974 pricelist revealed just a few options for new Stratocasters. Most of Fender's original Custom Colors had been discontinued in the late 60s and early 70s. By now the with-trem Strat was available in just six finishes: standard Sunburst ($405), or Blond, Black, White, Natural, and Walnut ($425). The regular model had the rosewood fingerboard of the period, but a maple board was an option for a few dollars more. Left-handers and trem-less versions were also available, in the same finish and board options.

The catalogue was settling down to a revised pattern. After the cold reception for the recent spate of 'new' humbucker-equipped Teles, Fender's taste for fresh designs slackened off considerably. A glance at the chronology assembled at the rear of this book tells its own story about the singular lack of new models in the 70s. It's clear that Fender was quite sensibly concentrating in general on its strengths – and as a result was enjoying its most successful period, producing a greater quantity of instruments than it had ever done in its entire history. "There were some improvements we wanted to make on the Stratocaster," said Freddie Tavares in 1979, when he was still a consultant to Fender's R&D department. "However, marketing's attitude was not to fool with success."[91]

Fender's UK distributor CBS/Arbiter was a joint venture formed with Ivor Arbiter, who had been the company's British agent since the mid 60s, when he'd taken over from Jennings and Selmer. Arbiter opened the Fender Soundhouse, a new instrument superstore in central London, toward the end of 1973. Sculptor Jon Douglas had worked at Arbiter's house, and Arbiter asked him to visit the store. When Douglas noted that most of the guitars looked boring, Arbiter invited him to do better. Douglas came up with a replacement Stratocaster body made from cold-cast bronze, employing a metallic layer over a fibreglass shell. A prototype was made, followed by six more models.

Each featured the sculpted body, in a variety of shades, and after a suggestion from Arbiter, Douglas set rhinestones into the body's surface, providing the instrument's name.

the stratocaster guitar book

■ A pair of typical 70s Strats: this **1973 Stratocaster** (left) is finished in Lake Placid Blue; the other **1973 Stratocaster** (right) is in Natural finish. It was time for a new catchphrase for Fender ads, and this **1974 ad** (bottom) showed a Strat ready for some classy speeding.

■ Two examples of 70s Stratmen at opposing ends of the musical spectrum: **Ritchie Blackmore** (opposite) was the classically-inspired technician whose six-string dexterity gave substance to Deep Purple's heavy rambles, while **Ernie Isley** (above) drew on Hendrix-like flavours to provide flowing melodies through The Isley Brothers' soul-pop-funk.

■ This **1975 Rhinestone Stratocaster** (main guitar) is one of the handful made with a bonded metal and fibreglass body by the British sculptor Jon Douglas especially for Fender's UK agent. It is in effect Fender's first 'art' guitar.

This small batch of Rhinestone Stratocasters was put on sale at the Soundhouse in 1975, but unfortunately a fire destroyed the premises soon afterward. It seems that two of the 'production' models had already been sold, but the other four probably perished in the flames. Douglas made fresh moulds for a further run of around 25 examples in the early 90s, some adapting old 70s parts, others with modern components, and all identified by a numbered plaque set into the moulding on the rear of the body. The originals were in effect the first of Fender's 'art guitars', a category that later would flourish at the Custom Shop from the 90s.

At the Fender factory a shortlived revival began in 1977 of the Antigua finish, a light-to-dark shaded brown colour that had first been offered as an option during the late 60s on some Coronado models. Back then, the finish was used as an emergency measure to disguise manufacturing flaws. This time around, for just a couple of years, it was used purely for the look. Also featured on the Antigua Strat was the new black hardware that Fender started to use from 1975. All the plasticware – knobs, pickup covers, switch caps – was black, and this certainly enhanced the overall look of the Antigua-finish instruments. It was also around this time that Fender replaced its tuners with closed-cover units bought in from the German Schaller company, a supplier used until 1983.

CBS was selling 40,000 Fender instruments a year by the end of the 70s. A further sign of such an enormously increased production rate was the end of the tradition for putting a date on an instrument's neck. Since the earliest days, workers had almost always pencilled and later rubber-stamped dates on the body-end of necks. It remains about the most reliable way to date a Fender of the period (leaving aside the question of fakes). But from 1973 to the early 80s Fender stopped doing it. Presumably they were simply too busy.

By 1976, Fender had a five-acre facility under one roof in Fullerton and employed over 750 workers. John Page, who would run Fender's Custom Shop from the late 80s until the early 2000s, started working for Fender in 1978. He spent some months on the production line before moving to R&D. There was rampant departmentalism at Fender in the late 70s, he recalled. "You couldn't even tell Purchasing what part you wanted or where you wanted it from; all you could tell them was the spec of the part you wanted," Page explained. "It was so compartmentalised, and virtually no one got to know anyone else in any of the other departments. There was no communication."

Page recalled his horror when he discovered one of the CBS executives cheerfully disposing of Fender's history. "This guy came through our office, and he was putting green dots on all our guitars. I asked what he was doing. 'Oh, well, I got this great programme: I'm gonna give these away to dealers, yes sir.' What! And before we were able to stop it, he had given away about 80 percent of our original prototypes and samples."[92]

Fender began to fit a five-way selector switch to the Stratocaster from 1977, replacing the old three-way unit. From its launch in 1954, the Strat had a selector pickup switch that offered three firm settings: neck pickup, or middle pickup, or bridge pickup. Almost immediately, some players began to discover that if the switch was lodged precariously between the official settings, two new combinations of pickups became available. A boost for the idea came when Eric Clapton mentioned it in a 1970 interview. "I just set the switch between the first and middle pickups. There is a little place where you can catch it so that you can get a special sound, somehow. I get a much more rhythm and blues or rock kind of sound that way."[93]

Lodging the three-way between neck and middle settings gave those two pickups combined, and similarly for middle and bridge. There was a change to the quality of the sound in these in-between positions, caused by phase cancellation, producing 'hollow' or 'honky' sounds – as well as a volume decrease – that could be quite useful musically. Players would sometimes loosen the spring inside the switch to make it easier to lodge the switch at in-between settings. Some accessory manufacturers spotted the trend and began to offer replacement five-way switches that gave the standard three positions plus two firm, clickable settings for the new sounds. That it took Fender until the late 70s to adopt the five-way says much for the firm's remoteness from players at the time.

One guitarist identified with these 'hollowed-out' tones was Mark Knopfler of Dire Straits, whose debut album of 1978 was awash with the sounds of in-between Strat pickups. Knopfler's Strat was a 1961, which when he bought it was stripped to natural wood, but he had it refinished in red, probably by London repairman Sam Li.

"The whole thing about a red Fender Strat is that it's kind of a joke," Knopfler said later. "It's such a ridiculous object, looked at in a certain way. It's the sort of thing that if you were a rock'n'roll star, and really into being a rock'n'roll star, that's the kind of thing you would play. And it was the sort of thing that me and my mates used to dream about, like the ultimate California hotrod machine. It really didn't look hardly like a musical instrument at all."[94]

By 1979, the Fender pricelist showed a basic Strat at $640 (rosewood board) or $680 (maple), with seven colour options: regular Sunburst, White, Black, Natural, Antigua, Wine, or Tobacco Sunburst. The Strats sat among seven other electric models: Bronco, Jazzmaster, Lead, Musicmaster, Mustang, Starcaster, and Telecaster.

Fender decided to celebrate the 25th anniversary of the introduction of the Stratocaster in 1979 with its first-ever anniversary model. Today, we might expect a nit-picking replica, accurate enough to satisfy the most anal of collectors. Not so in the late 70s. About the only concessions to the design specifics of a 1954 Strat were the fretted maple neck and the body-end truss-rod adjustment. Otherwise, what you got was a 1979 Stratocaster with a unique paint job, a cheesy anniversary logo on the upper horn, a celebratory neck-plate with special serial number, and locking Sperzel tuners.

Fender had shifted during 1979 from its multi-coat 'thick skin' polyester finish to a water-based paint. The earliest examples of the 25th Anniversary Strat used the new finish formulation, in Pearl White. Unfortunately this cracked spectacularly. Most were sent back to the factory by irate stores or owners, and Fender reverted to polyester paints. The main production of the 25th Anniversary was changed to a more appropriate Silver finish. "The

It's a soul machine.

It's a country machine.

It's a rock machine.

It's a business machine.

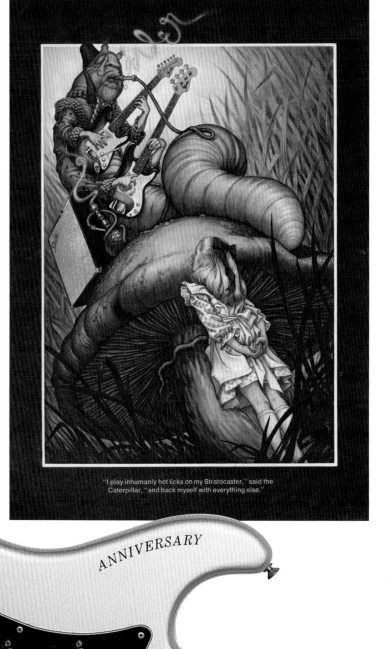

"I play inhumanly hot licks on my Stratocaster," said the Caterpillar, "and back myself with everything else."

■ More ads from Fender's 70s promo efforts are shown here. The **1978 ad** (above) has the R&D team at work, and the guitar they're holding features a fashionable combination at the time: a Stratocaster with natural finish and hardtail (non-vibrato) bridge. Meanwhile, this far-out **1976 ad** (right) has Alice in a somewhat disturbing Fenderland.

ANNIVERSARY

■ **Mark Knopfler** (left) rose to fame with Dire Straits, whose debut album appeared in 1978. Knopfler used his red Strat (with unmistakable black volume knob) for a delightful series of records that placed his deftly picked guitar at the centre of storytelling songs and a driving band sound.

■ Fender's first attempt to celebrate its own history came with this **1979 25th Anniversary Stratocaster** (main guitar). It was nothing like we'd expect today, with few stylistic links to the original 1954 guitar. The **1978 Antigua Stratocaster** (right) shows the Antigua sunburst finish offered for a few years, plus the new black hardware used on some guitars from 1975.

quantity, naturally, is limited," announced Fender, and during 1979 and 1980 the firm proceeded to make thousands of 25th Anniversary Stratocasters ($800 including case, virtually the same price as a standard model). "They went fast in '54. They'll go fast now," ran the insistent ad. An official estimate of production mentioned 10,000 units.

Most people tend to refer to a Stratocaster as a Strat, and in 1980 Fender finally used the abbreviation officially on a new model. It was designed by Gregg Wilson, who had come up with the budget-price Fender Lead models introduced the previous year. The new Strat combined regular Stratocaster looks with updated circuitry, a 'hot' bridge pickup, and fashionable heavy-duty brass hardware. Fender also offered the hardware separately as an after-market accessory line, called Original Brass Works, following the lead of various companies that popularised a craze for retrofit replacement parts. Larry DiMarzio was a leader in this new business, introducing his Super Distortion replacement pickup in 1975, with Mighty Mite, Seymour Duncan, and others soon following.

Fender intended with the Strat to re-introduce the old-style narrow headstock of the original Stratocasters. The broader type of the time had been in use since 1965. However, Fender used old worn-out tooling, and the result was not an entirely accurate re-creation. Smaller, certainly; accurate, no. A reversion to the four-bolt neck fixing and body-end truss-rod adjustment and the removal of the neck-tilt for the new Strat model implied that CBS were already aware of criticisms of 70s Stratocasters. A few brighter colours were offered for the Strat, too, reviving Lake Placid Blue, Candy Apple Red, and Olympic White. The model was significant as the first attempt at a modernised Strat. It retailed at $995, compared to $745 for the regular Stratocaster.

One further attempt in 1980 to provide something different for Strat fans was the Hendrix Stratocaster. It was something like a 25th Anniversary Strat in overall spec, but it had an inverted headstock and additional body contouring, and was only offered in white. It's another significant guitar, as it was the first Fender marketed to highlight an association with a musician, a sales technique that would become very important to the company from the late 80s. Only 25 or so were produced, and most if not all were marked as prototypes.

Colour schemes were brightened and expanded a little during the 80s, with the shortlived International Colors in 1981 and then the Custom Colors and Stratobursts of '82. Some of the new hues were distinctly lurid – such as Capri Orange, Aztec Gold, or Bronze Stratoburst – and they were not much liked at the time. In 1983, there was a short run of Marble or 'bowling ball' finishes, designed by Darren Johansen, in swirling Red, Blue, or Gold.

With generally trimmed model lines and a massive output from the factories at Fender, it was hard to resist the feeling as the 80s dawned that the newly-important calculations of the balance sheet were firmly established and took precedence over the company's former creativity. At the start of the decade, CBS management decided that they needed some new blood to help reverse a decline in Fender's image and finances. Income had been climbing spectacularly to 1980 – it had tripled in that year from 1971's $20 million – but re-investment in the company was wavering.

During 1981, key people were recruited from the American musical instrument division of Yamaha, the giant Japanese company. John McLaren was hired as head of CBS Musical Instruments, and among the other newcomers from Yamaha were Bill Schultz and Dan Smith. Schultz was hired as Fender president and Smith as director of marketing electric guitars. Smith recalled: "We were brought in to turn the reputation of Fender around and to get it so it was making money again. It was starting to lose money, and at that point in time everybody hated Fender. We thought we knew how bad it was. We took it for granted that they could make Stratocasters and Telecasters the way they used to make them. But we were wrong. So many things had been changed in the plant."[95]

One of the first improvements Smith made was to revise the Strat's overall specs, introducing the Stratocaster Standard as the new regular model. It reverted to body-end truss-rod adjustment, a revamped narrow headstock shape, and what was generally felt to be the more stable four-screw neck-to-body fixing. Schultz recommended a large investment package, primarily aimed at modernising the factory. This had the immediate effect of virtually stopping production while new machinery was brought in and workers were re-trained.

Schultz wanted to start alternative production of Fender guitars in Japan. The reason was relatively straightforward: Fender's sales were being hammered by the onslaught of copies produced in the orient. These Japanese copyists made the biggest profits in their own domestic market, so the best place to hit back at them was in Japan – by making and selling guitars there. A good deal of these instruments were copies of the Fender Stratocaster, which was enjoying renewed popularity.

In the early 70s, when the Japanese began manufacturing electric guitars in the style of classic American models, most Western makers didn't see much to worry about. Later, the quality of the Japanese instruments improved, but some American makers had their heads stuck firmly in the sand. Dave Gupton, vice president of Fender in 1978, said: "Fender is not adversely affected by the Japanese copies as perhaps some of the other major manufacturers, because we have been able to keep our costs pretty much in line."[96]

That casual attitude changed dramatically in a few short years. By the start of the 80s, the US dollar had increased in value relative to the Japanese yen. It shifted from a low in 1978, when a dollar was worth around 200 yen, to a high in 1982, when it rose to nearly 250 yen. Coupled with the high quality of many Japanese guitars, this meant that instruments built in the orient were making a notable impact on the international guitar market. Many of the copies emulated Fender and Gibson models.

"We had to stop this plethora of copies," said Smith. "A lot of these companies basically told Bill Schultz and me that they were going to bury us. They were ripping us off, and what we really needed to do was to get these guys where it hurt – back in their own marketplace."[97]

■ Fender offered a lurid selection of what it called **International Colors** in 1981, and a selection of Strats are pictured on this page. The hardtail **1981 Stratocaster** (main guitar) is finished in Capri Orange, while the two vibrato models are finished in Sahara Taupe (right) and Monaco Yellow (below). Strats from this period marked the last appearance, for now, of the big-headstock style, and the **1981 catalogue** cover (opposite) was one of the last pieces of Fender publicity to feature it. During 1981, Fender recruited new management personnel who would make a number of essential changes and improvements.

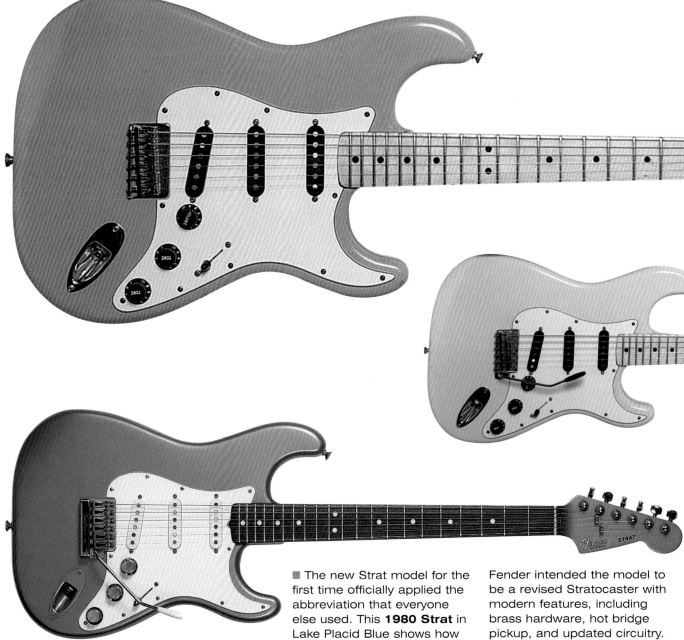

■ The new Strat model for the first time officially applied the abbreviation that everyone else used. This **1980 Strat** in Lake Placid Blue shows how Fender intended the model to be a revised Stratocaster with modern features, including brass hardware, hot bridge pickup, and updated circuitry.

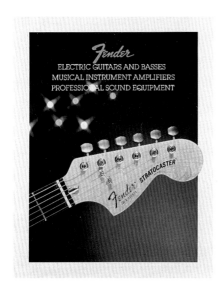

■ **Bonnie Raitt** (right) plays Old Brown, her favoured 1965 Strat. Well known to fellow guitarists as a great blues and slide player, she enjoyed wider fame in the late 80s with her bestselling Nick Of Time album. New Fender managers instigated a move to a more traditional look for the **1982 Stratocaster Standard** (below).

the stratocaster guitar book

With the blessing of CBS, negotiations began with two Japanese distributors, Kanda Shokai and Yamano Music, to establish the Fender Japan company. The joint venture was officially established in March 1982 combining the forces of Fender, Kanda, and Yamano. Fender USA licensed Fender Japan the right to have Fender guitars built within Japan for the Japanese market. After discussions with Tokai, Kawai, and others, the factory finally chosen to build guitars for Fender Japan was Fujigen, based in Matsumoto, some 130 miles north-west of Tokyo. Fujigen was best known in the West for the excellence of its Ibanez-brand instruments. Fujigen had been making Greco copies of Fender and Kanda Shokai had been selling them, so they were well prepared to make and sell Fender guitars.

Meanwhile, in the States the new management team was working on a strategy to return Fender to its former glory. The plan was, quite simply, for Fender to copy itself, by re-creating the guitars that, as we've seen, many players and collectors were spending increasingly large sums of money to acquire: the 'vintage' Fender guitars made back in the company's glory years in the 50s and 60s.

Freddie Tavares continued to work as a consultant to Fender R&D until his retirement in 1985. Around 1980, he began work on a Vintage Telecaster model, planned to be a re-creation of an original 1952 Tele. It became the first modern reissue of a vintage-style Fender guitar and prompted a wider look at the potential for a line of models. R&D man John Page travelled with marketing boss Dan Smith to a vintage-guitar dealer, Ax In Hand in Illinois, where they took measurements and photographs and paint-tests from a few old Fenders. They also bought some vintage Fender instruments. "We spent $5,600 on a '61 Strat, a '57 Precision, and a '60 Jazz Bass. Which for Fender at the time was ludicrous," laughed Smith. "That's right. We went out and bought back our own product!"[98]

Such industry resulted in Fender's first Vintage reissues. The models consisted of a maple-neck '57 and rosewood-board '62 Stratocaster, alongside the revised '52 Telecaster. Production of the Vintage series was planned to start in 1982 at Fender USA (Fullerton) and at Fender Japan (Fujigen), but the changes underway at the American factory meant that the US versions did not come properly on-stream until early 1983, and the factory there was not up to full speed until the start of '84.

The July 1983 pricelist pitched the '57 and '62 Strat reissues at $995, which was $345 more than the regular Strat. That same month, Guitar Trader, a dealer based in New Jersey and specialising in vintage instruments, offered an original '57 Stratocaster for $3,000. The most expensive Fender in its inventory, this Strat was, said Guitar Trader, an "exceptionally fine collectable specimen, factory two-tone sunburst lacquer, maple 'v-neck' construction, tremolo equipped, original and excellent throughout".[99]

Fender's Vintage Strat reproductions were not exact enough for some die-hard collectors, but the idea seemed sound enough. If there was a market for old guitars, then why not for guitars that looked like the old ones? Guitarists knew that the instruments had to feel and play right, too, however – the very attributes that made the older Strats so appealing. Clearly, Fender had more work to do. But they were definitely onto something.

Dan Smith and his colleagues at Fender USA received samples of the Japan-made Vintage reissues before American production started, and he remembered their reaction to the high quality of these oriental Fender re-creations. "Everybody came up to inspect them and the guys almost cried, because the Japanese product was so good. It was what we were having a hell of a time trying to do."[100]

As we've learned, Fender Japan's guitars at this stage were being made only for the internal Japanese market, but Fender's European agents were putting pressure on the Fullerton management for a budget-price Fender to compete with the multitude of exported models being sold in Europe and elsewhere by other Japanese manufacturers.

This led in 1982 to Fender Japan making some less costly versions of the Vintage Strat and Tele reissues for European distribution. At first they had a small extra Squier Series logo on the tip of the headstock. This was soon changed, with a large 'Squier' replacing the Fender logo. The Squier guitar brand was born. The name was much older, however. It came from a string-making company, V.C. Squier of Michigan, that Fender had acquired in the mid 60s. Victor Carroll Squier was born in 19th-century Boston, the son of an English immigrant, and became a violin maker, moving to Battle Creek, Michigan, where he founded his string-making firm in 1890. The company operated at the same Battle Creek building from 1927 to 1972, when CBS relocated the operation within the town.

Toward the end of 1983, with the US Fender factory still not up to the scale of production the team wanted, Schultz and Smith decided to have Fender Japan build some instruments for the US market, too. They approved Japanese production of a Squier-brand 70s-style Stratocaster and Telecaster. These, together with the earlier Squier Vintage-style Strats and Teles, marked the start of the sale of Fender Japan products around the world and the move by Fender to become an international manufacturer of guitars.

"It taught us, contrary to what the guys believed at Fender six or seven years before, that people would buy Fender guitars with 'made in Japan' on them," Smith said. "In fact, I really believe that our introduction of those instruments, worldwide and in the USA, was what legitimised buying Japanese guitars."[101] Certainly there had been a resistance by many musicians to the cheap image associated with Japan-made guitars, but the rise in quality of instruments from brands such as Ibanez, Yamaha, Fernandes, Aria, and Tokai – as well as Fender and Squier – wiped away a good deal of this prejudice and gave oriental guitars a new popularity and respectability.

At its US factory in 1983, Fender made some cost-cutting changes to the Standard Stratocaster and Telecaster. These were the result of the dollar's continuing strength and the consequent difficulty in selling US-made products overseas, where they were becoming increasingly high-priced. Savings had to be made, so the Strat lost a tone control and its distinctive jack plate. The revisions were ill-conceived, and many who had applauded the improvements made since 1981 groaned inwardly at the familiar signs of economics once again taking precedence over playability and sound. Fortunately, this mutant variety of Fender's key Stratocaster model lasted only until 1985.

■ Fender hit a high note with the vintage reissue series, with models like this **1988 '57 Stratocaster** (above). The series marked an attempt to reproduce classic models of the past. Less impressive was the shortlived and modified two-control **1983 Stratocaster Standard** (below).

■ Squier was a new brand, launched in 1982 when the newly established Fender Japan made some versions of the vintage reissues for Europe, like this **1982 Squier Series Stratocaster** (below). At first a small Squier logo was used on the tip of the headstock, but soon the brand was used prominently on instruments made in parallel with the Fender lines. Meanwhile, the explosive Strat-wielding guitarist **Yngwie Malmsteen** (right) released his powerful debut album.

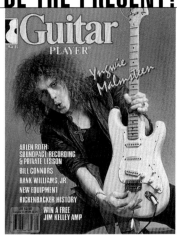

■ With the vintage series under way in the early 80s, Fender's **1983 catalogue** (right) emphasised the company's links to players old and new, and it included shots of Strat players from Jimi Hendrix and Eric Clapton to Steve Morse and Adrian Belew.

Another shortlived guitar from the same period was the Elite Stratocaster, and an accompanying Telecaster, intended as a radical new high-end version of the old faithful. The Elite listed for $999 and had new pickups designed for humbucking noise cancellation and single-coil brilliance, linked to active circuitry. This was a popular kind of system at the time, but it was a first for Fender. The guitar incorporated a battery-powered pre-amp to boost the signal and widen the tonal range – and only a few of these new sounds would be familiar to traditional Strat players.

There were good points – the new pickups, the effective active circuitry, and an improved truss-rod design – but they were mostly overlooked, because the vibrato-equipped Elite Strat came saddled with a terrible bridge, which is what most players recall when an Elite is mentioned. In-fighting at Fender had led to last-minute changes and the result was an unwieldy, unworkable piece of hardware. The Elite Strat also featured three pushbuttons for pickup selection, not to the taste of players brought up on the classic Fender switch. The model was dropped by the end of 1984.

Fender's business and production headaches didn't help them in the 80s, and new competing styles of solidbody electric guitars were appearing, notably in the superstrat style. The superstrat design was primarily devised by Grover Jackson, who headed the US Charvel/Jackson firm that manufactured in America and then Japan. The Jackson Soloist model, which appeared around 1983, was one of the first superstrats. Subsequently, many brands such as Washburn, Ibanez, Kramer, and others adopted elements of the design in various forms, often with notable success.

The idea of the superstrat was to take the classic Stratocaster as its basis but then square the body sides, stretch the horns, make the contouring bolder, and slim the overall shape. The revamped body was equipped with powerful combinations of single-coil and humbucker pickups, quickly evolving to the preferred combination of two single-coils plus a bridge humbucker. All this was partnered by a double-locking heavy-duty fine-tunable vibrato system, designed for extreme pitch shifting. Access to the highest of the 24 frets was improved with a through-neck and deeper cutaways, and the design popularised a drooping 'pointy' headstock.

Fender's first nod toward the style had been with 1985's Performer, but this had effectively been lost in the difficulties surrounding the sale of Fender by CBS. The Japan-made HM Strat series, which began in 1988, tried again. From the point of view of players of the traditional Stratocaster, these were not Strats at all. The HM name was a big clue: metal guitarists were the major players of such guitars, although more mainstream guitarists such as Jeff Beck were briefly seduced.

Then in 1989 came a line of US-made HM Strats, with most of the expected superstrat features on board, including a locking vibrato. These US models came with three different pickup configurations: two single-coils and a bridge humbucker; one Lace Sensor and a bridge humbucker; or two humbuckers. All were shortlived: it seemed that, generally, players still expected traditional Fenders from Fender.

Meanwhile, the US Contemporary Stratocaster, also new in 1989, put the locking vibrato system and two-single-coils-plus-humbucker scheme on a conventional Strat body and neck, but this too did not last long. This model did have some historical significance as the first relatively conventional looking Fender Stratocaster to be officially offered with a humbucker. A few years later, Fender tried with more Japan-made HMs, again without success. Another take on the idea was the Strat Ultra of 1990, which featured a twin-coil bridge pickup, controlled with an extra switch that allowed the player to mix in single-coil or humbucker tones. Arguably, however, it wasn't until the Floyd Rose Classic Stratocaster (1992–98) that Fender hit on a successful blend of traditional and new features.

Prominent Strat men of the 80s ranged from shred king Yngwie Malmsteen to David Gilmour, who had been playing Strats to great effect in Pink Floyd for some time – 1975's *Wish You Were Here* had underlined that. But Gilmour's solo on 'Comfortably Numb' from *The Wall*, and especially his live version at the summit of the bricks during the early-80s *Wall* shows, remains for many a definitively sublime Stratocaster moment.

Stevie Ray Vaughan brought the Stratocaster's capabilities spectacularly to notice in 1983 when the Texan blues-rocker made a surprisingly effective pairing with David Bowie on Bowie's *Let's Dance* album. Vaughan's own *Texas Flood* of the same year went on to reveal more of his abilities, including some inspired Hendrix-flavoured work. Vaughan died prematurely in a helicopter crash in 1990, but not before he redefined contemporary blues-rock guitar, mostly performed on his careworn Strat known as Number One.

Vaughan recalled his brother Jimmie Vaughan playing a Strat before he did. "I always really liked the tone he got out of it," Stevie Ray said in 1988. "I'd been using Telecasters and Epiphone Rivieras, different things, and I got a hold of a Stratocaster I really liked. However, I was having some problems with the intonation – it was driving me crazy."

He continued to describe a fortuitous acquisition in 1973. "I went down to this music store in Austin, Texas, called Ray Henning's, and in the window was this '59 Strat. It was already beat up. Soon as I saw the guitar I went: wait a minute – this is it. I walked in there with this black Stratocaster I had, and I said will you trade me this guitar for that guitar over there? Guy said yeah. I said give it to me. And I traded right then. Didn't have a case or anything. Walked over, plugged it in, and it sounded just like I wanted it to, and I've had the same one ever since. I've gotten many others, but that's still my first wife."

Vaughan called Number One a '59 because of a date he remembered seeing on the pickups, but in fact it had a late '62 neck and a '63 body, which is probably how it left the factory. He had a few other Strats, but Number One was his primary choice. "There are certain things on a Stratocaster that I really haven't found other guitars to do," said Vaughan. "Just the way they react. Even with all the new-fangled add-ons, still it seems to me that a Stratocaster, pretty much stock, for me is the best thing."[102]

Adrian Belew was known for deploying modified Stratocasters and Fender Mustangs to devastating effect with King Crimson, especially on the densely textured *Discipline* album of 1981, and on his own records, such as *Twang Bar King* (1983). Belew was a dab hand at

■ Fender's new Elite series was a shortlived attempt to make high-end versions of the old faithfuls. This **1983 Elite Stratocaster** (below) is finished in Blue Stratoburst. Closing in on the Elite Strat (bottom), the **1983 catalogue** highlighted the most criticised features: the poor Freeflyte vibrato bridge and the replacement of the pickup switch with three pushbuttons.

the stratocaster guitar book

■ **Stevie Ray Vaughan** used a number of Strats in his sadly shortlived career, including **Lenny** (main guitar), which he acquired in 1980 and named for his wife Lenora. Earlier, he'd bought Number One, with which he's pictured (below),

and that guitar remained a firm favourite until his untimely death in a helicopter accident in 1990. Stevie Ray's Double Trouble album was included among the collage of records by Fender players featured on this **1988 catalogue** cover (right).

conjuring noise and feedback, and also worked with Talking Heads, David Bowie, and others. "Feedback just seems so natural coming out of a Strat," he explained. "I can almost feel the wood of the guitar vibrate in sympathy to the note."[103]

At the big Live Aid event in 1985 there was much conspicuous Strat strumming on view to the millions watching around the world, not least by Eric Clapton, who performed on the Philadelphia stage, and Edge with U2, on the Wembley stage. Meanwhile, Bonnie Raitt had been known to blues fans for years, but the success of her *Nick Of Time* album in 1989 thrust her into the mainstream and showed many just what a fine guitarist she was, especially when she turned to her favourite '65 Strat, Old Brown. "There would be no rock'n'roll or rhythm & blues without Leo Fender's contribution," said Raitt. "The tone is everything."[104] Jonathan Richman even managed to write a song about the instrument, 'Fender Stratocaster', which appeared on his self-titled 1989 album. "It sounds so thin that it's barely there," he sang, "like a bitchy girl who just don't care."

For a variety of reasons, CBS decided during 1984 to sell Fender Musical Instruments. A newspaper report in January 1985 detailed the reasons. Essentially, CBS blamed Japanese competition for Fender's recent losses. "The Fullerton-based firm's last domestic guitar manufacturing unit, which employs 60 senior craftsmen who build top-of-the-line instruments for professional musicians, is scheduled to be shut down February 1," added the reporter.

"Company officials say tentative plans call for the continued manufacture of electric pianos until the end of February at the plant in this Orange County community 25 miles southeast of Los Angeles. The future of the company's famed product lines – the guitars pioneered by Leo Fender, pianos by Harold Rhodes, Rogers drums, and Squier guitar strings – will depend on Fender's new owner, who must decide which ones to continue and which, if any, will be made in the United States."

The report went on to explain that the Fender name and business were offered for sale separately from the manufacturing plant, which covered more than 250,000 square feet. "There are a lot of broken hearts around Fullerton," said former CBS Musical Instruments Division president John McLaren. The newspaper pointed out that McLaren and Bill Schultz and their team tried to turn the company around between 1981 and 1983. McLaren had left Fender in 1984. One estimate put sales of Fender guitars down 50 percent in the last three years. "CBS does not report financial statistics for its division separately," said the report, "but attributed an $8.3 million Columbia Group operating loss for the third quarter of 1984 in part to 'continued losses in the musical instruments business'."

The newspaper report speculated that the problems the US guitar industry faced were not due solely to the impact of the Japanese companies. It suggested that the baby-boom generation was past the prime instrument-buying age and, in a phrase still familiar to us today, that "today's young people seem to be more interested in video games and computers than guitars". The report also reckoned that some fault lay with the corporate giants who had begun snapping up the best instrument manufacturers during the 60s but were still "ill-suited to running businesses in which success depended so much on craftsmanship and personal service".[105]

CBS invited offers for Fender, and by the end of January 1985, almost exactly 20 years since it had acquired it, CBS confirmed that it would sell Fender to "an investor group led by William Schultz, president of Fender Musical Instruments". The contract was formalised in February and the sale completed in March for $12.5 million. This figure compared conspicuously with the $13 million that CBS originally paid for the company back in 1965.

With the hectic months of negotiations behind them, Schultz and his team could now get down to the equally tricky business of actually running Fender. The problems they faced were legion, but probably the most pressing was the fact that the Fullerton buildings were not included in the deal. So US production of Fenders stopped in February 1985 – although the new team had been stockpiling bodies and necks and had acquired some existing inventory of completed guitars as well as production machinery. The company went from employing over 800 people in early 1984 down to about 100 by early 1985.

George Blanda was a new arrival at Fender that year, and he later recalled the scene. "I don't think people realise what a little mom and pop business it was then. I'd seen the CBS gigantic building, 800 or so people. I was employee number 76. They envisioned they were going to be a distribution company of import instruments – which they were doing well with. They were going to have US production of just the vintage models, at a very small rate, like the Custom Shop does now."[106]

"Scary but exciting" is how Dan Smith described it at the time. "We're not going to be in the position to be able to make any mistakes," he said. "There'll be nobody behind us with a big cheque-book if we have a bad month."[107] Administration headquarters were established in Brea, California, not far from Fullerton. Six years later, Fender moved admin from Brea to Scottsdale, Arizona, where it remains today. A new factory had to be found, and Fender searched for a site in the Orange County area.

The Japanese operation became Fender's lifeline, providing much-needed product to a company that had no US factory. All the guitars in Fender's 1985 catalogue were made in Japan, including the new Contemporary Stratocasters and Teles, the first Fenders with the increasingly fashionable heavy-duty vibrato units and string-clamps.

Production in Japan was based on a handshake agreement that Fujigen would continue to supply Fender with guitars after CBS left the picture. One estimate put as much as 80 percent of the guitars that Fender USA sold from around the end of 1984 to the middle of 1986 as made in Japan.

Meanwhile, the dollar had started to weaken against other currencies, and Fender had trouble competing on price. So the firm looked to one of its offshore acoustic-guitar manufacturers, the Young Chang Akki Co of Seoul, South Korea, to make electric guitars. Smith remembered that Fender's first Korean guitars were pretty good: these were the Squier Standard Strats and Teles that began to appear in 1985 and lasted around three years. Fender would continue using Korea as a source for electrics until 2010, at which time it was making Squier-brand and Starcaster-brand electrics in China, India, and Indonesia and occasionally some Fender-brand electrics in Indonesia.

Back in the United States, Fender finally established its new factory at Corona, about 20 miles east of the defunct Fullerton site. Production started on a limited scale toward the end of 1985, building only about five guitars per day for the Vintage reissue series. But Smith and his colleagues wanted to re-establish the US side of Fender's production with a good, basic Stratocaster (and, of course, a Tele, P-Bass, and Jazz Bass). The attraction was that these guitars would involve very little new costs, and they would, the company hoped, be seen as a continuation of the very best of Fender's long-standing American traditions. The plan translated into the American Standard models.

The team had learned from recent mistakes, such as the Elite vibrato, and knew that the focus had to be on simplicity. The first result of their efforts appeared in 1986, the $589.99 American Standard Stratocaster. It was an efficacious piece of re-interpretation. Smith said they had in effect started the idea rolling with the first Standard models at the start of the 80s. "We wanted to make a good-quality standard instrument that better addressed modern playing styles, and at a reasonable price, so George Blanda and I began work on the American Standard Strat and its bridge design."[108] The American Standard drew from the best of the original Stratocaster, but was updated with a 22-fret neck, which had a slightly flatter fingerboard, and a revised vibrato unit.

The vibrato had twin knife-edge pivot points, which Fender claimed would provide increased stability, it had a smoother action, and much less opportunity for friction, the number-one enemy of vibrato bridges. The flat saddles, cast in stainless-steel, offered the most obvious visual clue to the presence of the new vibrato, while other technical changes allowed greater arm travel. "We needed something that was less expensive to make than the vintage-style with the bent saddles," said Blanda. "But also, at that time, almost every guitar selling had some kind of locking tremolo. The whole Floyd Rose thing was happening. Everybody wanted to do those extreme tremolo dives. So we modified the basic Stratocaster bridge so that it could do that. It did stay in tune pretty well, properly set up, more than a stock Strat, but of course it wasn't as good as a locking. But it did have more of the Strat tonality than any of the locking bridges."[109]

A new set of six colour options – Arctic White, Black, Brown Sunburst, Gun Metal Blue, Pewter, and Torino Red – was immediately available for the American Standard Strat, with changes and additions following. Once the Corona plant's production lines reached full speed, the American Standard proved to be a successful model for the revitalised Fender company. There was an early irony, as Blanda recalled. "It won Most Innovative Guitar Product at the *Music & Sound Retailer* Awards during the 1987 NAMM show … but it was anything but innovative! It was almost retro. However, it did make us realise that the industry was kind of rooting for Fender to build something in the US."[110] By the early 90s, the guitar had become a bestseller, notching up around 25,000 sales annually. In many markets today, including the United States, the various American Standard models continue to feature among the bestselling US-made Fender models.

In the mid 80s, Fender officially established a Custom Shop at the Corona plant. It began so that the company could build one-offs and special orders for players who had the money and the inclination. "We were only going to make ten Vintage pieces a day," said Dan Smith, "so we were going to start a Custom Shop to build special projects for artists, to make certain that the prestige was still there for the company."[111] That role remains – customers over the years have included everyone from Bob Dylan and Pops Staples to David Bowie and John Mayer – but today the Shop plays a much wider and more visible part in Fender's expanding business.

When guitar builder George Blanda joined Fender in 1985, he was recruited to make artist guitars, but a year later, as shifting exchange rates began to favour exports, demand for US-made product increased dramatically. Fender needed an R&D specialist to come up with new models, and the job fell to Blanda. He had the perfect combination for the post: an engineering capability, and a love of guitars. Blanda's move left the Custom Shop position vacant.

Fender discussed the idea with guitar makers Michael Stevens and John Carruthers, and also with former Fender R&D man John Page, who had left the company a year earlier to concentrate on his music. The result was that Stevens and Page joined Fender to start the Custom Shop in January 1987. The very first guitar the Shop completed was a Lake Placid Blue Stratocaster for the Ohio store chain Buddy Roger's Music. It was ordered in mid April and completed by John Page on June 8 1987.

Also among the earliest instruments made by the Shop were two prototypes of a new Strat Plus model, for display at that summer's NAMM show, one in Graffiti Yellow and the other in Surf Green. Jeff Beck had for now vetoed Fender's wish to produce a Beck signature edition Stratocaster, and the design intended for that purpose evolved into the Strat Plus. (A Jeff Beck signature Strat not dissimilar to the Plus finally appeared in 1991.)

Dan Smith said that the Strat Plus, introduced in 1987 and lasting a little over ten years in the line, followed on logically from the new company's important early developments: the vintage-style Fenders, the US-made American Standard models, and the establishment of Fender Japan. "The Strat Plus was a real modern guitar that addressed a lot of needs that modern players had but retained the integrity of the Stratocaster. That applied to the whole Plus series."[112]

The Strat Plus marked a willingness on Fender's part to work with outside designers: it had a roller nut by Trev Wilkinson and locking tuners by Bob Sperzel, fashionable features at the time that were designed to improve vibrato performance. It was also the first Fender with Lace Sensor pickups. Don Lace, an expert in magnetics, had tried to interest Fender in his designs before the CBS sale, and discussions reopened afterwards. Fender wanted to continue in the direction started with the Elite pickups, aiming for an ideal of low noise and low magnetic attraction while still delivering the classic single-coil sound.

The result was Lace Sensor pickups. While not to every player's taste, they proved to be a viable alternative to Fender's standard pickup designs, and were offered on various models following the debut on the Strat Plus. More pickups of various kinds have been offered since on some Fender models, either supplied by the better-known pickup brands or coming from the company's in-house designers and its own production lines.

The expansion of the Custom Shop's business prompted a move in 1993 to new buildings – still close to the Corona factory – providing extra space and improved efficiency. When Fender's new plant was unveiled five years later, the Custom Shop was at last shifted into the factory. At the start of the 90s, the Shop was building about 2,500 guitars a year, and by the middle of the decade that figure would rise to some 7,000 instruments annually. Fender will not discuss current numbers, but it's safe to assume they have not gone down.

The first signature guitar produced by Fender was the Eric Clapton Stratocaster. Signature models have become important to the firm in the years since, but at first this was another bonus brought about by the new Custom Shop, which was actively seeking pro players and pushing its services for building one-off instruments tailored to their individual requirements.

Clapton had discovered that his faithful old bitser Strat, Blackie, was coming to the end of its useful life, and he began talking to Fender about a modern replacement. "The big thing was the neck shape that Clapton wanted," George Blanda recalled. "Dan Smith and I made about a dozen neck samples for him to play. He ended up liking two and couldn't quite decide between them: one was like a pre-war Martin he had, with a very deep V shape; the other was a kind of soft 'rounded V' like Blackie, whose neck had become pretty thin through so many refrets."[113]

Fender had given Clapton an Elite Strat a few years before and he liked the sound of its active circuit. He wanted something similar, but with more boost, which he called compression. With all this in mind, Blanda and Smith delivered prototypes to Clapton in April 1986 while he was recording the *August* album at Sunset Sound in Los Angeles.

"Then he was on the road for some time, over a year, and we didn't hear much back," said Blanda. "At some point, he had a problem with the prototype he had been playing most, the one with the neck like the Martin with the deep V, and he sent it back to us to be fixed. We had done all our drawings and tooling and were ready to make this deep-V guitar, but then he started playing the other one, the one like Blackie – and he said yes, I like this guitar a lot better. So ... we ended up changing back to that for the signature model. It was a very long process, because he was on the road so much – his career was having a renaissance."[114]

The final design eventually went on sale to the public in 1988 as the Eric Clapton Stratocaster. Fender demonstrated to Clapton that Lace Sensor pickups and a midrange-boosting active circuit could deliver the 'compressed' sound he described as his aim. The production model even offered a blocked-off vintage-style vibrato unit, carefully duplicating that feature of Clapton's favoured set-up. He never used vibrato, but disliked the sound of hardtail (non-vibrato) Strats. Clapton retired Blackie around this time and soon began playing his new signature models.

Fender also released in 1988 a second signature model, the Yngwie Malmsteen Stratocaster. The most unusual aspect of the Swedish metal guitarist's instrument was its scalloped fingerboard. Malmsteen claimed that the absence of physical contact with the fingerboard enabled him to play even faster than his already lightning technique allows. A number of Fender signature models have followed – some made in the Custom Shop, others from Corona or further afield – and each one is endowed with features favoured by the named artist.

At various times, in addition to the Clapton and Malmsteen models, there have been signature Stratocasters named for Jeff Beck, Ritchie Blackmore, Billy Corgan, Robert Cray, Dick Dale, Tom Delonge, Jerry Donahue, Rory Gallagher, David Gilmour, Buddy Guy, Matthias Jabs, Eric Johnson, John Jorgensen, Mark Knopfler, Hank Marvin, John Mayer, Dave Murray, Bonnie Raitt, Chris Rea, Jim Root, Richie Sambora, Kenny Wayne Shepherd, Robin Trower, Jimmie Vaughan, and Stevie Ray Vaughan.

A new Fender factory was established in Ensenada, Mexico, in 1987, 180 miles south of Los Angeles, just across the California/Mexico border. (Non-American readers may be confused by references to Fender's 'Baja California' factory. This is the Mexican plant: Ensenada is in an area of Mexico sometimes known as Baja California.) The first Mexican Fender guitars began to appear in 1991, including the Standard Stratocaster as well as an equivalent Tele, P-Bass, and Jazz Bass. By early 1992, the Mexican factory was assembling around 175 Fender Standard Stratocasters each day, and by 1995 it had a daily capacity to produce 600 instruments.

Fender's 1988 pricelist included a case with everything and showed 12 Stratocasters: two signature models (Clapton and Malmsteen, each at $1,299), two $999.99 Vintage models (the '57 and '62), the US Strat Plus ($849.99), the American Standard ($649.99), Japan-made Paisley ($579.99), Blue Flower ($579.99), and '68 models ($509.99), the HM Strat (in three varieties, $589.99–$669.99), the Standard ($619.99), and the Strat XII ($719.99). The Strat XII was only the second solidbody electric 12-string produced by Fender, updating the Electric XII of the 60s into a modern Strat-style guitar.

The company was still faced with the 'un-Fender Fender' problem: it hardly ever succeeded with products that were not derived from the classic designs – and for guitars that meant primarily the Stratocaster and the Telecaster. Perhaps the answer was to use a completely different brandname for 'un-Fender' projects. Squier had become closely associated with Fender, so in 1989 the company concocted the Heartfield brand for a line of guitars considered too radical to be Fenders. These decidedly un-Strat and un-Tele designs were devised by Fender USA and Fender Japan and built at Fujigen in Japan. Some did have "Heartfield by Fender" logos, in a similar way to Squier, but the experiment was halted by 1993.

■ Diverse Stratmen: **Edge** from U2 (top left), in New York in 1992, and **Jimmie Vaughan** (top) in a **1997 ad** for the Tex-Mex Strat, a forerunner of his signature model. The **1990 ad** (above) from Japan promotes Fender's new Custom Shop.

the stratocaster guitar book

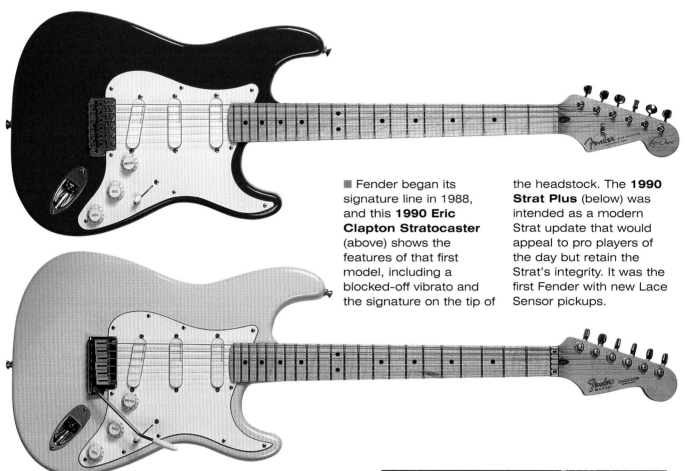

■ Fender began its signature line in 1988, and this **1990 Eric Clapton Stratocaster** (above) shows the features of that first model, including a blocked-off vibrato and the signature on the tip of the headstock. The **1990 Strat Plus** (below) was intended as a modern Strat update that would appeal to pro players of the day but retain the Strat's integrity. It was the first Fender with new Lace Sensor pickups.

■ Under new ownership in 1985, Fender swept away poor changes made to the Strat in the CBS years, re-establishing simplicity and playability. One result was the American Standard. This **1991 American Standard Stratocaster** (main guitar, below) is an example, finished in Frost Red. Meanwhile, Fender opened a new factory in Mexico in 1987, and its Standard Stratocaster appeared four years later, as in this **1995 catalogue** shot of a left-hander (right).

There was no shortage of good new Stratocaster players during the 90s – from Mike McCready of Pearl Jam and Billy Corgan of Smashing Pumpkins to John Frusciante and Dave Navarro of Red Hot Chili Peppers. When Frusciante left the Chili Peppers early in the decade, Dave Navarro eventually replaced him, and one of Navarro's first big performances with the band was at the Woodstock 94 festival. At the end of their set, each member came back on dressed more or less as Jimi Hendrix had at the original Woodstock, 25 years earlier: in blue jeans, white fringed top, and red headband. Navarro's Strat certainly suited the occasion, but it was still a bizarre if touching tribute to one of their heroes. Frusciante rejoined the band in time for their fine return to form on the 1999 album *Californication*.

There was an unmistakable whiff of Woodstock in the air. At Sotheby's auction house in London, England, in April 1990, a 1968 Fender Stratocaster was up for sale as the one that Jimi Hendrix played at the original Woodstock festival. The room was buzzing with excitement as lot 490 came around, which Sotheby's said "has belonged to [ex-Hendrix drummer] Mitch Mitchell since ... September 1970 and is now estimated to sell for £60,000–70,000".[115] The bidding began at £48,000 and then soared off to finish at £180,000, selling to one of two anonymous phone bidders. With the buyer's premium, that brought the price-tag to £198,000 (about $325,000 at the time).

It was by far the most money anyone had ever paid for an electric guitar, and later Paul Allen, the Microsoft co-founder, bought the instrument for his Experience Music Project museum in Seattle. The Hendrix guitar would not be upstaged until another Strat, Eric Clapton's Brownie, went for $497,500 (plus premium) some nine years later, also to Allen, and then a further six year after that, when Clapton's Blackie Stratocaster sold to Guitar Center for a staggering $959,500 (plus premium).

There were guitarists' guitarists about with Stratocasters in the 90s, too, notably Eric Johnson with his enviable tones all over the *Ah Via Musicom* album of 1990, while Eric Clapton played for a record-breaking 24 nights at London's Albert Hall the following year, Custom Shop replica of Blackie in tow and with some great Strat-wielding guests to hand, including Buddy Guy, Jimmie Vaughan, and Robert Cray.

Around the turn of the decade and into the 90s, it was grunge that emerged as a defining style for some guitarists, and for many fans it characterised this era of guitar playing. As with punk before, it was never quite that simple. Talented players made their own marks within and around the fashionable label. And also as with punk, the attraction of relatively cheap instruments – and of being seen *not* to play the old-school favourites like Strats and Teles – meant that Fender's apparent also-rans, models such as Jaguars, Jazzmasters, and Mustangs, made a good showing among some of the would-be fretmen of the time.

Leo Fender, who would probably have shuddered at the thought of his guitars as punk tools, was one of 12 music legends inducted into the Rock & Roll Hall Of Fame in January 1992, alongside Hendrix and others. Leo's second wife Phyllis was there for Leo, who had died the previous year. "When I accepted his award, I said that Leo truly believed that musicians were special angels, special envoys from the Lord," Mrs Fender told me later. "He believed he was put here to make the very best instruments in the world, because these special angels would help us get through this life, would ease our pain and ease our sadness, and help us celebrate."[116] Keith Richards also spoke on behalf of Leo, rather more prosaically. "He gave us the weapons," Richards told the Hall Of Fame gathering, leaving them with what he called the guitar players' prayer: "Caress it. Don't squeeze it."[117]

Richards was well aware how useful Fender's historical achievements could be to a musician. A common request at the time from some artists was for the Custom Shop to make a replica of a favourite old guitar, usually because the original was too valuable – financially and emotionally – to risk taking out on the road. The story goes, according to a Fender insider, that Richards thought some replicas the Shop made him for a Stones tour looked too new. "Bash 'em up a bit and I'll play 'em," he said. So the Shop began to include wear-and-tear distress marks to replicate the overall look of a battered old original. It was not a new idea, but certainly an effective one.

J.W. Black, a builder at the Custom Shop who had been working with the Stones, showed John Page an aged Fender that a friend, Vince Cunetto, had made. Black came up with the idea of offering aged replicas as regular Custom Shop catalogued items, called Relics. John Page admitted that it started out as "almost a tongue-in-cheek thing". He explained: "It was like worn-in Levis, or something. It would look cool – and in the first three rows it would look like you're playing a valuable Nocaster. But only you know that it's not really. That was how it started."

Black and Cunetto made two aged 50s-era samples: a 'Mary Kaye' Stratocaster (Blond body, gold-plated parts) and a Nocaster (nickname for the transitional Broadcaster/Telecaster). "We took them to the January 1995 NAMM trade show," recalled Page, "and put them under glass cases like they were pieces of art. Everyone came along and would say oh, that's really cool, you brought original ones as a tribute. And we were saying, er, yeah ... how many do you want? People went nuts! It was amazing."[118]

Soon the Custom Shop was reacting to the demand, offering a set line of three Relic Strats and a Relic Nocaster. At first, Cunetto worked off-site, at his workshop in Missouri, ageing the bodies, necks, and parts that Fender sent him, starting in summer 1995. Four years later, the work was all handled within the Custom Shop. The line was expanded in 1998, when Fender established three strands of these 're-creations' in what is now known as the Time Machine series. The original Relic style had 'aged' knocks and the look of heavy wear, as if the guitar had been out on the road for a generation or so; the Closet Classic was made to look as if it had been bought new way back when, played a few times, and then stuck in a closet; and N.O.S. (for 'New Old Stock') was like an instrument that had been bought brand new in the 50s or 60s and then put straight into a time machine that transported it to the present day. The kind of thing, in other words, that vintage guitar collectors and dealers regularly fantasise about but which rarely happens in real life.

■ **Billy Corgan** (right), pictured here at Lollapalooza in 1994, led Smashing Pumpkins to great success in the 90s, often with a Strat in tow. Back at Fender HQ, a new scheme was the Relic guitar, as featured in this **1996 catalogue** (below). The idea, which proved a surprise hit, was to 'age' new guitars so that they would look something like roadworn oldies.

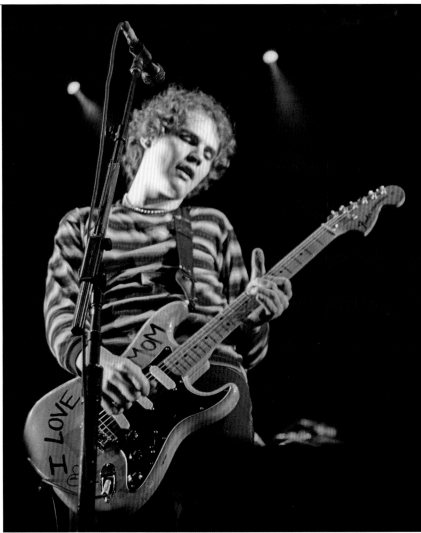

the stratocaster guitar book

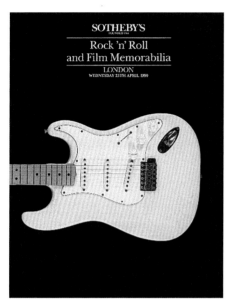

■ The **1990 catalogue** from Sotheby's (top left) shows the Strat played by Jimi Hendrix at Woodstock in 1969. It sold for £198,000, a record at the time. Squier (**1997 ad**, top right) continued to provide Fender's successful second-string budget line. Fender Japan had a new 12-string: this **1990 Strat XII** (above) is quite unlike Fender's Electric XII of the 60s. The Custom Shop continued to build fine vintage re-creations like this **1996 '60 Stratocaster** (right) in Shell Pink.

■ This **1997 Relic 50s Stratocaster** (main guitar) is an early example of the aged models that Fender's Custom Shop launched in 1995. This one, with its gold-plated hardware and blond finish, is known as the Mary Kaye style.

the stratocaster guitar book

By 2010, the Custom Shop's Time Machine series would include '59, '63, and '65 Stratocasters, and the ageing was limited to two of the original levels, Relic and N.O.S., although the '59 was offered only in a new Heavy Relic style, which Fender said shows the "wear and tear of years of heavy use". All of these models listed in 2010 at around the $3,500 mark. This may seem a high price, but when you compare what you might have to pay now for genuine originals – maybe tens of thousands of dollars for those earlier years – then the attraction becomes clearer.

Even if you could find originals, there's always the worry among collectors with a vintage piece about the veracity of this paint finish or that pickguard screw or those solder joints. The Time Machines at least take away any niggling doubts about originality. These Custom Shop specials appeal to guitar fans keen to acquire a new Fender with the feel and sound of an oldie – and in the case of the Relics they are made to look as if decades of wear-and-tear have stained the fingerboard, scuffed the body, and tarnished the hardware. The Time Machine series was a clever move, the nearest Fender had come with new instruments to the almost indefinable cool of vintage guitars. It was something that many thought was firmly and safely locked away in the past.

Floyd Rose, a guitar hardware designer known for his heavy-duty locking vibrato system, joined forces with Fender toward the end of 1991. Fender acquired the exclusive rights to Floyd Rose products bearing his name. Other makers could still buy licensed hardware, but Fender seemed to be more interested in gaining access to Rose's design skills as well as the assistance that his name brought to sell guitars to metal players.

To metal-heads and others interested in extreme wang-bar activity, 'Floyd Rose' was almost synonymous with the heavy-duty double-locking vibrato systems associated with a fast, intense, and highly-technical style of playing that peaked in popularity during the early 90s. By the middle of the decade, the locking vibrato had lost fashionable ground, and instead there was a marked return to simplicity amid moves to earlier retro designs and modern interpretations – all of which could hardly have been hindered by Fender's own emphasis on vintage-style vibratos. Fender's deal with Floyd Rose came to an amicable end in 2001, although Rose-licensed vibratos do appear occasionally on some Fender models at the time of writing.

Aside from a couple of shortlived models launched back in 1984 – the Esprit and the Flame – Fender had not strayed much from its customary bolt-on-neck construction. However, a new Set Neck Stratocaster in 1992 offered a glued joint, enabling a fashionable smooth heel-less junction where neck meets body, in the style traditionally used by Gibson and other makers. Some players find this more comfortable and usefully playable. "We always try to have something in our line to interest someone who likes Gibson," said Dan Smith.[119]

Following the success of the Vintage reissue series, introduced in the early 80s, Fender Japan began to issue more models that re-created real or imagined guitars from Fender's past, including a Paisley and Blue Flower Strat and a '68 Strat. In 1992, Fender USA came up with the series name Collectables to cover a selection of these Japanese instruments sold in the US, including various vintage-style Strats and Teles. In more recent years, the series names have changed again, and at the time of writing reissues were organised into the Classic and Road Worn series from Mexico, the American Vintage guitars from the US Corona factory, and the Time Machine models from the Custom Shop.

Fender's US-made 'hot' Texas Special Strat-type single-coils first appeared on 1992's new Stevie Ray Vaughan signature Strat. The model had been agreed before Vaughan's tragic death in 1990 in a helicopter accident, when the guitarist's career was at a peak. The signature model was based on Vaughan's well-used Stratocaster, known as Number One, and duplicated the original instrument's substantial SRV logo on the pickguard. It featured an unusual left-handed vibrato system, as favoured by right-handed Vaughan, a result of his strong stylistic link with left-hander Jimi Hendrix. The idea was that a left-handed vibrato would provide a right-handed player with similar tonal peculiarities that a right-handed vibrato would give to a left-hander.

The Custom Shop's 'catalogue' items expanded with the introduction of the American Classic Stratocaster in 1992, effectively an upscale Shop version of the factory's best-selling American Standard Strat. Further from home, Korea was a new production source for Fender-brand instruments, providing 1992's Squier Series Standard Strat and Tele models, each of which had a regular Fender logo plus small 'Squier Series' on the headstock.

The idea of the signature guitar seems to have taken quite a hold at Fender in the 90s following the first models for Eric Clapton and Yngwie Malmsteen in the late 80s. There were signature Strats for Jeff Beck (1991), Robert Cray and Stevie Ray Vaughan (1992), Richie Sambora (1993), Dick Dale (1994), Bonnie Raitt and Buddy Guy (1995), Hank Marvin (1996), Jimmie Vaughan and Ritchie Blackmore (1997), Matthias Jabs (1998), and Chris Rea (1999). Sambora's Strat had a Floyd Rose double-locking vibrato, a DiMarzio bridge humbucker plus Texas Special single-coils, and a flatter, wider fingerboard. A personal touch from the fiery Bon Jovi guitarist was the series of stars he had inlaid into the fingerboard instead of regular position markers. Dick Dale's Strat re-created the surf king's personal guitar, which he affectionately referred to as The Beast.

A related series began in 1995 with the Freddie Tavares Stratocaster, Fender's first limited edition model designed to honour one of the men who helped establish the original company back in the 50s. Further Custom Shop Strats named for George Fullerton and Bill Carson followed in later years.

In 1994, the Corona factory rather than the Custom Shop produced the 40th Anniversary 1954 Stratocaster, a numbered limited edition. There was also a 40-only run of a Custom Shop Concert Edition. Appropriately, exactly 1,954 of the factory 40th Strat were made, and the regular American Standard Stratocaster gained a small 40th Anniversary headstock medallion to mark this special year. Still in a historical mood, Fender marked its 50th anniversary in 1996. As you may recall from many pages back, in 1946 Leo Fender parted company with his original partner, Doc Kauffman. Leo dissolved

■ During the 90s, Fender settled into three main strands for the Strat lines: modern interpretations of the classics; signature models; and vintage-flavoured guitars. The **Strat Ultra** (**1990 ad**, below) was in the first category: it was developed from an Anniversary model and featured upscale appointments and four Lace Sensor pickups switchable in various combinations. Signature Strats abounded in the 90s, and one unmistakable model was that for Bon Jovi's guitarist **Richie Sambora** (**1996 catalogue**, below). The vintage reissue business was as busy as ever, underlined in this **1994 ad** (below) where guitarists were invited to travel through time.

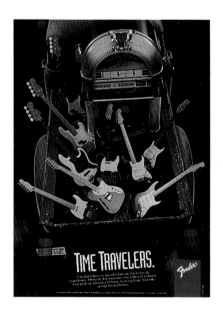

■ This **1992 Stevie Ray Vaughan Stratocaster** (main guitar) is a signature model based on the great Texan guitarist's best-known Fender, complete with that instrument's substantial SRV logo on the pickguard. The guitar was first issued in 1992 as a tribute to the lauded bluesman who had died tragically two years earlier. One of the most unusual features of the SRV signature Strat is the left-handed vibrato, as favoured by Vaughan, some of whose work revealed a stylistic link to that of the left-hander Jimi Hendrix.

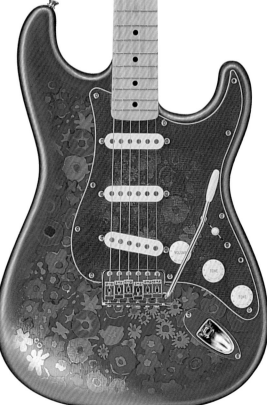

■ Fender Japan, established in 1982, continued to make guitars exclusively for the domestic Japanese market as well as for export to the US and elsewhere. Among the export models was this **1992 Blue Flower Stratocaster** (far right). Over at the US Custom Shop, the new **American Classic** series was featured in this **1999 ad** (right) from Japan, an important market for Custom Shop instruments. The Classics were upscale Custom Shop versions of the American Standard models.

FENDER CLASSIC SERIES

新しいフェンダー・クラシック・シリーズは、選び抜かれたトラディショナル・ヴィンテージ・モデルへのトリビュート。歴史が物語るオリジナルの特色を忠実に再現。

their K&F company, called his revised operation Fender Manufacturing, and then renamed it the Fender Electric Instrument Co in December 1947.

The modern company celebrated what it called "50 Years of Excellence" in 1996 with some factory-made limited-edition anniversary models – the apparently timeless quartet of Stratocaster, Telecaster, Precision Bass, and Jazz Bass – each with a special commemorative neckplate. Fender also attached a 50th Anniversary decal to many products sold that year. Also in 1996, the new Lone Star Strat was an example of how Fender in recent years has taken core products and subtly (and not-so-subtly) modified them to create 'new' models based on players' changing tastes. With the Lone Star, Fender worked with an American Standard Strat as the base model, changing the pickup configuration to a Seymour Duncan Pearly Gates Plus humbucker at the bridge plus two of Fender's 'hot' Texas Special single-coils. (The Lone Star Strat was renamed as the American Fat Strat Texas Special in 2000 and prompted the Mexico-made Deluxe Lone Star Strat of 2008.)

In 1997, 30 years since Jimi Hendrix's career had blossomed with his debut album, Fender launched a couple of Hendrix-related US-made Strats, from the Custom Shop and the factory. Corona's contribution was the simply-named Jimi Hendrix Stratocaster, but the thinking behind the model was anything but simple. Fender had the go-ahead to make an official model in tribute to Hendrix, the best-known Strat player ever. But Jimi was a left-hander and, despite at least ten per cent of us sharing that trait, the majority of potential customers for such a guitar would want a right-handed machine.

Hendrix would take a regular right-handed Strat, turn it upside down, and re-string it – all to accommodate his left-handedness. So Fender decided to make a completely reversed version of one of Jimi's typical late-60s Strats. The result was a guitar that right-handed players needed to consider as a 'regular' left-handed guitar turned upside down and re-strung, recreating Jimi's experience in reverse, as it were. As if this was not befuddling enough, Fender added a final flourish. So that the adoring owner could pose to full effect with the new acquisition in front of the mirror, the headstock logo was applied completely in reverse. In the mirror, the owner was Jimi.

The Jimi Hendrix Stratocaster lasted in the line until 2000, although in 1998 Fender issued a more straightforward Jimi-for-right-handers, the Voodoo Stratocaster, which had a left-handed neck on a right-handed body with a reverse-angled bridge pickup. The similar '68 Reverse Strat Special followed in 2002.

The second Hendrix model of 1997 was more specific. The Custom Shop's Jimi Hendrix Monterey Strat re-created the hand-painted Strat that Jimi played briefly at the June 1967 Monterey Pop festival, the one that he famously burned on-stage. Careful examination of pictures taken at the show, pre-conflagration, enabled artist Pamelina Hovnatanian to reconstruct Hendrix's decorative flowers-and-hearts painting, with some embellishments of her own, for the limited edition of 210 guitars. "For almost 30 years, Jimi has been unofficially associated with Fender Stratocasters and has influenced countless thousands

the stratocaster guitar book

of guitar players," said Fender marketing man Jack Shelton in a press release. "I think nearly every electric guitar player thinks of Jimi whenever they see a white Strat. He's made a huge impact on our company and on the world. We're very honoured and excited to be able, after all these years, to officially recognise Jimi's contributions."

Away from the glare of big-name endorsers, dead or alive, Fender continued to try out different pickup configurations. In 1997, the new Big Apple was the first two-humbucker Strat – a pickup combination that in earlier decades would have been seen as the antithesis of Stratocaster, but which now provided players with a range of tones from single-coil scratch to humbucker raunch (the model was renamed the American Double Fat Strat in 2000). The Roadhouse Strat featured three Texas Special single-coils (it was renamed the American Strat Texas Special in 2000), and the California series added Tex Mex pickups to US Strats, Teles, and Precisions. The Stratacoustic was a new thinline Strat-shaped electro-acoustic with spruce top and fibreglass back and sides.

Fender's 1998 pricelist had 32 Stratocasters: Standard $399.99; Richie Sambora Standard $599.99; 50s $599.99; 60s $599.99; Deluxe Powerhouse Strat $649.99; Jimmie Vaughan Tex-Mex $649.99; '68 $689.99; Deluxe Super Strat $699.99; Standard Roland-Ready $749.99; California Strat $799.99; California Fat Strat $849.99; American Standard $979.99; Mathias Jabs $1,099.99; Hellecasters Jerry Donahue $1,149.99; Roadhouse Strat $1,149.99; Lone Star Strat $1,199.99; Strat Plus $1,199.99; Big Apple Strat $1,249.99; Hellecasters John Jorgenson $1,299.99; Jimi Hendrix Voodoo $1,299.99; Floyd Rose Classic $1,379.99; Bonnie Raitt $1,499.99; Deluxe Strat Plus $1,499.99; Jimi Hendrix Tribute $1,499.99; '57 $1,499; '62 $1,499; Buddy Guy $1,599.99; Eric Clapton $1,599.99; Jeff Beck $1,599.99; Stevie Ray Vaughan $1,599.99; Yngwie Malmsteen $1,599.99; Strat Ultra $1,799.99; Richie Sambora $1,899.99.

A big event was the opening of a new factory in November 1998, still in Corona, California. The company proudly described the impressive state-of-the-art plant as the world's most expensive and automated guitar factory. Since starting production at the original Corona factory back in 1985, Fender had grown to occupy 115,000 square feet in ten buildings across the city. Such a rambling spread proved increasingly inefficient, and Fender began to plan a centralised factory during the early 90s. The new $20 million plant provided a potentially growing production capacity for the future. Some models were reorganised into new series in 1998, with new high-end US models grouped as American Deluxes and reissues brought together as American Vintages.

Simplicity and accessibility seemed the rationale behind the Tom Delonge Stratocaster, launched in 2001 to match the guitar that Delonge used regularly with his band blink-182. The Mexico-made production model duplicated his straightforward requirement of a single Seymour Duncan humbucker, a large 70s-style headstock, and just the one control knob – for volume, of course. Delonge explained that he didn't need more pickups or extra knobs, that he liked to keep his rig as simple as possible. Admirably, he just wanted to plug straight in and play.

■ Ever more aware of the value of its history, Fender devised this series of gorgeous **1998 ads** (above) with the simple but apposite tagline: "The Sounds That Create Legends." Four key Stratocaster players were featured in the series (left to right): **Jeff Beck** with his signature model; **Hendrix** with black Strat; **Stevie Ray Vaughan** with Number One; and **Eric Clapton** with his personal signature Strat.

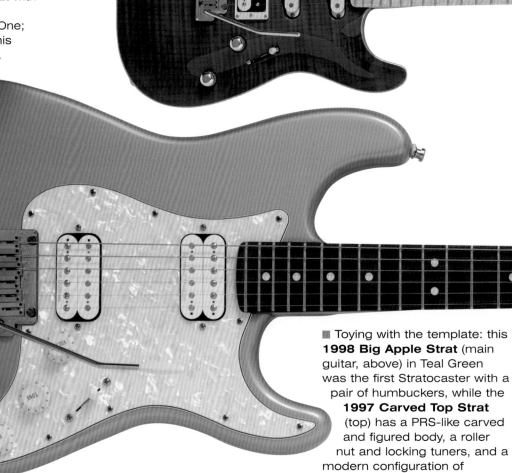

■ Toying with the template: this **1998 Big Apple Strat** (main guitar, above) in Teal Green was the first Stratocaster with a pair of humbuckers, while the **1997 Carved Top Strat** (top) has a PRS-like carved and figured body, a roller nut and locking tuners, and a modern configuration of pickups and controls.

the stratocaster guitar book

■ Fender celebrated 50 years since Leo founded his original firm with this **1996 ad** (top). The **1997 Monterey Stratocaster** (bottom) was based on the Strat that Jimi Hendrix burned at the 1967 pop festival, while a Hendrix signature model (**1997 ad**, below right) also appeared. **Tom Delonge** (right) of blink-182 used a simple custom Strat with one pickup and one knob.

the stratocaster guitar book

Up at the legendary end of Fender's signature series, two Strats had a change of pickups in 2001, which, said Fender, reflected alterations made by the artists themselves to their own guitars. The Eric Clapton model gained Vintage Noiseless pickups, while the Jeff Beck was fitted with Ceramic Noiseless units, in both cases replacing the existing Lace Sensors.

The Noiseless pickups were among Fender's recent developments in stacked-pickup design. They were by ex-EMG man Bill Turner, and were joined in 2010 by the new alnico N3 Noiseless pickups. More stacked types followed in 2004, the SCN (Samarium Cobalt Noiseless) pickups, designed with the help of pickup legend Bill Lawrence. Fender's Noiseless and SCN pickups both aim for the dream combination – vintage sound and low noise – but tackle the problems using different technical solutions. A new switching system, known as S-1, enhanced the new pickup capabilities. The S-1 is a simple push-pull option on the master volume knob of selected Strat models, but the results seem to be as complex as the player might want, adding a number of new pickup combinations.

The main signs of the 50th birthday of the Stratocaster in 2004 came with four special anniversary models and a celebratory concert. Fender's four 50th anniversary Strats were crowned by a no-detail-spared Custom Shop replica 1954 Stratocaster, listed as a Limited Release at an appropriate if lofty $5,400. "Every deep body contour, pickup magnet, and screw is a replica of a 1954 Strat," said Fender. Down a notch came two more birthday Strats, an American Series model and an American Deluxe 50th Anniversary, both with identifying neckplates and assorted modern features, while the Deluxe had suitable gold-plated hardware. Last, there was the Mexico-made 50th Anniversary Golden Stratocaster, which lived up to its name by featuring an Aztec Gold finish, gold-plated hardware, and a gold-anodised pickguard.

The Stratocaster's 50th birthday show at London's Wembley Arena was a curious affair. Two worthy guests were David Gilmour and Hank Marvin, but also on hand were a good number of other guitarists less well-known for their Strat associations. Some of the audience might have expected to see Eric Clapton or Jeff Beck but instead were offered Amy Winehouse, Paul Rodgers, Theresa Andersson, Jamie Cullum, and others. Phil Palmer did a fine job as musical director, and Gary Moore thrashed a long 'Red House' into eventful submission.

The most significant moment at Wembley came when Gilmour strode on with one of his best-known Stratocasters, the one that famously bears serial 0001. This instrument's neck date of June 1954 and body date of September 1954 mean that it certainly wasn't the first Strat ever made. However, putting the serial number aside, it is at the very least an interesting early Strat from the first year of production. Gilmour rose above the historical debate and had no trouble at all making his famous instrument sound wonderful. And there it was, at last, in this birthday concert: 50 years of the Stratocaster before your very eyes and ears.

Eric Clapton may not have been at the Wembley event, but that same year he did sell his most famous Stratocaster, Blackie, for a record-breaking sum, at auction. As we learned earlier, Clapton made Blackie in 1970 by putting together some bits and pieces from a number of 50s Strats. Guitar Center, the US music-store chain, bought Blackie at Christie's in New York City in 2004 for a record-breaking $959,000 (plus buyer's premium), benefiting Clapton's Crossroads charity.

A special entry in Fender's Tribute Series came two years later, in 2006, the Eric Clapton Blackie Stratocaster. Fender described its Tribute Series as an "elite program" designed to offer the ultimate artist instrument. Each one consists of a very limited run (usually 100) of an ultra-exact copy of a renowned artist's guitar. It's like an extreme version of the regular signature-model idea. Examples so far have included Rory Gallagher's battered Strat, Andy Summers's careworn Tele Custom, Mary Kaye's gleaming Blond-body/gold-hardware Strat, Jeff Beck's early-days Esquire, and Yngwie Malmsteen's bashed-up '71 Strat.

For the Clapton Tribute, Guitar Center allowed the Custom Shop access to the guitar so that Fender could nit-pickingly spec this historic Strat for an exacting replica. Just 275 were made, of which 185 were sold through Guitar Center and the rest through Fender's international channels. Guitar Center sold all theirs in one day, with 106 going in the first two minutes. The suggested retail price was a hefty $24,000 each, with a portion donated to the Crossroads Centre in Antigua and to a new facility in Delray Beach, Florida.

Fender Japan was reorganised early in 2005 when a new company, Dyna Boeki, was formed to produce Fender's Japanese instruments. Fender said that this was simply a tidying-up of the business arrangements and that nothing about the physical production of the guitars changed. At the same time, distribution was simplified: all Japan-made instruments were distributed in Japan by Kanda Shokai, while the rest of the Fender and Squier catalogue made in the USA and elsewhere was distributed by Yamano Music. Meanwhile, fewer Japan-made Fenders have been sold outside Japan in recent years, indicating that Fender is content to rely on its two main sources, the US and Mexico factories, to provide instruments for Western markets.

In the boardroom, Bill Schultz stepped down as Fender CEO in 2005, staying on as chairman of the board of directors, and Bill Mendello became CEO. Sadly, Schultz died in September 2006. Dan Smith waved goodbye to Fender that same year after 25 remarkable years with the company, his era including the crucial management buy-out from CBS in 1985 and the creative struggle through the years following. "Part of being able to retire," Smith said, "was that I knew we'd accomplished a lot. And the heart of the company is always the product. I could walk away proud, knowing Fender was so far ahead of where it had been, in terms of technology and training and people, and that it was going to continue and go way beyond that."[120] Mendello retired in 2010, replaced as CEO by Larry Thomas.

Today, one of the recurring aims at Fender is to make what everyone seems to want: a vintage-style instrument with features to suit the modern player. The first part will always remain more or less the same, but the second is ever-shifting, and it's the job of Fender's R&D department to track and react to those changes as accurately and efficiently as possible. "Every few years, in every era in music, it's like players will say we want the Strat

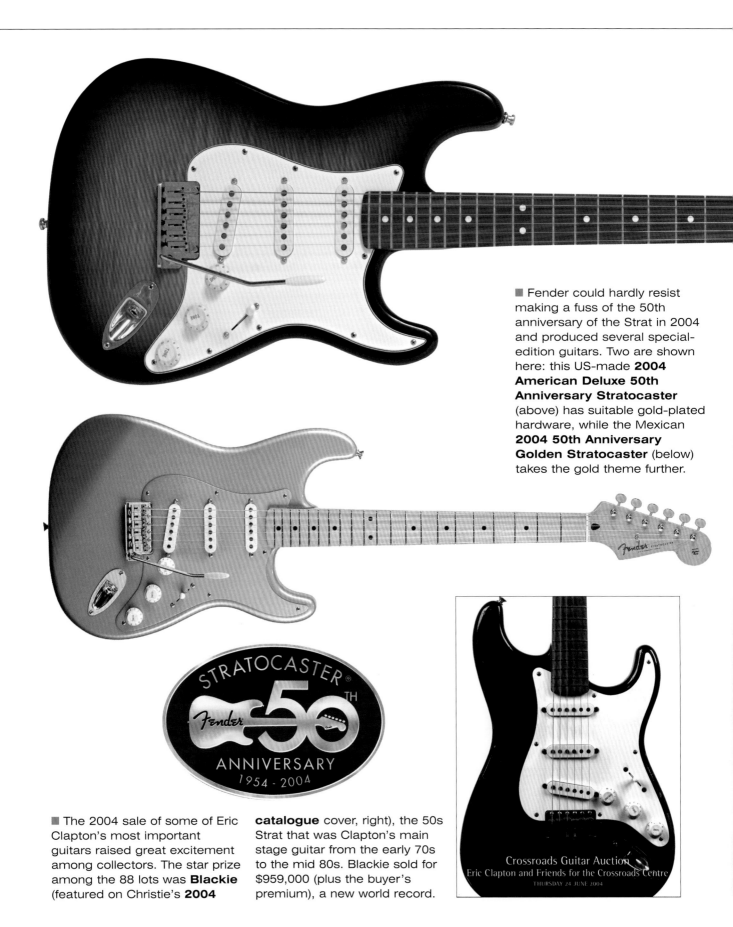

■ Fender could hardly resist making a fuss of the 50th anniversary of the Strat in 2004 and produced several special-edition guitars. Two are shown here: this US-made **2004 American Deluxe 50th Anniversary Stratocaster** (above) has suitable gold-plated hardware, while the Mexican **2004 50th Anniversary Golden Stratocaster** (below) takes the gold theme further.

■ The 2004 sale of some of Eric Clapton's most important guitars raised great excitement among collectors. The star prize among the 88 lots was **Blackie** (featured on Christie's **2004 catalogue** cover, right), the 50s Strat that was Clapton's main stage guitar from the early 70s to the mid 80s. Blackie sold for $959,000 (plus the buyer's premium), a new world record.

Crossroads Guitar Auction
Eric Clapton and Friends for the Crossroads Centre
THURSDAY 24 JUNE 2004

the stratocaster guitar book

■ Fender was keen to fly the flag on this **2000 catalogue** cover (right) as it revamped its US-made American Standard models. By now the company was making guitars at its US and Mexico factories, Fender Japan still made guitars there, and other sources included Korea, Indonesia, and elsewhere. From its first tentative steps in the 80s, Fender was now a truly international guitar maker.

■ **David Gilmour** (below) was a star guest at the special 50th anniversary concert for the Stratocaster at London's Wembley Arena. Suitably, he's playing his 1954 Strat with serial number 0001 (see page 35), which is also projected on to the screen behind him.

exactly like it was … except these one or two things," said George Blanda, Fender R&D's chief design engineer. "For a while it was the flatter fretboard; and then, no, we don't want that any more. Now we want the humbucker pickups, or the locking tremolo. It's almost like the demand arises for one kind of feature, because of music or style, and then it resets a little, and some of the other features go back to the original. The market kind of changes en masse – all of a sudden everyone wants whatever it is this year. I'm sure the Strat will continue to evolve back and forth like this, between some limits."[121]

In 2006, the Classic Player series built on the idea of adding fashionable modern twists to a vintage-flavoured core, combining Custom Shop know-how with Mexico production. The budget Squier brand's Vintage Modified series had similar intentions. A year later, it was the turn of the higher-end, with the new US-made Vintage Hot Rod guitars. These were based on US-made vintage reissues but offered thin-skin lacquer finishes, flatter fingerboards, bigger frets, modern pickups, and custom wiring. The series kicked off with a '57 and '62 Strat as well as a '52 Tele.

It's always difficult to put the most recent music into any kind of context, and reporting on the state of current Strat popularity is no exception – so for once we won't itemise our favourite players, because you'll doubtless have your own decent (and forever changing) list of top Strat people. Stratocasters today continue to attract guitarists at all levels. But the picture is less clear than in was in earlier years and decades, when it was easier to identify this or that player as a firm Strat fan, often to the exclusion of other models. It's much more common today for a guitarist to shift around from model to model and brand to brand. In part, that's because there are now so many viable alternatives. Simply, there are more good guitars to choose from today, and for some players it doesn't make a lot of sense to keep still for too long.

Modelling was a new technology applied to guitar-playing as musicians entered the 21st century. This now widespread idea is based on the provision of digital re-creations of classic guitar and amp sounds. California-based Line 6 was the innovator, and its Vetta amps and Pod boxes showed what could be done. Other amp makers followed and, naturally, they leaned heavily on the sounds of classic Fender models. Line 6 launched a modelling guitar, the Variax, in 2003, and among the sounds included onboard were, of course, Fender imitations.

It was inevitable that Fender itself would enter this brave new world, which it did first in 2001 with the Cyber Twin, Fender's particular take on the idea of multiple amp sounds. Meanwhile, ex-Steely Dan guitarist Jeff Baxter was working closely with Roland, the Japanese music technology pioneer. Around 2003, Baxter went to Ikutaro Kakehashi, founder and chairman of Roland, and suggested a Fender–Roland modelling guitar – which became the American VG Stratocaster, launched in 2007 with a list price of $2,429 (about $1,100 more than a regular American Stratocaster).

Two Fender–Roland Strats had appeared in the late 90s, the shortlived American Standard Roland GR-Ready model and its 1998 replacement, the Mexico-made Standard

Roland Ready Stratocaster. Both required an external synth of some sort in order to get new sounds, with Roland's VG-88 modelling module of 2000 a popular choice for this purpose. Unlike some competitors, Fender made everything happen inside the VG Strat. The only connection the guitarist needed was through the regular jack to a regular amp. No external synth or box: the modelling was done onboard. But the guitar could still play and sound exactly like a Strat, if you wanted, using the regular Strat magnetic pickups and controls. The bonus seemed clear: a fall-back to Strat sounds and playability if the player tired of the guitar's modelled sounds (or if the batteries ran out).

Two extra knobs controlled the new sounds, together with a small LED and a Roland GK bridge pickup. The Mode Control knob provided five sound settings: N for Normal (the regular Strat); S for modelled Stratocaster; T for modelled Telecaster; H for modelled Humbucking Pickups (which a player would call Les Paul mode); and A for modelled Acoustic. The five-way selector gave logical variations within each setting. Then there was the Tuning Control knob, which provided regular six-string tuning plus four alternative tunings and a simulated 12-string. Despite all this innovation – or perhaps because of it – the brave VG lasted only a couple of years in the catalogue following its launch in 2007, apparently another victim of the way players reject most ideas they see as too extreme from Fender.

With so many different models in the current catalogue, it can be daunting trying to navigate your way around the Fender lines. At the time of writing, Fender's pricelist had no fewer than 56 individual Fender-brand Stratocaster models plus 11 Squier-brand models. They ranged in list-price from a China-made Squier Bullet Strat at $199.99 ("the perfect choice for a first guitar") to the Custom Shop's David Gilmour Signature Stratocaster Relic for $4,800.

Fender defended the vast array in a recent catalogue. "So, why do we make so many models of Fender electric guitars? Because there are so many different styles of music, and even more individual artists playing them!" Fair point: but with all that choice – and usually with nothing more on the guitar than "Fender" and "Stratocaster" – it can sometimes be difficult to know for sure what you're looking at. For example, you might be buying a secondhand guitar, an area of the market where people have been known to blur the truth. It's time Fender began identifying the precise model name somewhere on the instrument itself. Leo would have dismissed such an idea as red tape – but then Leo only had one Stratocaster model to deal with, not 67.

By 2010, Fender organised its line of factory-made Stratocasters into 12 series: American Deluxe; American Vintage; American Special; American Standard; Artist; Classic; Classic Player; Deluxe; Highway One; Road Worn; Standard; and Vintage Hot Rod. Justin Norvell, director of marketing for Fender Electrics, described how they are divided. "The American Standard guitars are the modern interpretations of the Strat, but in more of a regular package. They have modern fingerboard radiuses and hardware, but with more of a traditional nod than the Deluxe."

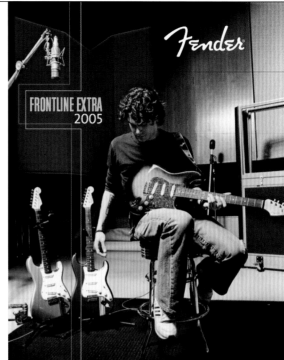

■ This **2005 Deluxe Players Strat** (main guitar) in Sapphire Blue was part of the Deluxe line, the Mexico factory's upscale series that goes beyond its regular Standard models. A new Classic Player series (**2006 ad**, top left) mixed the design know-how of the Shop's master builders with Mexican production. **John Mayer** (seen on the **2005 catalogue** cover, top right) is among the most talented of recent Strat players, and his new-for-2005 signature Stratocaster was a noteworthy catch for Fender.

the stratocaster guitar book

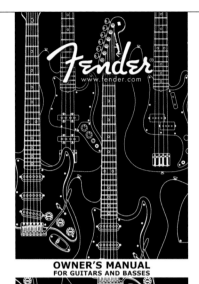

■ Fans of the traditional look of the Stratocaster must have been perplexed by the four controls of the American VG Strat (**2007 catalogue** cover, above right). The reason was that this was a modelling guitar, bringing digital re-creations of a variety of guitar tones and sounds thanks to onboard circuitry. Sadly, the brave experiment was not a success with players, and the VG was discontinued within two years. This **owner's manual** (top left) came with most new Fender guitars and basses from 2002 and offered a wide-ranging guide to features and usage.

■ The Custom Shop produces true one-offs alongside its other roles, including this odd Strat (above). It has an aluminium body that has coloured chambers with liquid inside that shifts around as the guitar is moved. The **2007 Vintage Hot Rod '57 Strat** (below) had an interesting mix of classic styling and new features: note the bridge 'blade' pickup.

The American Deluxe models first appeared in 1998, with two major upgrades since then. Norvell said they are intended as modern instruments for the contemporary player, featuring roller nuts (on some), S-1 switching (push-pull volume knob giving extra sound options), locking tuners, and flashier cosmetics. The series was last relaunched in 2010, with Fender's next-generation N3 Noiseless pickups, a compound fingerboard radius (nine-and-a-half inches at the nut to a flatter fourteen inches at the body), and new colours such as Tungsten and Sunset Metallic. "The new pickups have better noiseless properties and reintroduce the sweetness of alnico magnets for the best of both worlds," said Norvell. "We went through dozens of pickup sets and actually settled on a combination of different ones for the Strat, featuring an Alnico 3 in the neck, an Alnico 2 in the middle, and an Alnico 5 in the bridge."

American Vintage and Artist guitars are what you'd expect: US-made period-style and star-specific instruments. The American Special Strats were launched in 2010, and Norvell said these build on Fender's long-held position as a maker of the workingman's guitar. "They're a US-made guitar for those on a budget. They are striking, with 70s-era big headstocks and black pickguards on many of the models. Although built for value, they are hardly stripped down, and we offered several key upgrades like our popular Texas Special pickups and jumbo frets."

The Classic series, introduced in 1999, are Mexico-made vintage-style guitars, while the Classic Player models that first appeared in 2006 are, said Norvell, the Mexican Classic series upgraded and made over by specific Custom Shop Master Builders. "They allow for cool, unique instruments and Custom Shop mojo at an affordable price," he said.

Deluxe models are heavily upgraded versions of Mexico's basic Standard series, often with high-end electronics, including boost circuits and Noiseless pickups. They first began to appear on Fender pricelists in 1998, while the Highway One series was launched in 2002. "The Highway Ones have been made over into upgraded, hot-rodded instruments," said Norvell, "with new pickups, narrower string spacing, jumbo frets, and a thin satin nitro-cellulose lacquer. They're true road dogs, built for modern performance in a low profile package. Throw them in the back of the car night after night! The last place this guitar should live is in a glass case above the fireplace."

Norvell said the new-for-2009 Road Worn series acknowledged the desirability of Vintage and Custom Shop Relic instruments. "They're more affordable versions of classic styled instruments," he explained, "billed as 'broken-in without breaking the bank'. They're built and skilfully aged, with Custom Shop advisors in assistance, to be strong on comfort and feel, like a favourite old T-Shirt or pair of jeans, and they feature thin nitro finishes and Tex Mex pickups for great tone. They'll continue to age and wear as they're played over time – we just provide a head start on history."

The Vintage Hot Rod models appeared in 2007 and are, Norvell concluded, similar to the Classic Players in that they are vintage-based models with player-friendly upgrades. "They're based on the US-made vintage reissues and offer thin-skin lacquer finishes, flatter

the stratocaster guitar book

radiuses, bigger frets, modern pickups, custom wiring, and more. Everyone likes the look and feel of a vintage Fender, but many want it to play like a modern instrument. Plus, many vintage guitar owners are hesitant to reduce the value by making the desired modifications, so here's a guitar that solves that problem outright."[122]

The Custom Shop's products today are divided into three different areas. First, it produces small runs and limited releases, which are special and often numbered runs of anything from a handful to hundreds of a specific model. The first of these was the 40th Anniversary Telecaster back in 1988, and the first Stratocaster, the HLE or Haynes Limited Edition followed a year later in a run of 500 instruments. More numbered editions have continued to appear from the Custom Shop.

The Shop also builds special limited runs for retailers and distributors, recently naming these the Dealer Select models. Some US music-store chains are regular customers, and overseas agents, too, such as Yamano in Japan are often treated to special models. In fact, Yamano remains the single largest customer for Custom Shop guitars at the time of writing, although the domestic US market is catching up.

The second type of production by the Custom Shop today is a general line of catalogued models, which began in 1992. By 2010, the catalogue items were divided into three further series: Custom Artist; Limited Collection; and Time Machine. Mike Eldred, director of marketing at Fender Custom Division, described Custom Artist guitars as "patterned after a specific artist's instrument," the Custom Shop equivalent of Signature models. Limited Collection guitars are offered only briefly and then retired. We met the aged and exacting Time Machine models – the Relics, Heavy Relics, N.O.S.s, and Closet Classics – earlier in the book.

All of this is not to say that the Custom Shop has abandoned the third strand of its business, which is its role as a true custom-builder. One-offs, or Master Built guitars as the Shop calls them, are the third strand of its production. These projects are exactly what most people would understand as the work of a custom shop: instruments made by a single person – one of the Shop's Master Builders or Senior Master Builders – with acute attention to detail and a price to match. "They're still extremely important to the Custom Shop," said Eldred. "This is where we get to push ourselves, and from these types of projects, newer designs emerge."

At the time of writing, the Shop had eight builders who individually make the one-off instruments. There were five Master Builders – John Cruz, Greg Fessler, Dennis Galuszka, Jason Smith, and Paul Waller – and three Senior Master Builders – Todd Krause, Yuriy Shishkov, and Stephen Stern. The one-offs they build include guitars made on the whim of a customer – maybe a vintage reproduction with absolutely dead-on accuracy, enough to satisfy the most nit-picking Fender-obsessed collector – or 'quasi-exact' reproductions of classic Fenders, with player-defined modifications on top of a vintage vibe.

There is also the exclusive fantasy guitar. Eldred remembered a good example. "There was a contest with a guitar magazine in which people were encouraged to design a

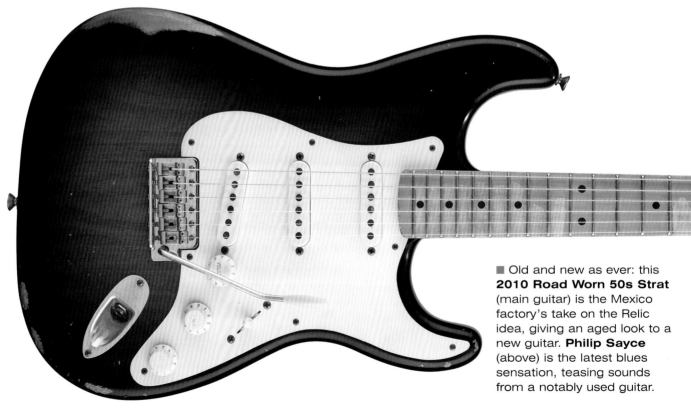

■ Old and new as ever: this
2010 Road Worn 50s Strat
(main guitar) is the Mexico
factory's take on the Relic
idea, giving an aged look to a
new guitar. **Philip Sayce**
(above) is the latest blues
sensation, teasing sounds
from a notably used guitar.

WINTER 2010 CUSTOM COLLECTION
PRICES EFFECTIVE JANUARY 1, 2010 | MSRP FOR FENDER® CUSTOM SHOP INSTRUMENTS

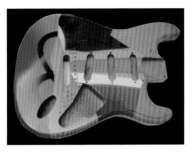

■ Fender's Custom Shop (**2010 catalogue**, top right) takes an important role alongside the US and Mexican factories, offering one-offs, catalogue models, and special editions. Senior Master Builder **Todd Krause** (above left) is seen working on a new instrument, while the multi-coloured Strat body (above right) was the first of a series of 50 in the Shop's 'art' line, created by **Crash**, whose painted guitar designs have been used by Eric Clapton. Back at the US factory, this **2009 Highway One HSS Stratocaster** (right) shows how Fender continues to mix old and new features, retaining some of the integrity of the classic design but at the same time trying to appeal to modern playing trends. That balance of old versus new will determine the future of the Stratocaster.

Stratocaster guitar to be built at the Shop. Many designs were submitted, and the magazine chose one which had an aluminium body with plastic chambers that held multi-coloured liquid, which moved when the guitar moved. It was the hardest guitar that the shop ever built." Other whacky constructions have included luxuriously appointed Rolls-Royce versions of traditional guitars, eight-string Strats, and weirdoes like an electric banjo with pedal-steel footpedals.

Such outlandishly peculiar orders are rare, however, and the truly bizarre one-offs now tend to come from the Master Builders' own imaginations, effectively creating a further sub-division of the one-offs, the Custom Shop's 'art guitars'. Master Builder Fred Stuart's Egyptian Telecaster, made in 1994, was the first Fender art guitar. It had pyramids, snakes, and runes hand-carved by George Amicay into a finish of Corian synthetic stone. Another was the 2005 Fender Memorabilia Set created by artist Dave Newman for a Stratocaster made by Master Builder Chris Fleming. The Strat and its companion Blues Junior amp were covered in a fascinating collage of vintage Fender catalogues and ads.

These are expensive items. The Shop apparently turned down $75,000 for an Aztec Telecaster and $50,000 for a Bird-o-Fire Strat some years ago. Meanwhile, the trend has developed today. "We've worked with several artists," said Eldred, "in order to really make the 'art guitar' moniker more true. Shepard Fairey, Pamelina, Shag, and Crash are just some of the artists we continue to work with, offering them a new and unique palette. The artists now usually do a matching amp with the guitar, too."[123]

John 'Crash' Matos found particular fame when Eric Clapton began using Stratocasters with bodies painted by Crash, and in 2004 the Custom Shop commissioned the artist to make a limited run of 50 bodies, each with individual artwork. "I love the challenge of trying to create 50 unique pieces," Crash wrote in his regular *Modern Guitars* column. "Also, I like calling them 'pieces' instead of Strats because that is what they are, pieces, as in 'master pieces' – graffiti lingo talk. They will be here long after we have departed."[124] Clapton has quite a few more Custom Shop art guitars, including Strats painted by D'Zine, She 1, Futura, Next Sky, Kaws, and Daze.

According to Eldred, the Custom Shop today sits at the pinnacle of the company. "The focus of the Shop is to assist in creating and developing new brands, designs, and techniques for all of our brands and facilities. We send builders to our Mexico, Tacoma [acoustic], and Japan facilities to teach as well as to learn. People do things differently all over the world, so why not look at those instances and possibly learn or develop something completely new? We maintain much of the original tooling, and we still use it to create some of the best instruments available. We offer a unique experience for the end user, whether that is John Mayer, Eric Clapton, Jeff Beck, or just a guy who likes a good guitar. They all have an opportunity to have a small team of builders make an instrument they have always dreamed of owning."[125]

Fender tried to trademark its three most famous body shapes, including the Stratocaster, in legal action starting in 2003. The claims were opposed by 17 other makers, and pickup-maker Jason Lollar summed up the opposition when he said that industry-wide replication of the Fender shapes "has caused those body styles to become generic".[126] Fender's position was that it had established common-law trademark rights over the body shapes of the Stratocaster, Telecaster, and Precision Bass, and that it was now seeking to obtain federal legal rights to those particular designs. The company already had federal trademark registrations for a number of its headstock shapes, but in 2009 the body-shape claims were rejected by the US Trademark Trial And Appeal Board. The Board concluded that Fender "failed to establish that the configurations involved in the applications before us have acquired distinctiveness".[127]

That must have been a blow to Fender's plans. But it certainly hasn't dented the popularity of the company's guitars, with the Stratocaster as prominent as ever on stages, in bedrooms, in studios, and online. Fender's factory in Corona, California, may be some 20 miles from Fullerton and Leo Fender's original workshops, but it's a universe away from the humble steel shacks that were home to Fender production and the birthplace of those first Stratocasters back in the early years of the 50s.

Leo loved few things more than gadgets, and he would have been enthralled by the present-day Fender plant – not least its automated conveyors that shift guitar components from storage area to production line. However, Leo would be looking most keenly at what tomorrow might bring. Fender now has no option but to acknowledge its rich history, full of great guitars and even greater players. But it must continue to attract the musicians of today and tomorrow.

In 1954, Don Randall wrote in Fender's original publicity: "For tone, appearance, and versatility, the Stratocaster has been engineered to give the player every possible advantage." Today, guitarists continue to exploit that advantage, wherever music is made. For David Gilmour, it's a personal matter. "The Stratocaster is the most versatile guitar ever made," he said. "It has this funny way of making you sound like yourself."[128]

ENDNOTES

1   Author's interview February 6 1992
2   *Guitar Player* October 1982
3   Author's interview February 10 1992
4   *Bay Area Music* August 29 1980
5   Author's interview with Karl Olmsted February 5 1992
6   *Guitar Player* September 1971
7   Author's interview February 5 1992
8   Author's interview February 8 1992
9   Author's interview February 10 1992
10   Author's interview with Forrest White February 5 1992
11   Author's interview February 10 1992
12   Author's interview February 5 1992
13   *Daily News Tribune* November 8 1949
14   Author's interview February 10 1992
15   *Guitar Player* September 1971
16   *Washington Post* December 17 1972
17   *Guitar Player* May 1978
18   Author's interview February 6 1992
19   Author's interview February 10 1992
20   Author's correspondence May 13 2010
21   *Guitar Player* July 1979
22   Author's interview with Bill Carson September 6 1991
23   *Los Angeles Times* April 3 1955
24   *The Music Trades* June 1953
25   Author's interview February 5 1992
26   Author's interview February 5 1992
27   Author's interview February 5 1992
28   *Guitar Player* July 1979
29   Author's interview February 10 1992
30   *Bay Area Music* August 29 1980
31   Author's interview with Bill Carson September 6 1991
32   Author's interview February 10 1992
33   Author's interview February 8 1992
34   Author's interview September 6 1991
35   Author's interview February 10 1992
36   Author's interview September 6 1991
37   Author's interview February 5 1992
38   Author's interview February 10 1992
39   Author's interview February 8 1992
40   Author's interview September 6 1991
41   *Rolling Stone* May 15 2003
42   Wheeler *Stratocaster Chronicles*
43   Author's interview February 10 1992
44   Author's interview February 5 1992

45   *La Habra Journal* March 8 2001
46   Author's interview February 5 1992
47   Author's interview February 10 1992
48   Author's interview November 15 2007
49   Goldrosen *Buddy Holly*
50   *The Austin Chronicle* October 15 2004
51   Author's interview February 10 1992
52   Author's interview February 8 1992
53   *Vintage Guitar* August 2003
54   Author's interview February 8 1992
55   Author's interview February 10 1992
56   *Guitar Player* November 1994
57   Author's interview February 10 1992
58   Balmer *Stratocaster Handbook*
59   *The Strat Pack* (BBC Radio 1, 1988)
60   Author's interview February 10 1992
61   *The Music Trades* January 1965
62   *The Music Trades* January 1965
63   *International Musician* August 1978
64   Author's interview February 10 1992
65   Author's interview February 10 1992
66   Author's interview February 5 1992
67   Author's interview February 8 1992
68   Author's interview February 10 1992
69   Author's interview February 10 1992
70   Smith *Fender: The Sound Heard*
71   Author's interview February 5 1992
72   Author's interview February 10 1992
73   *Los Angeles Free Press* August 25 1967
74   *Clapton: The Autobiography*
75   *Guitar Player* July 1985
76   *Beat Instrumental* October 1967
77   *Guitar Player* June 1970
78   *Clapton: The Autobiography*
79   *Crossroads Guitar Auction* Christie's catalogue 2004
80   Author's interview February 10 1992
81   *Q* July 1990
82   Author's interview April 27 2005
83   Author's interview January 25 1984
84   Author's interviews January 25 1984 & April 27 2005
85   Author's interview January 25 1984
86   *Music Maker* May 1967
87   *Washington Post* December 17th 1972
88   *Rolling Stone* February 13 1975
89   *Guitar Player* December 1976
90   Author's correspondence May 13 2010

91   *Guitar Player* July 1979
92   Author's interview February 5 1992
93   *Guitar Player* June 1970
94   *The Strat Pack* (BBC Radio 1, 1988)
95   Author's interview February 4 1992
96   *Guitar Player* May 1978
97   Author's interview February 4 1992
98   Author's interview February 4 1992
99   *Guitar Trader Vintage Guitar Bulletin* Vol.2 No.7 July 1983
100   Author's interview February 4 1992
101   Author's interview February 4 1992
102   *The Strat Pack* (BBC Radio 1, 1988)
103   Author's interview January 26 1984
104   *Guitar Player* May 1977
105   *San Francisco Chronicle* January 15 1985
106   Author's interview May 11 2010
107   Author's interview February 11 1985
108   Author's interview June 2 2005
109   Author's interview May 11 2010
110   Author's interview May 11 2010
111   Author's interview February 4 1992
112   Author's interview March 30 2007
113   Author's interview May 11 2010
114   Author's interview May 11 2010
115   *Rock'n'Roll And Film Memorabilia* Sotheby's catalogue 1990
116   Author's interview February 6 1992
117   *New York Times* January 16 1992
118   Author's interview December 2 1997
119   Author's interview June 2 2005
120   Author's interview March 30 2007
121   Author's interview May 11 2010
122   Author's interviews March 15 2007 & June 4 2010
123   Author's interviews March 27 2007 & June 8 2010
124   modernguitars.com January 2005
125   Author's interviews March 27 2007 & June 8 2010
126   forbes.com June 22 2004
127   United States Patent And Trademark Office, Trademark Trial And Appeal Board, Application serial no. 76516127, Opinion by Kuhlke, Administrative Trademark Judge, March 25 2009
128   *Guitar Player* January 2009

THE
REFERENCE
LISTING

How to use the reference listing

The main Reference Listing offers a simple, condensed format to convey a large amount of information about every Fender Stratocaster and related models made between 1954 and early 2010. The notes here are intended to ensure that you gain the most from this unique inventory.

The list covers all the production Fender-brand Stratocasters and related models made by Fender US between 1954 and early 2010, the output of Fender Mexico between 1991 and early 2010, the export models of Fender Japan issued from 1982 to early 2010, and the few Fender-brand models made in Korea between 1992 and 2008. Models by Squier and other Fender-related brands are beyond the detailed scope of this Reference Listing, although there is a brief summary for Squier. Most limited editions and other special runs from the Custom Shop issued in small numbers are also beyond the scope of this Listing.

The listings

The five main sections within the Reference Listing are: US-made Stratocasters; Mexico-made Stratocasters; Japan-made Stratocasters; Korea-made Stratocasters; and a brief round-up of Squier. Each model is listed under the various headings by the alphabetical order of its model name. Where a model name is also a person's name, the first word still supplies the alphabetical order. For example, the Billy Corgan Stratocaster is listed under B, not C. The exception to alphabetical order is found under the US 'Regular' grouping, where the models are shown in chronological order for ease of reference.

Reading the entries

At the head of each entry in the main listing is the model name in bold type, followed by a date or range of dates showing the production period of the instrument. It's worth stressing here that these dates are approximate. In many cases it's virtually impossible to pinpoint with complete accuracy the period during which a model was in production at the factory. For example, Fender's dated promo material does not always reflect what was being made at that precise time. Naturally our extensive research has resulted in the most accurate dates possible – but please treat them as approximate, because that is all they can be.

Following the model name and production date(s) is a brief one-sentence identification of the guitar in question, in italic type, intended to help you recognise a specific model at a glance. To do this we have noted elements of the guitar's design that are unique to that particular model.

For some guitars there may be a sentence below the heading text that reads "Similar to ... except:" which will refer to another model entry and then itemise any differences between the two.

Common features

To avoid repetition, we have considered a number of features to be common to all models, and these are not shown in the main listings. You can always presume the following:

■ Metal tuner buttons unless stated.

■ Standard Fender headstock shape unless stated.

■ Four-screw neckplate unless stated.

■ Bolt-on neck unless stated.

■ Scale length of twenty-five-and-a-half inches, and a total of twenty-one frets, unless stated.

■ Fingerboard with dot markers unless stated.

■ Single-coil pickups unless stated.

■ Nickel or chrome-plated hardware unless stated.

Specification points

In most guitar entries there follows a series of bullet points. This list of specification points, separated into groups, provides details of the particular model's features. In the order listed the points refer to:

● Neck, fingerboard, headstock.

● Body.

● Pickguard.

● Pickups.

● Bridge.

● Controls.

● Hardware finish.

Not every model will need all seven points. Some models were made in a number of variations, and where applicable these are listed (beginning *Also...*) after the specification points, in italic type. Any other general comments are made in this position, and a Custom Shop model is identified as such here.

Some models have only a short listing, all in italic type. This is often because the model is a 'replica' of an earlier guitar. The listing usually refers you to the entry for the original instrument.

This information is designed to tell you more about your Fender Stratocaster or related model. By using the general information and illustrations earlier in the book combined with the knowledge contained in this unique reference section, you should be able to build up a very full picture of your instrument and its pedigree.

US-MADE STRATOCASTERS

US-made Stratocasters are divided into three sections: US Regular; US Replica; and US Revised.

US REGULAR STRATOCASTERS

Listed here in chronological order are the models we regard as the standard versions of the Stratocaster.

STRATOCASTER pre-CBS 1954–65 *21 frets, small headstock, one string guide, four-screw neckplate, three controls.*
● Fretted maple neck (maple neck with rosewood fingerboard from 1959); truss-rod adjuster at body end; one string-guide.
● Body sunburst or colours.
● Three white six-polepiece pickups (bridge pickup angled).
● Three controls (volume, two tone) and three-way selector, all on pickguard; jack socket in body face.
● Eight-screw white plastic or anodised metal pickguard (11-screw white or tortoiseshell laminated plastic from 1959).
● Six-saddle small bridge with through-body stringing or six-pivot bridge/vibrato unit.
Some examples with gold-plated hardware (when with blond body unofficially known as Mary Kaye model).
Succeeded by STRATOCASTER CBS Sixties (1965–71).

STRATOCASTER CBS Sixties 1965–71 *21 frets, enlarged headstock, one string-guide, four-screw neckplate, three controls.*

- Maple neck with rosewood fingerboard (maple option 1967–69, replaced by fretted maple neck from 1969); truss-rod adjuster at body end; one string-guide; enlarged headstock.
- Body sunburst or colours.
- Three white six-polepiece pickups (bridge pickup angled).
- Three controls (volume, two tone) and three-way selector, all on pickguard; jack socket in body face.
- 11-screw white or tortoiseshell laminated plastic pickguard (only white from 1967).
- Six-saddle small bridge with through-body stringing or six-pivot bridge/vibrato unit.

Early examples with STRATOCASTER PRE-CBS small headstock. Some examples with bound rosewood fingerboard. Succeeded by STRATOCASTER CBS Seventies (1971–81).

STRATOCASTER CBS Seventies 1971–81 *21 frets, enlarged headstock, two string-guides, three-screw neckplate, three controls.*

- Fretted maple neck, or maple neck with rosewood finger-board; 'bullet' truss-rod adjuster at headstock end; two string-guides; enlarged headstock; three-screw neckplate.
- Body sunburst or colours.
- Three white (1971–75 and 1979–81) or black (1975–81) six-polepiece pickups (bridge pickup angled).
- Three controls (volume, two tone) and three-way selector (five-way from 1977), all on pickguard; jack socket in body face.
- 11-screw white (1971–75 and 1981) or black (1975–81) laminated pickguard.
- Six-saddle small bridge with through-body stringing or six-pivot bridge/vibrato unit.

Some late examples with truss-rod adjuster at body end and four-screw neckplate.
Also ANTIGUA STRATOCASTER, with white/brown shaded body finish and matching-colour laminated plastic pickguard (1977–79).
Also INTERNATIONAL COLOR STRATOCASTER, with special colour finishes, white laminated plastic pickguard, and black-plated pickguard screws (1981).
Succeeded by STRATOCASTER STANDARD first version (1981–83).

STRATOCASTER STANDARD first version 1981–83 *21 frets, small headstock, two string-guides, four-screw neckplate, three controls.*

- Fretted maple neck, or maple neck with rosewood fingerboard; truss-rod adjuster at body end; two string-guides; small headstock.
- Body sunburst or colours.
- Three white six-polepiece pickups (bridge pickup angled).
- Three controls (volume, two tone) and five-way selector, all on pickguard; jack socket in body face.
- 11-screw white or black laminated plastic pickguard.
- Six-saddle small bridge with through-body stringing or six-pivot bridge/vibrato unit.

Succeeded by STRATOCASTER STANDARD second version (1983–84).

STRATOCASTER STANDARD second version 1983–84
21 frets, small headstock, two string-guides, four-screw neckplate, two controls.
- Fretted maple neck only; truss-rod adjuster at headstock end; two string-guides; small headstock.
- Body sunburst or colours.
- Three white six-polepiece pickups (bridge pickup angled).
- Two controls (volume, tone) and jack socket, all on pickguard.
- 12-screw white plastic pickguard.
- Re-designed six-saddle bridge/tailpiece or single-pivot bridge/vibrato unit.

Also in red, yellow, or blue streaked Marble finish, unofficially known as MARBLE or BOWLING BALL STRATOCASTER (1984). Succeeded by AMERICAN STANDARD STRATOCASTER first version (1986–2000).

AMERICAN STANDARD STRATOCASTER first version
1986–2000 22 frets, small headstock, two string-guides, four-screw neckplate, three controls.
- Fretted maple neck, or maple neck with rosewood fingerboard; 22 frets; truss-rod adjuster at headstock end; two string-guides.
- Body sunburst or colours.
- Three white six-polepiece pickups (bridge pickup angled).
- Three controls (volume, two tone) and five-way selector, all on pickguard; jack socket in body face.
- 11-screw white laminated plastic pickguard.
- Two-pivot bridge/vibrato unit.

Also with 40th Anniversary medallion on headstock and commemorative neckplate (1994).
Also with anodised aluminium hollow-body option (1994–95).
Succeeded by AMERICAN STRATOCASTER (2000–07).

AMERICAN STANDARD STRATOCASTER HARD-TAIL
1998–2000 22 frets, small headstock, two string-guides, four-screw neckplate, three controls, six-saddle bridge with through-body stringing.
Similar to AMERICAN STANDARD STRATOCASTER (see previous listing), except:
- Six-saddle small bridge with through-body stringing.

AMERICAN STRATOCASTER 2000–07 *22 frets, small headstock, one string-guide, four-screw neckplate, three controls.*
- Fretted maple neck, or maple neck with rosewood fingerboard; 22 frets; truss-rod adjuster at headstock end; staggered-height tuners; one string-guide.
- Body sunburst or colours.
- Three white six-polepiece pickups (bridge pickup angled).
- Three controls (volume, two tone) and five-way selector, all on pickguard; jack socket in body face.
- 11-screw white laminated plastic pickguard.

● Two-pivot bridge/vibrato unit.
Succeeded by AMERICAN STANDARD STRATOCASTER second version (2008–current).

AMERICAN STRATOCASTER HARD-TAIL 2000–06 *22 frets, small headstock, one string-guide, four-screw neckplate, three controls, six-saddle bridge with through-body stringing.* Similar to AMERICAN STRATOCASTER (see previous listing), except:
● Six-saddle small bridge with through-body stringing.

AMERICAN STANDARD STRATOCASTER second version 2008–current *22 frets, small headstock, one string-guide, four-screw neckplate, three controls, bent-steel bridge saddles.*
● Fretted maple neck, or maple neck with rosewood fingerboard; 22 frets; truss-rod adjuster at headstock end; one string-guide.
● Body sunburst or colours.
● Three white six-polepiece pickups (bridge pickup angled).
● Three controls (volume, two tone) and five-way selector, all on pickguard; jack socket in body face.
● 11-screw off-white laminated plastic pickguard.
● Two-pivot bridge/vibrato unit; bent steel saddles.

US REPLICA STRATOCASTERS

Listed here in alphabetical order are the models that replicate various standard-version US Regular Stratocasters.

AMERICAN VINTAGE '57 STRATOCASTER 1998–current *Replica of 1957-period original (see STRATOCASTER PRE-CBS listing in earlier US Regular Stratocasters section).*

AMERICAN VINTAGE '62 STRATOCASTER 1998–current *Replica of 1962-period original (see STRATOCASTER PRE-CBS listing in earlier US Regular Stratocasters section).*

AMERICAN VINTAGE 70s STRATOCASTER 2006–current *Replica of 1970s-period original (see STRATOCASTER CBS SEVENTIES listing in earlier US Regular Stratocasters section).*

N.O.S. STRAT 1998 *Replica of 1965-period original (see STRATOCASTER CBS SIXTIES listing in earlier US Regular Stratocasters section). Custom Shop production.*

RELIC 50s STRATOCASTER 1996–98 *Distressed-finish replica of 1950s-period original (see STRATOCASTER PRE-CBS listing in earlier US Regular Stratocasters section). Gold-plated hardware option. Custom Shop production.*

RELIC 60s STRATOCASTER 1996–98 *Distressed-finish replica of early 1960s-period original (see STRATOCASTER PRE-CBS listing in earlier US Regular Stratocasters section). Gold-plated hardware option. Custom Shop production.*

'54 STRATOCASTER 1992–98 *Replica of 1954-period original (see STRATOCASTER PRE-CBS listing in earlier US Regular Stratocasters section). Gold-plated hardware option. Custom Shop production.*

'56 STRATOCASTER 1999–current *Replica of 1956-period original (see STRATOCASTER PRE-CBS listing in earlier US Regular Stratocasters section). Available with three levels of finish distress: N.O.S., Closet Classic, and Relic. Gold-plated hardware option. Custom Shop production.*

'57 STRATOCASTER 1983–85, 1986–98 *Replica of 1957-period original (see STRATOCASTER PRE-CBS in earlier US Regular Stratocasters section). Gold-plated hardware option.*

'57 STRATOCASTER HEAVY RELIC 2007 *Heavily-distressed-finish replica of 1957-period original (see STRATOCASTER PRE-CBS listing in earlier US Regular Stratocasters section). Custom Shop production.*

'58 STRATOCASTER 1996–98 *Replica of 1958-period original (see STRATOCASTER PRE-CBS listing in earlier US Regular Stratocasters section). Gold-plated hardware option. Custom Shop production.*

'59 STRATOCASTER HEAVY RELIC 2010–current *Heavily-distressed-finish replica of 1959-period original (see STRATOCASTER PRE-CBS listing in earlier US Regular Stratocasters section). Custom Shop production.*

'60 STRATOCASTER first version 1992–98 *Replica of 1960-period original (see STRATOCASTER PRE-CBS listing in earlier US Regular Stratocasters section). Gold-plated hardware option. Custom Shop production.*

'60 STRATOCASTER second version 1999–current *Revised replica of 1960-period original (see STRATOCASTER PRE-CBS listing in earlier US Regular Stratocasters section). Available 2003–06 with three levels of finish distress (N.O.S., Closet Classic, and Relic) and from 2010 with two levels of finish distress (N.O.S. and Relic). Custom Shop production.*

'62 STRATOCASTER 1983–85, 1986–98 *Replica of 1962-period original (see STRATOCASTER PRE-CBS in earlier US Regular Stratocasters section). Gold-plated hardware option.*

'62 STRATOCASTER HEAVY RELIC 2007 *Heavily-distressed-finish replica of 1962-period original (see STRATOCASTER PRE-CBS listing in earlier US Regular Stratocasters section). Custom Shop production.*

'63 STRATOCASTER 2010–current *Replica of 1963-period original (see STRATOCASTER PRE-CBS listing in earlier US Regular Stratocasters section). Available with two levels of finish distress: N.O.S. and Relic. Custom Shop production.*

'65 STRATOCASTER 2003–06, 2010–current *Replica of 1965-period original (see STRATOCASTER CBS SIXTIES listing in earlier US Regular Stratocasters section). Available 2003–06 with three levels of finish distress (N.O.S., Closet Classic, and Relic) and from 2010 with two levels of finish distress (N.O.S. and Relic). Custom Shop production.*

'66 STRATOCASTER 2004–08 *Replica of 1966-period original (see STRATOCASTER CBS SIXTIES listing in earlier US Regular Stratocasters section). Available with three levels of finish distress: N.O.S., Closet Classic, and Relic. Custom Shop production.*

'69 STRATOCASTER first version 1996–98 *Replica of 1969-period original (see STRATOCASTER CBS SIXTIES listing in earlier US Regular Stratocasters section). Custom Shop production.*

'69 STRATOCASTER second version 1999–current *Revised replica of 1969-period original (see STRATOCASTER CBS SIXTIES listing in earlier US Regular Stratocasters section). Available 2003–06 with three levels of finish distress (N.O.S., Closet Classic, and Relic) and from 2010 with two levels of finish distress (N.O.S. and Relic). Custom Shop production.*

US REVISED STRATOCASTERS

Listed here in alphabetical order are the models we regard as revised and adapted versions of the standard-version US Regular Stratocasters.

ALUMINUM-BODY STRATOCASTER 1994–95 *Anodised aluminium hollow-body option offered on AMERICAN STANDARD STRATOCASTER, STRAT PLUS, STRAT PLUS DELUXE, and STRAT ULTRA (see relevant listings).*

AMERICAN CLASSIC STRATOCASTER 1992–99 *Two-pivot vibrato, one string-guide.*
Similar to AMERICAN STANDARD STRATOCASTER first version (see listing in earlier US Regular Stratocasters section), except:
● One string-guide; 11-screw white pearl or tortoiseshell laminated plastic pickguard.
Gold-plated hardware option. Custom Shop production.

AMERICAN DELUXE ASH STRATOCASTER 2004–current *Three white single-coils, staggered-height locking tuners, two-pivot vibrato, ash body.*
Similar to AMERICAN DELUXE STRATOCASTER second version (see later listing), except:
● Ash body.
● 11-screw white or black laminated plastic pickguard.

AMERICAN DELUXE FAT STRAT 1998–2003 *Two Noiseless logo white pickups and one white humbucker, staggered height locking tuners, two-pivot vibrato.*

Similar to AMERICAN DELUXE STRATOCASTER first version (see later listing), except:
● No string-guide; roller nut.
● Two Noiseless logo white six-polepiece pickups and one white coverless humbucker (at bridge).

AMERICAN DELUXE FAT STRAT/LOCKING TREM
1998–2003 *Two Noiseless logo white pickups and one white humbucker, staggered height locking tuners, two-pivot locking vibrato.*
Similar to AMERICAN DELUXE STRATOCASTER first version (see later listing), except:
● No string-guide; roller nut.
● Two Noiseless logo white six-polepiece pickups and one white coverless humbucker (at bridge).
● Two-pivot locking bridge/vibrato unit.

AMERICAN DELUXE STRATOCASTER first version
1998–2003 *Three Noiseless logo white pickups, staggered height locking tuners, two-pivot vibrato.*
● Fretted maple neck, or maple neck with rosewood fingerboard; 22 frets; truss-rod adjuster at headstock end; staggered height locking tuners; one string-guide.
● Body sunburst or colours.
● Three Noiseless logo white six-polepiece pickups (bridge pickup angled).
● Three controls (volume, two tone) and five-way selector, all on pickguard; jack socket in body face.
● 11-screw white laminated plastic pickguard.
● Two-pivot bridge/vibrato unit.

AMERICAN DELUXE STRATOCASTER second version
2004–current *Three white or black single-coils, staggered-height locking tuners, two-pivot vibrato.*
Similar to AMERICAN DELUXE STRATOCASTER first version (see previous listing), except:
● Three white or black six-polepiece pickups (bridge pickup angled).
● Three controls (volume with push-switch, two tone) and five-way selector, all on pickguard.
● 11-screw white, tortoiseshell or black pearl laminated plastic pickguard, or gold plastic pickguard.

AMERICAN DELUXE STRATOCASTER FMT HSS
2004–09 *Figured-top body, no pickguard, two black single-coils and one black humbucker.*
● Maple neck with ebony fingerboard; 22 frets; truss-rod adjuster at headstock end; staggered height locking tuners; roller nut.
● Body with figured top; sunburst or colours.
● Two black six-polepiece pickups and one black coverless humbucker (at bridge).
● Two controls (volume with push-switch, tone) and five-way selector, all on body; jack socket in body face.
● No pickguard.
● Two-pivot bridge/vibrato unit.

Also AMERICAN DELUXE STRATOCASTER QMT HSS, with figured-top body (2004–09).

AMERICAN DELUXE STRATOCASTER HSS 2004–current
Two white or black single-coils and one white or black humbucker, staggered-height locking tuners, two-pivot vibrato.
Similar to AMERICAN DELUXE STRATOCASTER second version (see earlier listing), except:
● No string-guide; roller nut.
● Two white or black six-polepiece pickups and one white or black coverless humbucker (at bridge).

AMERICAN DELUXE STRATOCASTER HSS LT 2004–06
Two white or black single-coils and one white or black humbucker, staggered-height locking tuners, two-pivot locking vibrato.
Similar to AMERICAN DELUXE STRATOCASTER second version (see earlier listing), except:
● No string-guide; roller nut.
● Two white or black six-polepiece pickups and one white or black coverless humbucker (at bridge).
● Two-pivot locking bridge/vibrato unit

AMERICAN DELUXE STRATOCASTER QMT HSS *See earlier AMERICAN DELUXE STRATOCASTER FMT HSS listing.*

AMERICAN DELUXE STRATOCASTER 'V' NECK
2004–current *Three white single-coils, staggered-height locking tuners, two-pivot vibrato, fretted maple neck with 'V' profile.*
Similar to AMERICAN DELUXE STRATOCASTER second version (see previous listing), except:
● Fretted maple neck only, 1950s-period 'V'-shaping.
● 11-screw white, gold or copper plastic pickguard.
Also 'Crew' neck and 'Polo' neck options.

AMERICAN DELUXE 50th ANNIVERSARY STRATOCASTER 2004 *Commemorative neckplate, staggered-height locking tuners, gold-plated hardware.*
Similar to AMERICAN DELUXE STRATOCASTER second version (see earlier listing), except:
● Fretted maple neck only; commemorative neckplate.
● Body sunburst only.
● 11-screw white plastic pickguard.
● Gold-plated hardware.

AMERICAN DOUBLE FAT STRAT 2000–03 *White pearl or tortoiseshell pickguard, two Seymour Duncan logo white humbuckers.*
Similar to AMERICAN STRATOCASTER (see listing in earlier US Regular Stratocasters section), except:
● Two Seymour Duncan logo white coverless humbuckers.
● 11-screw white pearl or tortoiseshell laminated plastic pickguard.

AMERICAN DOUBLE FAT STRAT HARD-TAIL 2000–03
One string-guide, white pearl or tortoiseshell pickguard, two
Seymour Duncan logo white humbuckers, six-saddle bridge with through-body stringing.
Similar to AMERICAN STRATOCASTER (see listing in earlier US Regular Stratocasters section), except:
● Two Seymour Duncan logo white coverless humbuckers.
● 11-screw white pearl or tortoiseshell laminated plastic pickguard.
● Six-saddle small bridge with through-body stringing.

AMERICAN FAT STRAT TEXAS SPECIAL 2000–03 *White pearl or tortoiseshell pickguard, two white single-coils and one Seymour Duncan logo white humbucker.*
Similar to AMERICAN STRATOCASTER (see listing in earlier US Regular Stratocasters section), except:
● Two white six-polepiece pickups and one Seymour Duncan logo white coverless humbucker (at bridge).
● 11-screw white pearl or tortoiseshell laminated plastic pickguard.

AMERICAN SPECIAL STRATOCASTER 2010–current *22 frets, large headstock, two string-guides.*
● Fretted maple neck; 22 frets; truss-rod adjuster at headstock end; two string-guides; large headstock.
● Body sunburst or red.
● Three white six-polepiece pickups (bridge pickup angled).
● Three controls (volume, two tone) and five-way selector, all on pickguard; jack socket in body face.
● 11-screw white laminated plastic pickguard.
● Six-pivot bridge/vibrato unit.

AMERICAN SPECIAL STRATOCASTER HSS
2010–current *Two black single-coils and one black humbucker, 22 frets, large headstock, two string-guides.*
Similar to AMERICAN SPECIAL STRATOCASTER (see previous listing), except:
● Maple neck with rosewood fingerboard.
● Body sunburst or black.
● Two black six-polepiece pickups and one black coverless humbucker (at bridge).
● 11-screw black laminated plastic pickguard.

AMERICAN STANDARD DELUXE STRATOCASTER
1989–90 *Two-pivot vibrato, two string-guides, three white plain-top pickups.*
Similar to AMERICAN STANDARD STRATOCASTER (see listing in earlier US Regular Stratocasters section), except:
● Three white plain-top Lace Sensor pickups (bridge pickup angled).

AMERICAN STANDARD ROLAND GR-READY STRATOCASTER 1995–98 *Two-pivot vibrato, two string-guides, extra slim white pickup at bridge.*
Similar to AMERICAN STANDARD STRATOCASTER (see listing in earlier US Regular Stratocasters section), except:
● Additional slim white plain-top Roland synthesiser pickup (at bridge)

- Three controls (volume, tone, synth volume), five-way selector, two pushbuttons and mini-switch, all on pickguard; jack socket in body face; side-mounted multi-pin synth output.

AMERICAN STANDARD STRATOCASTER HSS

2008–current *Two white single-coils and one white humbucker, staggered-height tuners, two-pivot vibrato, bent steel bridge saddles, one string-guide.*
Similar to AMERICAN STANDARD STRATOCASTER second version (see listing in earlier US Regular Stratocasters section), except:
- Two white six-polepiece pickups and one white coverless humbucker (at bridge).

AMERICAN STRAT TEXAS SPECIAL

2000–03 *White pearl or tortoiseshell pickguard, three white single-coils.*
Similar to AMERICAN STRATOCASTER (see listing in earlier US Regular Stratocasters section), except:
- 11-screw white pearl or tortoiseshell laminated plastic pickguard.

Fitted with different-specification visually similar pickups.

AMERICAN STRATOCASTER HH

2003–06 *One string-guide, black pickguard, two black humbuckers.*
Similar to AMERICAN STRATOCASTER (see listing in earlier US Regular Stratocasters section), except:
- Two black coverless humbuckers.
- Three controls (volume with push switch, two tone) and five-way selector, all on pickguard.
- 11-screw black laminated plastic pickguard.

AMERICAN STRATOCASTER HH HARD-TAIL

2003–05 *One string-guide, black pickguard, two black humbuckers, six-saddle bridge with through-body stringing.*
Similar to AMERICAN STRATOCASTER (see listing in earlier US Regular Stratocasters section), except:
- Two black coverless humbuckers.
- Three controls (volume with push switch, two tone) and five-way selector, all on pickguard.
- 11-screw black laminated plastic pickguard.
- Six-saddle small bridge with through-body stringing.

AMERICAN STRATOCASTER HSS

2003–07 *One string-guide, black pickguard, two black single-coils and one black humbucker.*
Similar to AMERICAN STRATOCASTER (see listing in earlier US Regular Stratocasters section), except:
- Two black six-polepiece pickups and one black coverless humbucker (at bridge).
- Three controls (volume with push switch, two tone) and five-way selector, all on pickguard.
- 11-screw black laminated plastic pickguard.

AMERICAN VG STRATOCASTER

2007–09 *Extra slim white pickup at bridge, two large and two small controls.*
Similar to AMERICAN STRATOCASTER (see listing in earlier US Regular Stratocasters section), except:
- Extra slim white plain-top Roland synthesiser pickup (at bridge).
- Four controls (two large: Volume, Tone; two small: M [Mode], T [Tuning]), five-way selector and LED, all on pickguard; jack socket in body face; side-mounted multi-pin synth output.

AMERICAN VINTAGE 1957 COMMEMORATIVE STRATOCASTER

2007 Similar to AMERICAN VINTAGE '57 STRATOCASTER (see listing in earlier US Replica Stratocasters section), except:
- Commemorative neckplate.
- Body white only.
- Gold-plated hardware.

AMERICAN 50th ANNIVERSARY STRATOCASTER

2004 *Commemorative neckplate, locking tuners.*
Similar to AMERICAN STRATOCASTER (see listing in earlier US Regular Stratocasters section), except:
- Fretted maple neck only; commemorative neckplate.

AMERICAN 60th ANNIVERSARY STRATOCASTER

2006 *Commemorative neckplate, maple neck with rosewood fingerboard.*
Similar to AMERICAN STRATOCASTER (see listing in earlier US Regular Stratocasters section), except:
- Maple neck with rosewood fingerboard only; commemorative headstock logo with jewel inlay; commemorative neckplate.

ANTIGUA STRATOCASTER

See STRATOCASTER CBS SEVENTIES listing in earlier US Regular Stratocasters section.

BIG APPLE STRAT

1997–2000 *Two-pivot vibrato, two string-guides, two white humbuckers.*
Similar to AMERICAN STANDARD STRATOCASTER (see listing in earlier US Regular Stratocasters section), except:
- Two white coverless humbuckers.
- 11-screw white pearl or tortoiseshell laminated plastic pickguard.

BIG APPLE STRAT HARD-TAIL

1998–2000 *Two string-guides, two white humbuckers, six-saddle bridge with through-body stringing.*
Similar to BIG APPLE STRAT (see previous listing), except:
- Six-saddle small bridge with through-body stringing.

BILLY CORGAN STRATOCASTER

2009–current *Signature on back of headstock.*
- Fretted maple neck; 22 frets; truss-rod adjuster at headstock end; two string-guides; Billy Corgan signature on back of large headstock.
- Body satin black or satin white.
- Three black twin-blade pickups (bridge pickup angled).

- Three controls (volume, two tone) and five-way selector, all on pickguard; jack socket in body face.
- 11-screw black or white laminated plastic pickguard.
- Six-saddle small bridge with through-body stringing.

BONNIE RAITT STRATOCASTER 1995–2001 *Signature on headstock.*
- Narrow maple neck with rosewood fingerboard; 22 frets; truss-rod adjuster at headstock end; one string-guide; Bonnie Raitt signature on large headstock.
- Body sunburst or blueburst.
- Three white six-polepiece pickups (bridge pickup angled).
- Three controls (volume, two tone) and five-way selector, all on pickguard; jack socket in body face.
- 11-screw white pearl laminated plastic pickguard.
- Six-pivot bridge/vibrato unit.
Also Custom Shop limited edition.

BOWLING BALL STRATOCASTER (also known as Marble Stratocaster) *See* STRATOCASTER STANDARD second version *listing in earlier US Regular Stratocasters section.*

BUDDY GUY STRATOCASTER 1995–2009 *Signature on headstock.*
- Fretted maple neck; 22 frets; truss-rod adjuster at headstock end; one string-guide; Buddy Guy signature on headstock.
- Body sunburst or blond.
- Three white plain-top Lace Sensor pickups (bridge pickup angled).
- Three controls (volume, tone, boost), five-way selector and mini-switch, all on pickguard; jack socket in body face; active circuit.
- Eight-screw (11-screw from 2000) white pearl or tortoiseshell laminated plastic pickguard.
- Six-pivot bridge/vibrato unit.

CALIFORNIA FAT STRAT 1997–98 *Six-pivot vibrato, 'California Series' on headstock, two white singles-coils and one white humbucker.*
- Fretted maple neck, or maple neck with rosewood fingerboard; truss-rod adjuster at headstock end; one string-guide; California Series on headstock.
- Body sunburst or colours.
- Two white six-polepiece pickups and one white coverless humbucker (at bridge).
- Three controls (volume, two tone) and five-way selector, all on pickguard; jack socket in body face.
- 11-screw white laminated plastic pickguard.
- Six-pivot bridge/vibrato unit.

CALIFORNIA STRAT 1997–98 *Six-pivot vibrato, 'California Series' on headstock, three white single-coils.*
Similar to CALIFORNIA FAT STRAT, except:
- Three white six-polepiece pickups (bridge pickup angled).

CARVED TOP STRAT 1995–98 *Two-pivot vibrato, no string-guides, two single-coils and one humbucker, figured carved-top body.*
- Fretted maple neck, or maple neck with rosewood fingerboard; 22 frets; truss-rod adjuster at headstock end; locking tuners; roller nut.
- Body with figured carved top; sunburst or colours.
- Two cream six-polepiece pickups and one black/cream coverless humbucker (at bridge).
- Two controls (volume, tone) and five-way selector, all on body; side-mounted jack socket.
- No pickguard.
- Two-pivot bridge/vibrato unit.
Known as CARVED TOP STRAT HSS (1998).
Custom Shop production.

CARVED TOP STRAT HH 1998 *Carved top, two metal-cover humbuckers.*
Similar to CARVED TOP STRAT (see earlier listing), except:
- Two metal-cover humbuckers.

CARVED TOP STRAT HSS *See earlier CARVED TOP STRAT listing.*

CLASSIC HBS-1 STRATOCASTER 2009–current *22 frets, six-pivot vibrato, two white single-coils and one black humbucker.*
- Fretted maple neck; truss-rod adjuster at headstock end; one string-guide.
- Body sunburst or black.
- Two white six-polepiece pickups and one Seymour Duncan logo black coverless humbucker (at bridge).
- Three controls (volume, two tone - one with push-switch) and five-way selector, all on pickguard; jack socket in body face.
- 11-screw white laminated plastic pickguard.
- Six-pivot bridge/vibrato unit.
Available with two levels of finish distress: N.O.S. and Relic.
Custom Shop production.

CLASSIC PLAYER STRAT 1998–2005 *Custom Shop headstock logo, two-pivot vibrato, no string-guides, three Noiseless logo white pickups.*
- Fretted maple neck, or maple neck with rosewood fingerboard; 22 frets; truss-rod adjuster at headstock end; staggered-height locking tuners.
- Body sunburst or colours.
- Three Noiseless logo white six-polepiece pickups (bridge pickup angled).
- Three controls (volume, two tone) and five-way selector, all on pickguard; jack socket in body face.
- Eight-screw white laminated plastic or anodised metal pickguard.
- Two-pivot bridge/vibrato unit.
Custom Shop production.

COLLECTORS EDITION STRATOCASTER 1997 *Six-pivot vibrato, '1997' inlay at 12th fret position.*
- Maple neck with rosewood fingerboard; truss-rod adjuster at body end; one string-guide; oval-shape 1997 inlay at 12th fret.
- Body sunburst only.
- Three white six-polepiece pickups (bridge pickup angled).
- Three controls (volume, two tone) and five-way selector, all on pickguard; jack socket in body face.
- 11-screw tortoiseshell laminated plastic pickguard.
- Six-pivot bridge/vibrato unit.
- Gold-plated hardware.

Numbered factory production run of 1,997.

CONTEMPORARY STRAT 1995–98 *Two-pivot vibrato, no string-guides, two white single-coils and one white humbucker, smaller body with slimmer horns.*
- Fretted maple neck, or maple neck with rosewood fingerboard; 22 frets; truss-rod adjuster at headstock end; locking tuners; roller nut.
- Smaller body with slimmer horns; sunburst or colours.
- Two white six-polepiece pickups and one white coverless humbucker (at bridge).
- 11-screw white pearl laminated plastic pickguard.
- Two-pivot bridge/vibrato unit.

Also CONTEMPORARY STRAT FMT with figured-top body and two-pivot locking bridge/vibrato unit (1995–98).
Custom Shop production.

CONTEMPORARY STRAT FMT *See previous listing.*

CUSTOM CLASSIC STRAT 1999–2008 *22 frets, Custom Shop headstock logo, two-pivot vibrato, three white single-coils.*
Similar to AMERICAN STANDARD STRATOCASTER (see listing in earlier US Regular Stratocasters section), except:
- Custom Shop logo on headstock.

Custom Shop production.

CUSTOM DELUXE STRATOCASTER 2009–current *22 frets, two-pivot vibrato, staggered-height locking tuners, Custom Shop logo on headstock.*
- Fretted maple neck, or maple neck with rosewood fingerboard; 22 frets; truss-rod adjuster at headstock end; staggered-height locking tuners.
- Body sunburst or colours.
- Three white six-polepiece pickups (bridge pickup angled).
- Three controls (volume, two tone) and five-way selector, all on pickguard; jack socket in body face.
- 11-screw white laminated plastic pickguard.
- Two-pivot bridge/vibrato unit.

Custom Shop production.

DAVE MURRAY STRATOCASTER 2009–current *Signature on back of headstock.*
- Fretted maple neck; truss-rod adjuster at body end; one string-guide; Dave Murray signature on back of headstock.

- Body black only.
- Two white coverless humbuckers (with chrome-plated surrounds) and one white six-polepiece pickup in centre.
- Three controls (volume, two tone) and three-way selector, all on pickguard; jack socket in body face.
- Eight-screw white plastic pickguard.
- Six-pivot bridge/vibrato unit.

DAVID GILMOUR STRATOCASTER N.O.S. 2008–current
Black body, black pickguard, mini-switch, short vibrato arm.
- Fretted maple neck; truss-rod adjuster at body end; one string-guide.
- Body black only.
- Three white six-polepiece pickups (bridge pickup angled).
- Three controls (volume, two tone), five-way selector and mini-switch, all on pickguard; jack socket in body face.
- 11-screw black plastic pickguard.
- Six-pivot bridge/vibrato unit, short vibrato arm.

Also DAVID GILMOUR STRATOCASTER RELIC with distressed finish (2008–current).
Custom Shop production.

DAVID GILMOUR STRATOCASTER RELIC See previous listing.

DICK DALE STRATOCASTER 1994–current *Signature on headstock.*
- Maple neck with rosewood fingerboard; truss-rod adjuster at body end; two string-guides; Dick Dale signature on reverse headstock.
- Body gold only.
- Three white six-polepiece pickups (bridge pickup reverse-angled).
- One control (volume), three-way selector and two-way switch, all on pickguard; jack socket in body face.
- 11-screw white laminated plastic pickguard, metal covers over three 'spare' holes.
- Six-pivot bridge/vibrato unit.

Custom Shop production.

ELITE STRATOCASTER 1983–84 *Single-pivot vibrato, three pushbutton switches.*
- Fretted maple neck, or maple neck with rosewood fingerboard; truss-rod adjuster at headstock end; two string-guides.
- Body sunburst or colours.
- Three white plain-top pickups (bridge pickup angled).
- Three controls (volume, two tone) and three pushbutton selectors, all on pickguard; side-mounted jack socket; active circuit.
- 11-screw white laminated plastic pickguard.
- Re-designed six-saddle bridge/tailpiece or single-pivot bridge/vibrato unit.

Also GOLD ELITE STRATOCASTER, with pearl tuner buttons and gold-plated hardware (1983–84).
Also WALNUT ELITE STRATOCASTER, with walnut neck and

ebony fingerboard, walnut body, pearl tuner buttons and gold-plated hardware (1983–84).

ERIC CLAPTON SIGNATURE STRATOCASTER

2004–current *Signature on headstock rear, three Noiseless logo white pickups, Custom Shop headstock logo.*
Similar to ERIC CLAPTON STRATOCASTER first version (see earlier listing), except:
● Eric Clapton signature and Custom Shop logo on back of headstock.
● Three Noiseless logo white six-polepiece pickups.
● No active circuit.
Custom Shop production.

ERIC CLAPTON STRATOCASTER first version

1988–2001 *Signature on headstock, three white plain-top pickups, active circuit.*
● Fretted maple neck; 22 frets; truss-rod adjuster at headstock end; one string-guide; Eric Clapton signature on headstock.
● Body various colours.
● Three white plain-top Lace Sensor pickups (bridge pickup angled).
● Three controls (volume, two tone) and five-way selector, all on pickguard; jack socket in body face; active circuit.
● Eight-screw white plastic pickguard.
● Six-pivot bridge/vibrato unit.
Earliest examples with 21 frets and/or mini-switch.

ERIC CLAPTON STRATOCASTER second version

2001–current *Signature on headstock, three Noiseless logo white pickups, active circuit.*
Similar to ERIC CLAPTON STRATOCASTER first version (see previous listing), except:
● Three Noiseless logo white six-polepiece pickups.

ERIC JOHNSON STRATOCASTER MAPLE 2005–current

Engraved neckplate, fretted maple neck.
● Fretted maple neck; truss-rod adjuster at body end; staggered-height tuners; engraved neckplate.
● Body sunburst or colours.
● Three white six-polepiece pickups (bridge pickup angled).
● Three controls (volume, two tone) and five-way selector, all on pickguard; jack socket in body face.
● 8-screw white plastic pickguard.
● Six-pivot bridge/vibrato unit.

ERIC JOHNSON STRATOCASTER ROSEWOOD

2009–current *Engraved neckplate, maple neck with rosewood fingerboard.*
Similar to ERIC JOHNSON STRATOCASTER MAPLE (see previous listing), except:
● Maple neck with rosewood fingerboard.
● Body colours only.
● 8-screw white laminated plastic pickguard.

FLOYD ROSE CLASSIC STRAT HH 1998–2002 *Two-pivot locking vibrato system, two white humbuckers, three-screw fixing for each humbucker.*

Similar to FLOYD ROSE CLASSIC STRAT HSS (see later listing), except:
● Two white coverless humbuckers.
Known as STRAT SPECIAL WITH LOCKING TREMOLO HH (2002).

FLOYD ROSE CLASSIC STRAT HSS 1998–2002 *Two-pivot locking vibrato system, two white single-coils and one white humbucker, three-screw fixing for humbucker.*

Similar to FLOYD ROSE CLASSIC STRATOCASTER (see later listing), except:
● Three-screw fixing for humbucker.
● No curved-ends humbucker cut-out in pickguard.
Known as STRAT SPECIAL WITH LOCKING TREMOLO HSS (2002).

FLOYD ROSE CLASSIC STRATOCASTER 1992–98 *Two-pivot locking vibrato system, two white single-coils and one white humbucker, curved-ends humbucker cut-out in pickguard.*

● Fretted maple neck, or maple neck with rosewood fingerboard; 22 frets; truss-rod adjuster at headstock end; single-bar string-guide; locking nut.
● Body sunburst or colours.
● Two white six-polepiece pickups and one white coverless humbucker (at bridge).
● Three controls (volume, two tone) and five-way selector, all on pickguard; jack socket in body face.
● 11-screw white laminated plastic pickguard.
● Two-pivot locking bridge/vibrato unit.
Replaced by FLOYD ROSE CLASSIC STRAT HSS (1998).

GOLD ELITE STRATOCASTER See earlier ELITE STRATOCASTER listing.

GOLD/GOLD STRATOCASTER 1981–83 *Six-pivot vibrato, gold body and hardware.*

Similar to STRAT (see later listing), except:
● Fretted maple neck only; 'Stratocaster' logo on headstock.
● Body gold only.
● Three controls (volume, two tone) and five-way selector.
● Normal-type six-pivot bridge/vibrato unit.
● Gold-plated hardware.
Some examples with pearl fingerboard position markers.

HENDRIX STRATOCASTER 1980 *Six-pivot vibrato, large inverted headstock, normal logo.*

● Fretted maple neck; truss-rod adjuster at body end; two string-guides; large reverse headstock; four-screw neckplate.
● Body with additional front contouring; white only.
● Three white six-polepiece pickups (bridge pickup angled).
● Three controls (volume, two tone) and five-way selector, all on pickguard; jack socket in body face.

- 11-screw white laminated plastic pickguard.
- Six-pivot bridge/vibrato unit.

Only 25 produced; most marked as prototypes.

HIGHWAY ONE STRATOCASTER first version 2002–06

Satin body finish, white pickguard, three white single-coils, small headstock.

- Fretted maple neck, or maple neck with rosewood fingerboard; 22 frets; truss-rod adjuster at headstock end; two string-guides.
- Body various colours, satin finish.
- Three white six-polepiece pickups (bridge pickup angled).
- Three controls (volume, two tone) and five-way selector, all on pickguard; jack socket in body face.
- 11-screw white laminated plastic pickguard.
- Six-pivot bridge/vibrato unit.

HIGHWAY ONE STRATOCASTER second version

2006–current Satin body finish, white pickguard, three white single-coils, large headstock.
Similar to HIGHWAY ONE STRATOCASTER first version (see previous listing), except:
- Large headstock.

HIGHWAY ONE STRATOCASTER HSS first version

2003–06 Satin body finish, large headstock, white pickguard, two white single-coils and one black humbucker.
Similar to HIGHWAY ONE STRATOCASTER first version (see earlier listing), except:
- Maple neck with rosewood fingerboard only; large headstock.
- Two white six-polepiece pickups and one black coverless humbucker (at bridge).

HIGHWAY ONE STRATOCASTER HSS second version

2006–current Satin body finish, large headstock, white pickguard, two black single-coils and one black humbucker.
Similar to HIGHWAY ONE STRATOCASTER HSS first version (see previous listing), except:
- Two black six-polepiece pickups and one black coverless humbucker (at bridge).
- Black plastic knobs.

HM STRAT first type 1989–90 *Two-pivot locking vibrato system, two black single-coils and one black humbucker, black-face headstock.*

- Fretted maple neck, or maple neck with rosewood fingerboard; 25-inch scale, 24 frets; truss-rod adjuster at headstock end; locking nut; large flamboyant 'Strat' logo on black-face headstock.
- Smaller body; various colours.
- Two black six-polepiece pickups and one black coverless humbucker (at bridge).
- Three controls (volume, two tone), five-way selector and coil-switch, all on body; side-mounted jack socket.
- No pickguard.

- Two-pivot locking bridge/vibrato unit.
- Black-plated hardware.

HM STRAT second type 1989–90 *Two-pivot locking vibrato system, one angled black plain-top pickup and one black humbucker.*

Similar to HM STRAT first type, except:
- Maple neck with rosewood fingerboard only.
- One angled black plain-top Lace Sensor and one black coverless humbucker (at bridge).
- Two controls (volume, tone), three-way selector and coil-switch, all on body.
- Black laminated plastic pickguard.

HM STRAT third type 1989–90 *Two-pivot locking vibrato system, two black humbuckers.*

Similar to HM STRAT first type, except:
- Maple neck with rosewood fingerboard only.
- Two black coverless humbuckers.
- Two controls (volume, tone), three-way selector and coil-switch, all on body.

HM STRAT fourth type 1989–90 *Two-pivot locking vibrato system, one black humbucker.*

Similar to HM STRAT first type, except:
- Maple neck with rosewood fingerboard only.
- One black coverless humbucker (at bridge).
- Two controls (volume, tone) and coil-switch, all on body.

HM STRAT ULTRA 1990–92 *Two-pivot locking vibrato system, four black plain-top pickups.*

Similar to HM STRAT first type, except:
- Ebony fingerboard with split-triangle markers.
- Four black plain-top Lace Sensor pickups (two at bridge).

INTERNATIONAL COLOUR STRATOCASTER *See STRATOCASTER CBS SEVENTIES listing in earlier US Regular Stratocasters section.*

JEFF BECK SIGNATURE STRATOCASTER 2004–current

Signature on headstock rear, Custom Shop logo on headstock.
Similar to JEFF BECK STRATOCASTER second version, except:
- Jeff Beck signature and Custom Shop logo on back of headstock.

Custom Shop production.

JEFF BECK STRATOCASTER first version 1991–2001

Signature on headstock, four white plain-top pickups.
- Maple neck with rosewood fingerboard; 22 frets; truss-rod adjuster at headstock end; locking tuners; roller nut; Jeff Beck signature on headstock.
- Body white, green or purple.
- Four white plain-top Lace Sensor pickups (two at bridge).
- Three controls (volume, two tone), five-way selector and pushbutton coil-switch, all on pickguard; jack socket in body face.

- 11-screw white laminated plastic pickguard.
- Two-pivot bridge/vibrato unit.

JEFF BECK STRATOCASTER second version
2001–current *Signature on headstock, three Noiseless logo white pickups.*
Similar to JEFF BECK STRATOCASTER first version (see previous listing), except:
- Body green or white.
- Three Noiseless logo white six-polepiece pickups (bridge pickup angled).
- Three controls (volume, two tone), five-way selector and push-switch, all on pickguard; jack socket in body face.

JIM ROOT STRATOCASTER 2010–current *Signature on back of headstock.*
- Fretted maple neck, or maple neck with ebony fingerboard, no front position markers; 22 frets; truss-rod adjuster at headstock end; locking tuners; one string-guide; signature on back of large headstock.
- Hard-edge body; satin black or satin white.
- Two black plain-top active humbuckers.
- One control (volume) and three-way selector, all on pickguard; jack socket in body face.
- 11-screw black laminated plastic pickguard.
- Six-saddle small bridge with through-body stringing.
- Black-plated hardware.

JIMI HENDRIX STRATOCASTER 1997–2000 *Mirror-image Fender Stratocaster logo on large inverted headstock.*
- Fretted maple neck; truss-rod adjuster at body end; one string-guide; mirror-image Fender Stratocaster logo on large reverse headstock.
- Left-handed body; white only.
- Three white six-polepiece pickups (bridge pickup reverse-angled).
- Three controls (volume, two tone) and five-way selector, all on pickguard; jack socket in body face.
- Left-handed 11-screw white laminated plastic pickguard.
- Left-handed six-pivot bridge/vibrato unit.

JOHN MAYER STRATOCASTER 2005–current *Signature on back of headstock.*
- Maple neck with rosewood fingerboard; truss-rod adjuster at body end; one string-guide (further up headstock); John Mayer signature on back of headstock.
- Body sunburst, gold with stripes, or white.
- Three white six-polepiece pickups (bridge pickup angled).
- Three controls (volume, two tone) and five-way selector, all on pickguard; jack socket in body face.
- 11-screw white or tortoiseshell laminated plastic pickguard.
- Six-pivot bridge/vibrato unit.

LONE STAR STRAT 1996–2000 *Two-pivot vibrato, two string-guides, two white single-coils and one white humbucker.*

Similar to AMERICAN STANDARD STRATOCASTER (see listing in earlier US Regular Stratocasters section), except:
- Two white six-polepiece pickups and one Seymour Duncan-logo white coverless humbucker (at bridge).
- 11-screw white pearl or tortoiseshell laminated plastic pickguard.

MARBLE STRATOCASTER (also known unofficially as Bowling Ball Stratocaster) *See STRATOCASTER STANDARD second version listing in earlier US Regular Stratocasters section.*

MARK KNOPFLER STRATOCASTER 2003–current
Signature on headstock.
- Maple neck with rosewood fingerboard; truss-rod adjuster at body end; one string-guide; Mark Knopfler signature on headstock.
- Body red only.
- Three white six-polepiece pickups (bridge pickup angled).
- Three controls (volume, two tone) and five-way selector, all on pickguard; jack socket in body face.
- 11-screw white laminated plastic pickguard.
- Six-pivot bridge/vibrato unit.

MARY KAYE STRATOCASTER *See STRATOCASTER PRE-CBS listing in earlier US Regular Stratocasters section.*

RELIC FLOYD ROSE STRATOCASTER 1998 *Two-pivot locking vibrato system, two white single-coils and one black humbucker, large headstock.*
- Fretted maple neck, or maple neck with rosewood fingerboard; truss-rod adjuster at body end; single-bar string-guide; locking nut; large headstock.
- Body black or white, distressed finish.
- Two white six-polepiece pickups and one black coverless humbucker (at bridge).
- Three controls (volume, two tone) and five-way selector, all on pickguard; jack socket in body face.
- 11-screw white laminated plastic pickguard.
- Two-pivot locking bridge/vibrato unit.
Custom Shop production.

RHINESTONE STRATOCASTER 1975 *Based on STRATOCASTER CBS SEVENTIES (see listing in earlier US Regular Stratocasters section) but with replacement bonded metal and fibreglass body from British sculptor Jon Douglas and specially ordered by Fender's UK agent in 1975. Front has heavy relief floral leaf scroll design, inset with rhinestones on some examples. Very small quantity produced. Unauthorised 1990s versions are identifiable by a plaque on back of body.*

RICHIE SAMBORA STRATOCASTER first version
1993–99 *Signature on headstock.*
- Fretted maple neck, star position markers; 22 frets; truss-rod adjuster at headstock end; single-bar string-guide; locking nut; Richie Sambora signature on headstock.
- Body sunburst or white.

- Two white six-polepiece pickups and one white coverless humbucker (at bridge).
- Three controls (volume, two tone), five-way selector and push-switch, all on pickguard; jack socket in body face; active circuit.
- 11-screw white laminated plastic pickguard.
- Two-pivot locking bridge/vibrato unit.

RICHIE SAMBORA STRATOCASTER second version
1999–2002 Star position markers, three Noiseless logo white pickups.
- Fretted maple neck, star position markers; 22 frets; truss-rod adjuster at headstock end.
- Body sunburst, red or white.
- Three Noiseless logo white six-polepiece pickups (bridge pickup angled).
- Three controls (volume, two tone), five-way selector and push-switch, all on pickguard; jack socket in body face; active circuit.
- 11-screw white laminated plastic pickguard.
- Six-pivot bridge/vibrato unit.

RITCHIE BLACKMORE STRATOCASTER 1999–2005
Signature on headstock, two white plain-top pickups.
- Maple glued-in neck with rosewood fingerboard, with scalloping between frets; 22 frets; "bullet" truss-rod adjuster at headstock end; locking tuners; Ritchie Blackmore signature on large headstock.
- Body white only.
- Two white plain-top Lace Sensor pickups (bridge pickup angled).
- Three controls (volume, two tone) and five-way selector, all on pickguard; jack socket in body face.
- 11-screw white laminated plastic or anodised metal pickguard.
- Two-pivot bridge/vibrato unit.
Roland GK-2 synth pickup system option.
Custom Shop production.

ROADHOUSE STRAT 1997–2000 *Two-pivot vibrato, two string-guides, three white single-coils, white pearl or tortoiseshell pickguard.*
Similar to AMERICAN STANDARD STRATOCASTER (see listing in earlier US Regular Stratocasters section), except:
- Visually similar pickups but different specification.
- 11-screw white pearl or tortoiseshell laminated plastic pickguard.

ROBERT CRAY STRATOCASTER 1992–current *Signature on headstock.*
- Maple neck with rosewood fingerboard; truss-rod adjuster at body end; one string-guide; Robert Cray signature on headstock.
- Body sunburst, silver or violet.
- Three white six-polepiece pickups (bridge pickup angled).
- Three controls (volume, two tone) and five-way selector, all on pickguard; jack socket in body face.

- 11-screw white laminated plastic pickguard.
- Six-saddle small bridge with through-body stringing.
Also gold-plated hardware (1998–current).
Custom Shop production.

ROBIN TROWER STRATOCASTER 2005–current *Signature on back of large headstock.*
- Fretted maple neck only; "bullet" truss-rod adjuster at headstock end; one string-guide; Robin Trower signature on back of large headstock.
- Body various colours.
- Three white six-polepiece pickups (bridge pickup angled).
- Three controls (volume, two tone) and five-way selector, all on pickguard; jack socket in body face.
- 11-screw white laminated plastic pickguard.
- Six-pivot bridge/vibrato unit.
Custom Shop production.

RORY GALLAGHER STRATOCASTER 2004–current *Ultra-distressed finish, one mismatching tuner.*
- Maple neck with rosewood fingerboard; truss-rod adjuster at body end; one mismatching tuner; two string-guides.
- Body sunburst, ultra-distressed finish.
- Three white six-polepiece pickups (bridge pickup angled).
- Three controls (volume, two tone) and five-way selector, all on pickguard; jack socket in body face.
- 11-screw white laminated plastic pickguard.
- Six-pivot bridge/vibrato unit.
Custom Shop production.

SET NECK STRATOCASTER first version 1992–1995
Two-pivot vibrato, no string-guides, four white plain-top pickups (two at bridge), glued-in neck.
- Maple glued-in neck with ebony fingerboard; 22 frets; truss-rod adjuster at headstock end; locking tuners; roller nut.
- Body with figured top; sunburst or colours.
- Four white plain-top Lace Sensor pickups (two at bridge).
- Three controls (volume, two tone), five-way selector and coil-switch, all on pickguard; jack socket in body face.
- 11-screw white laminated plastic pickguard.
- Two-pivot bridge/vibrato unit.
Custom Shop production. Also Custom Shop limited edition.

SET NECK STRATOCASTER second version 1995–98
Two-pivot vibrato, no string-guides, two white single-coils and one white humbucker, glued-in neck.
Similar to SET NECK STRATOCASTER first version, except:
- Rosewood fingerboard.
- Sunburst or natural.
- Two white six-polepiece pickups and one white coverless humbucker (at bridge).
Custom Shop production.

SET NECK FLOYD ROSE STRATOCASTER 1992–95 *Two-pivot locking vibrato system, two black single-coils and one black humbucker, reverse headstock, glued-in neck.*

the stratocaster guitar book

- Maple glued-in neck with ebony fingerboard; 22 frets; truss-rod adjuster at headstock end; locking nut; black-face reverse headstock.
- Smaller body; sunburst or colours.
- Two black six-polepiece pickups and one black coverless humbucker (at bridge).
- Two controls (volume, tone) and five-way selector, all on body; side-mounted jack socket.
- No pickguard.
- Two-pivot locking bridge/vibrato unit.
- Black-plated or gold-plated hardware.

Custom Shop production.

SPECIAL EDITION 1993 STRATOCASTER 1993
Commemorative neckplate.
Similar to AMERICAN STANDARD STRATOCASTER (see listing in earlier US Regular Stratocasters section), except:
- Commemorative neckplate.
- 11-screw white pearl laminated plastic pickguard.
- Gold-plated hardware.

SPECIAL EDITION 1994 STRATOCASTER 1994
Commemorative neckplate.
Similar to AMERICAN STANDARD STRATOCASTER (see listing in earlier US Regular Stratocasters section), except:
- Commemorative neckplate.
- Body black or blond.
- 11-screw grey pearl or tortoiseshell laminated plastic pickguard.

STEVIE RAY VAUGHAN STRATOCASTER 1992–current
Signature on headstock.
- Maple neck with pao ferro fingerboard; truss-rod adjuster at body end; one string-guide; Stevie Ray Vaughan signature on headstock.
- Body sunburst only.
- Three white six-polepiece pickups (bridge pickup angled).
- Three controls (volume, two tone) and five-way selector, all on pickguard; jack socket in body face.
- Eight-screw black laminated plastic pickguard with 'SRV' engraving.
- Left-handed six-pivot bridge/vibrato unit.
- Gold-plated hardware.

STRAT 1980–83 *Six-pivot vibrato, 'Strat' logo on headstock.*
- Fretted maple neck, or maple neck with rosewood fingerboard; truss-rod adjuster at body end; two string-guides; 'Strat' logo on re-styled headstock with face matching body colour.
- Body red, blue or white.
- Three white six-polepiece pickups (bridge pickup angled).
- Three controls (volume, tone, two-way rotary switch) and five-way selector, all on pickguard; jack socket in body face.
- 11-screw white laminated plastic pickguard.
- Re-designed six-pivot bridge/vibrato unit.

- Gold-plated brass hardware (early examples have chrome machine heads and polished brass hardware).

Also WALNUT STRAT, with fretted walnut neck (some with walnut neck, ebony fingerboard), walnut body, black laminated plastic pickguard, and gold-plated hardware (1981–83).

STRAT-O-SONIC DVI 2003–04 *Model name on headstock, one large black six-polepiece pickup.*
- Maple neck with rosewood fingerboard; 22 frets; truss-rod adjuster at headstock end; staggered-height locking tuners; black-face headstock.
- Semi-solid body; sunburst, blonde or red.
- One large black six-polepiece pickup (at bridge).
- Two controls (volume, tone) on body; side-mounted jack socket.
- Six-screw black laminated plastic pickguard.
- Six-saddle wrapover bridge/tailpiece.

STRAT-O-SONIC DVII 2003–06 *Model name on headstock, two large black six-polepiece pickups.*
Similar to STRAT-O-SONIC DVI (see previous listing), except:
- Two large black six-polepiece pickups.
- Two controls (volume, tone) and three-way selector, all on body.

STRAT-O-SONIC HH 2005–06 *Model name on headstock, two black humbuckers.*
Similar to STRAT-O-SONIC DVII (see previous listing), except:
- Two black coverless humbucker pickups.

STRAT PLUS 1987–98 *Two-pivot vibrato, no string-guides, three same-type white plain-top pickups.*
- Fretted maple neck, or maple neck with rosewood fingerboard; 22 frets; truss-rod adjuster at headstock end; locking tuners; roller nut.
- Body sunburst or colours.
- Three same-type white plain-top Lace Sensor pickups (bridge pickup angled).
- Three controls (volume, two tone) and five-way selector, all on pickguard; jack socket in body face.
- 11-screw white or white pearl laminated plastic pickguard.
- Two-pivot bridge/vibrato unit.

Also with anodised aluminium hollow body option (1994–95).

STRAT PLUS DELUXE 1989–98 *Two-pivot vibrato, no string-guides, three differing white plain-top pickups.*
Similar to STRAT PLUS, except:
- Three differing white plain-top Lace Sensor pickups (bridge pickup angled).
- 11-screw white, white pearl or tortoiseshell laminated plastic pickguard.
- Two-pivot bridge/vibrato unit.

Also with anodised aluminium hollow body option (1994–95).

STRAT PRO 2006–08 *Large headstock, roller nut, two-pivot vibrato.*

- Fretted maple neck, or maple neck with rosewood fingerboard; 22 frets (from 2007); truss-rod adjuster at body end; roller nut; large headstock.
- Body black or white, distressed finish.
- Three white six-polepiece pickups (bridge pickup angled).
- Three controls (volume, two tone) and five-way selector, all on pickguard; jack socket in body face.
- 11-screw white laminated plastic pickguard.
- Two-pivot bridge/vibrato unit.
Custom Shop production.

STRAT SPECIAL WITH LOCKING TREMOLO HH *See earlier FLOYD ROSE CLASSIC STRAT HH listing.*

STRAT SPECIAL WITH LOCKING TREMOLO HSS *See earlier FLOYD ROSE CLASSIC STRAT HSS listing.*

STRAT ULTRA 1990–98 *Two-pivot vibrato, no string-guides, four white plain-top pickups (two at bridge), bolt-on neck.*
- Maple neck with ebony fingerboard; 22 frets; truss-rod adjuster at headstock end; locking tuners; roller nut.
- Body sunburst or colours.
- Four white plain-top Lace Sensor pickups (two at bridge).
- Three controls (volume, two tone), five-way selector and coil-switch, all on pickguard; jack socket in body face.
- 11-screw white or white pearl laminated plastic pickguard.
- Two-pivot bridge/vibrato unit.
Also with anodised aluminium hollow body option (1994–95).

STRATOCASTER PRO RELIC 2009–current *Three Noiseless logo white pickups, staggered-height locking tuners, two-pivot vibrato, roller nut.*
- Fretted maple neck, or maple neck with rosewood fingerboard; 22 frets; truss-rod adjuster at headstock end; staggered-height locking tuners; roller nut.
- Body sunburst or red, distressed finish.
- Three Noiseless logo white six-polepiece pickups (bridge pickup angled).
- Three controls (volume, two tone) and five-way selector, all on pickguard; jack socket in body face.
- 11-screw white laminated plastic pickguard.
- Two-pivot bridge/vibrato unit.
Custom Shop production.

SUB-SONIC STRATOCASTER HH baritone 2000–01 *Sub-Sonic on headstock, long-scale neck, white pearl pickguard, two white humbuckers.*
Similar to SUB-SONIC STRATOCASTER HSS baritone first version (see next listing), except:
- Two white coverless humbuckers.
Custom Shop production.

SUB-SONIC STRATOCASTER HSS baritone first version 2000–01 *'Sub-Sonic' on headstock, long-scale neck, white pearl pickguard, two Noiseless-logo white single-coils and one white humbucker.*

- Fretted maple neck, or maple neck with rosewood fingerboard; 27-inch scale, 22 frets; truss-rod adjuster at body end; one string-guide; Sub-Sonic on headstock.
- Body sunburst or colours.
- Two Noiseless logo white six-polepiece pickups and one white coverless humbucker (at bridge).
- Three controls (volume, two tone) and five-way selector, all on pickguard; jack socket in body face.
- 11-screw white pearl laminated plastic pickguard.
- Six-saddle small bridge with through-body stringing.
Custom Shop production.

SUB-SONIC STRATOCASTER HSS baritone second version 2001 *'Sub-Sonic' on headstock, long-scale neck, white pickguard, two white single-coils and one white humbucker.*
- Fretted maple neck, or maple neck with rosewood fingerboard; 27-inch scale, 22 frets; truss-rod adjuster at body end; one string-guide.
- Body sunburst or colours.
- Two white six-polepiece pickups and one white coverless humbucker (at bridge).
- Three controls (volume, two tone) and five-way selector, all on pickguard; jack socket in body face.
- 11-screw white laminated plastic pickguard.
- Six-saddle small bridge with through-body stringing.

US CONTEMPORARY STRATOCASTER 1989–91 *Two-pivot locking vibrato system, two white single-coils and one white humbucker, straight-sided humbucker cut-out in pickguard.*
- Maple neck with rosewood fingerboard; 22 frets; truss-rod adjuster at headstock end; locking nut.
- Body sunburst or colours.
- Two white six-polepiece pickups and one white coverless humbucker (at bridge).
- Three controls (volume, two tone) and five-way selector, all on pickguard; jack socket in body face.
- 11-screw white laminated plastic pickguard.
- Two-pivot locking bridge/vibrato unit.

VINTAGE HOT ROD '57 STRAT 2007–current *Two white six-polepiece pickups and one white twin-blade pickup.*
- Fretted maple neck; truss-rod adjuster at body end; one string-guide.
- Body sunburst, black or red.
- Two white six-polepiece pickups and one white twin-blade pickup (angled at bridge).
- Three controls (volume, two tone) and five-way selector, all on pickguard; jack socket in body face.
- Eight-screw white plastic pickguard.
- Six-pivot bridge/vibrato unit.

VINTAGE HOT ROD '62 STRAT 2007–current *Circuitry modifications.*
- Maple neck with rosewood fingerboard; truss-rod adjuster at body end; one string-guide.

- Body sunburst, white or green.
- Three white six-polepiece pickups (bridge pickup angled).
- Three controls (volume, two tone) and five-way selector, all on pickguard; jack socket in body face.
- 11-screw white laminated plastic pickguard.
- Six-pivot bridge/vibrato unit.

Circuitry modifications as standard.

VOODOO STRATOCASTER 1998–2000 *Large inverted headstock, reverse-angled bridge pickup, Jimi Hendrix image engraved neckplate.*

- Maple neck with maple or rosewood fingerboard; truss-rod adjuster at body end; one string-guide; Jimi Hendrix image engraved neckplate; large reverse headstock.
- Body sunburst, black or white.
- Three white six-polepiece pickups (bridge pickup reverse-angled).
- Three controls (volume, two tone) and five-way selector, all on pickguard; jack socket in body face.
- 11-screw white laminated plastic pickguard.
- Six-pivot bridge/vibrato unit.

WALNUT ELITE STRATOCASTER *See earlier ELITE STRATOCASTER listing.*

WALNUT STRAT *See earlier STRAT listing.*

YNGWIE MALMSTEEN STRATOCASTER first version
1988–98 *Signature on small headstock, two-pivot vibrato.*

- Fretted maple neck, or maple neck with rosewood fingerboard, both with scalloping between frets; truss-rod adjuster at body end; one string-guide; brass nut; Yngwie Malmsteen signature on headstock.
- Body red, white or blue.
- Three white six-polepiece pickups (bridge pickup angled).
- Three controls (volume, two tone) and five-way selector, all on pickguard; jack socket in body face.
- 11-screw white laminated plastic pickguard.
- Two-pivot bridge/vibrato unit.

YNGWIE MALMSTEEN STRATOCASTER second
version 1998–2006 *Signature on large headstock, six-pivot vibrato.*

Similar to YNGWIE MALMSTEEN STRATOCASTER first version (see previous listing), except:

- Yngwie Malmsteen signature on large headstock.
- Three controls (volume, two tone) and three-way selector, all on pickguard.
- Six-pivot bridge/vibrato unit.

YNGWIE MALMSTEEN STRATOCASTER third version
2007–current *Signature on large headstock, six-pivot vibrato, "bullet" truss-rod adjuster.*

Similar to YNGWIE MALMSTEEN STRATOCASTER second

version (see previous listing), except:

- 'Bullet' truss-rod adjuster at headstock end.

25th ANNIVERSARY STRATOCASTER 1979–80
'Anniversary' logo on body.

Similar to STRATOCASTER CBS SEVENTIES (see listing in earlier US Regular Stratocasters section), except:

- Fretted maple neck only; truss-rod adjuster at body end; commemorative four-screw neckplate.
- Body silver (earliest examples white) with black 'Anniversary' logo.
- Six-pivot bridge/vibrato unit only.

40th ANNIVERSARY 1954 STRATOCASTER 1994 *Replica of 1954-period original (see STRATOCASTER PRE-CBS listing in earlier US Regular Stratocasters section) but with commemorative neckplate. Numbered factory production run of 1,954.*

50th ANNIVERSARY STRATOCASTER 1996
Commemorative neckplate.

Similar to AMERICAN STANDARD STRATOCASTER (see listing in earlier US Regular Stratocasters section), except:

- Maple neck with rosewood fingerboard only; commemorative neckplate.
- Body sunburst only.
- Gold-plated hardware.

Numbered factory production run of 2,500. Also Custom Shop limited editions.

'54 STRATOCASTER FMT 1995–98 *Replica of 1954-period original (see STRATOCASTER PRE-CBS listing in earlier US Regular Stratocasters section) but with figured body top. Gold-plated hardware option. Custom Shop production.*

'57 COMMEMORATIVE STRATOCASTER 2007 *Replica of 1957-period original (see STRATOCASTER PRE-CBS listing in earlier US Regular Stratocasters section) but with commemorative neckplate. Blond finish, gold-plated hardware.*

'60 STRATOCASTER FMT 1995–98 *Replica of 1960-period original (see STRATOCASTER PRE-CBS listing in earlier US Regular Stratocasters section) but with figured body top. Gold-plated hardware option. Custom Shop production.*

'68 REVERSE STRAT SPECIAL 2002 *Large inverted headstock, reverse-angled bridge pickup.*

- Maple neck with maple fingerboard; truss-rod adjuster at body end; one string-guide; large reverse headstock.
- Body sunburst, black or white.
- Three white six-polepiece pickups (bridge pickup reverse-angled).
- Three controls (volume, two tone) and five-way selector, all on pickguard; jack socket in body face.
- 11-screw white laminated plastic pickguard.
- Six-pivot bridge/vibrato unit.

60s CLOSET CLASSIC COMPETITION STRIPE STRATOCASTER 2007 *Three Noiseless logo white pickups, staggered-height locking tuners, two-pivot vibrato, roller nut. Distressed finish replica of 1960-period original (see STRATOCASTER PRE-CBS listing in earlier US Regular Stratocasters section). Stripes on body. Custom Shop production.*

CUSTOM SHOP

The Fender Custom Shop was officially established in 1987. It now produces three broad types of instruments: one-offs or 'Master Built' guitars; numbered limited-edition guitars; and catalogued general-production instruments. Guitars in the latter category are noted here in the main US listing, indicated as "Custom Shop production". Most of the one-offs and limited editions are beyond the scope of this reference section. All official Custom Shop instruments carry an appropriate identifying logo on the rear of the headstock.

MEXICO-MADE STRATOCASTERS

Mexican Stratocasters are divided into two sections: Mexico Replica; and Mexico Revised. Each guitar has 'Made In Mexico' somewhere on the instrument.

MEXICO REPLICA STRATOCASTERS

Listed here in alphabetical order are the Mexico-made models that replicate various standard-version US-made Stratocasters (see earlier US-made Regular Stratocasters section).

CLASSIC 50s STRATOCASTER 1999–current *Replica of 1950s-period original (see STRATOCASTER PRE-CBS listing in earlier US Regular Stratocasters section).*

CLASSIC 60s STRATOCASTER 1999–current *Replica of 1960s-period original (see STRATOCASTER PRE-CBS listing in earlier US Regular Stratocasters section).*

CLASSIC 70s STRATOCASTER 1999–current *Replica of 1970s-period original (see STRATOCASTER CBS listing in earlier US Regular Stratocasters section).*

ROAD WORN 50s STRATOCASTER 2009–current *Distressed-finish replica of 1950s-period original (see STRATOCASTER PRE-CBS listing in earlier US Regular Stratocasters section).*

ROAD WORN 60s STRATOCASTER 2009–current *Distressed-finish replica of 1960s-period original (see STRATOCASTER PRE-CBS listing in earlier US Regular Stratocasters section).*

MEXICO REVISED STRATOCASTERS

Listed here in alphabetical order are the models we regard as revised and adapted versions of the standard-version US-made Stratocasters (see earlier US-made Regular Stratocasters section).

BUDDY GUY POLKA DOT STRAT 2002–current *Signature on headstock, black/white polka dot body finish.*
Similar to STANDARD STRATOCASTER (see later listing), except:
● Buddy Guy signature on headstock.
● Body black/white polka dot finish only.
● Three black six-polepiece pickups.
● Eight-screw black laminated plastic pickguard.

CHRIS REA CLASSIC STRATOCASTER 1999 *Signature on headstock.*
Similar to CLASSIC 60s STRATOCASTER (see listing in earlier Mexico Replica Stratocasters section), except:
● Chris Rea signature on headstock.
● Body red only.

CLASSIC PLAYER 50s STRATOCASTER 2006–current *Maple fingerboard, locking tuners, two-pivot vibrato.*
Similar to CLASSIC 50s STRATOCASTER (see listing in earlier Mexico Replica Stratocasters section), except:
● Locking tuners; neckplate with 'Custom Shop designed' logo.
● Body sunburst or gold.
● Two-pivot bridge/vibrato unit.

CLASSIC PLAYER 60s STRATOCASTER 2006–current *Rosewood fingerboard, locking tuners, two-pivot vibrato.*
Similar to CLASSIC 60s STRATOCASTER (see listing in earlier Mexico Replica Stratocasters section), except:
● Locking tuners; neckplate with 'Custom Shop designed' logo.
● Body sunburst or blue.
● Two-pivot bridge/vibrato unit.

CONTEMPORARY STRATOCASTER *See later STRAT SPECIAL listing.*

DELUXE BIG BLOCK STRATOCASTER 2005–06 *Block markers, black headstock face, chrome pickguard.*
● Maple neck with rosewood fingerboard, block markers; truss-rod adjuster at headstock end; one string-guide; black-face headstock.
● Body black only.
● Two black six-polepiece pickups and one black coverless humbucker (at bridge).
● Two controls (volume, tone) and five-way selector, all on pickguard; jack socket in body face.
● 11-screw chrome plastic pickguard.
● Six-pivot bridge/vibrato unit.

DELUXE DOUBLE FAT STRAT 1999–2004 *Six-pivot vibrato, two black humbuckers, black pickguard, large headstock.*
Similar to DELUXE FAT STRAT first version (see later listing), except:
● Two black coverless humbuckers.
Known as DELUXE DOUBLE FAT STRAT HH (2002–03).
Known as DELUXE STRAT HH (2004).

DELUXE DOUBLE FAT STRAT FLOYD ROSE 1998–2004
Two-pivot locking vibrato system, two black humbuckers, black pickguard, large headstock.
Similar to DELUXE FAT STRAT (see later listing), except:
● Single-bar string-guide; locking nut.
● Two black coverless humbuckers.
● Two-pivot locking bridge/vibrato unit.
Known as DELUXE DOUBLE FAT STRAT HH WITH LOCKING TREMOLO (2002–03).
Known as DELUXE STRAT HH WITH LOCKING TREMOLO (2004).

DELUXE DOUBLE FAT STRAT HH WITH LOCKING TREMOLO *See previous DELUXE DOUBLE FAT STRAT FLOYD ROSE listing.*

DELUXE FAT STRAT first version 1999–2006 *Six-pivot vibrato, two black single-coils and one black humbucker, black pickguard, large headstock.*
● Maple neck with rosewood fingerboard; truss-rod adjuster at headstock end; one string-guide; large headstock.
● Body black or white.
● Two black six-polepiece pickups and one black coverless humbucker (at bridge).
● Three controls (volume, two tone) and five-way selector, all on pickguard; jack socket in body face.
● 11-screw black laminated plastic pickguard.
● Six-pivot bridge/vibrato unit.
Known as DELUXE FAT STRAT HSS (2002–03).
Known as DELUXE STRAT HSS (2004–06).

DELUXE FAT STRAT second version 2008–09 *Six-pivot vibrato, two black single-coils and one black humbucker, white pickguard, large headstock.*
Similar to DELUXE FAT STRAT first version (see previous listing), except:
● 11-screw white laminated plastic pickguard.

DELUXE FAT STRAT FLOYD ROSE 1998–2005 *Two-pivot locking vibrato system, two black single-coils and one black humbucker, black pickguard, large headstock.*
Similar to DELUXE FAT STRAT first version, except:
● Single-bar string-guide; locking nut.
● Two-pivot locking bridge/vibrato unit.
Known as DELUXE FAT STRAT HSS WITH LOCKING TREMOLO (2002–03).
Known as DELUXE STRAT HSS WITH LOCKING TREMOLO (2004–05).

DELUXE FAT STRAT HSS WITH LOCKING TREMOLO
See previous DELUXE FAT STRAT FLOYD ROSE listing.

DELUXE LONE STAR STRATOCASTER 2008–current *Two white single-coils and one Seymour Duncan-logo white humbucker, tortoiseshell pickguard, six-pivot vibrato.*
Similar to STANDARD STRATOCASTER (see later listing), except:
● Maple neck with rosewood fingerboard only.
● Body sunburst, black or white.
● Two white six-polepiece pickups and one Seymour Duncan-logo white coverless humbucker (at bridge).
● 11-screw tortoiseshell laminated plastic pickguard.

DELUXE PLAYERS STRAT 2004–current *Gold-plated hardware, push-switch, three Noiseless logo white pickups.*
Similar to STANDARD STRATOCASTER (see later listing), except:
● Three Noiseless logo white six-polepiece pickups.
● Three controls (volume, two tone), five-way switch and push-switch, all on pickguard.
● 11-screw tortoiseshell pickguard.
● Gold-plated hardware.

DELUXE POWER STRATOCASTER 2006–current *Fishman Powerbridge vibrato, two volume controls, one tone control.*
Similar to STANDARD STRATOCASTER (see later listing), except:
● Two white six-polepiece pickups and one white coverless humbucker (at bridge).
● Three controls (volume, tone, piezo volume) and five-way switch, all on pickguard.
● 11-screw tortoiseshell pickguard.
● Six-pivot Fishman Powerbridge vibrato with six piezo pickup bridge saddles.

DELUXE POWERHOUSE STRAT 1997–2007 *White pearl pickguard, active circuit.*
Similar to *STANDARD STRATOCASTER* (see later listing), except:
● Body various colours.
● Three controls (volume, tone, boost) and five-way selector, all on pickguard; active circuit.
● 11-screw white pearloid plastic pickguard.

DELUXE ROADHOUSE STRATOCASTER 2008–current *Modern-style 'thick' Fender headstock logo in silver, six-pivot vibrato, tortoiseshell pickguard.*
Similar to STANDARD STRATOCASTER (see later listing), except:
● Fretted maple neck only.
● Body sunburst, black or white.
● Visually similar pickups but different specification.
● 11-screw tortoiseshell laminated plastic pickguard.

DELUXE STRAT HH *See earlier DELUXE DOUBLE FAT STRAT listing.*

DELUXE STRAT HH WITH LOCKING TREMOLO *See earlier DELUXE DOUBLE FAT STRAT FLOYD ROSE listing.*

DELUXE STRAT HSS *See earlier DELUXE FAT STRAT listing.*

DELUXE STRAT HSS WITH LOCKING TREMOLO *See earlier DELUXE FAT STRAT FLOYD ROSE listing.*

DELUXE SUPER STRAT 1997–2004 *Gold-plated hardware, push-switch.*
Similar to STANDARD STRATOCASTER (see earlier listing), except:
● Three controls (volume, two tone), five-way selector and push-switch, all on pickguard.
● 11-screw tortoiseshell laminated plastic pickguard.
● Gold-plated hardware.

FLOYD ROSE STANDARD STRATOCASTER 1994–98
Two-pivot locking vibrato system, two white single-coils and one white humbucker, white pickguard, small headstock, two controls.
Similar to STANDARD STRATOCASTER (see later listing), except:
● Single-bar string-guide; locking nut.
● Body black or white.
● Two white six-polepiece pickups and one white coverless humbucker (at bridge).
● Two controls (volume, tone) and five-way selector, all on pickguard.
● Two-pivot locking bridge/vibrato unit.
Also known as SQUIER SERIES FLOYD ROSE STANDARD STRATOCASTER, with small Squier Series logo on headstock (1994–96).

GOLD SISTER STRATOCASTER 2007 *Gold body and headstock face*
Similar to STANDARD STRATOCASTER HSS (see later listing) except:
● Fretted maple neck only; gold-faced headstock.
● Body gold only.
● Two black six-polepiece pickups and one black coverless humbucker (at bridge).
● Two controls (volume, tone) and five-way selector, all on pickguard.
● Chromed pickguard.

HANK MARVIN CLASSIC STRATOCASTER 2000
Signature on headstock.
Similar to CLASSIC 50s STRATOCASTER (see listing in earlier Mexico Replica Stratocasters section), except:
● Hank Marvin signature on headstock.
● Body red only.
● Six-pivot bridge/vibrato unit with special design vibrato arm.
Limited edition of 250.

HANK MARVIN STRATOCASTER 1997 *Signature on body.*
Similar to TRADITIONAL STRATOCASTER (see later listing), except:

● Fretted maple neck only; Hank Marvin signature on body.
● Body red only.
Limited edition of 300.

JIMMIE VAUGHAN TEX-MEX STRATOCASTER
1997–current *Signature on back of headstock.*
Similar to STANDARD STRATOCASTER (see later listing), except:
● Fretted maple neck only; Jimmie Vaughan signature on back of headstock.
● 11-screw white plastic pickguard.
● Modified control operation.

KENNY WAYNE SHEPHERD STRATOCASTER
2010–current *Signature on back of headstock.*
Similar to CLASSIC 60s STRATOCASTER (see listing in earlier Mexico Replica Stratocasters section), except:
● Kenny Wayne Shepherd signature on back of headstock.
● Body sunburst, black with silver stripes or white with black cross.
● 11-screw black or white laminated plastic pickguard.

RICHIE SAMBORA STANDARD STRATOCASTER
1994–2002 *Signature on headstock.*
Similar to STANDARD STRATOCASTER (see later listing), except:
● Maple neck with rosewood fingerboard only; single-bar string-guide; locking nut; Richie Sambora signature on headstock.
● Body various colours.
● Two white six-polepiece pickups and one white coverless humbucker (at bridge).
● Two-pivot locking bridge/vibrato unit.

RITCHIE BLACKMORE STRATOCASTER 2009–current
Signature on headstock.
Similar to CLASSIC 70s STRATOCASTER (see listing in earlier Mexico Replica Stratocasters section), except:
● Maple neck with scalloped rosewood fingerboard only; Ritchie Blackmore signature on large headstock.
● Body white only.
● Two black six-polepiece pickups (bridge pickup angled); centre pickup missing, cover only installed.
● Three controls (volume, two tone) and three-way selector, all on pickguard; jack socket in body face.

ROBERT CRAY STRATOCASTER 2003–current *Signature on headstock.*
Similar to CLASSIC 60s STRATOCASTER (see listing in earlier Mexico Replica Stratocasters section), except:
● Robert Cray signature on headstock.
● Body sunburst, silver or violet.
● Six-saddle bridge with through-body stringing.

SILVER SISTER STRATOCASTER 2007 *Silver body and headstock face*
Similar to STANDARD STRATOCASTER HSS (see later listing) except:

- Maple neck with rosewood fingerboard only; silver-faced headstock.
- Body silver only.
- Gold anodised metal pickguard.

SPECIAL STRATOCASTER See later STANDARD STRATOCASTER listing.

SPLATTER STRATOCASTER 2003 Coloured splatter finish on body and pickguard.
Similar to STANDARD STRATOCASTER (see later listing), except:
- Body various colours, splatter finish.
- 11-screw plastic pickguard in splatter finish matching body colour.

SQUIER SERIES FLOYD ROSE STANDARD STRATOCASTER See earlier FLOYD ROSE STANDARD STRATOCASTER listing.

SQUIER SERIES STANDARD STRATOCASTER See later TRADITIONAL STRATOCASTER listing.

STANDARD FAT STRAT 1999–current Modern-style 'thick' Fender headstock logo in silver, two single-coils and one humbucker, six-pivot vibrato.
Similar to STANDARD STRATOCASTER (see later listing), except:
- Two white six-polepiece pickups and one white coverless humbucker (at bridge).
Known as STANDARD STRATOCASTER HSS (2004–current).

STANDARD FAT STRAT FLOYD ROSE 1999–current Two-pivot locking vibrato system, two white single-coils and one white humbucker, white pickguard, small headstock, three controls.
Similar to STANDARD STRATOCASTER (see later listing), except:
- Maple neck with rosewood fingerboard only; single-bar string-guide; locking nut.
- Two white six-polepiece pickups and one white coverless humbucker (at bridge).
- Two-pivot locking bridge/vibrato unit.
Known as STANDARD FAT STRAT WITH LOCKING TREMOLO (2002–03).
Known as STANDARD STRATOCASTER HSS WITH LOCKING TREMOLO (2004–current).

STANDARD FAT STRAT WITH LOCKING TREMOLO See previous STANDARD FAT STRAT FLOYD ROSE listing.

STANDARD ROLAND READY STRAT 1998–current Six-pivot vibrato, one string-guide, extra slim white pickup at bridge.
Similar to STANDARD STRATOCASTER (see later listing), except:

- Maple neck with rosewood fingerboard only.
- Additional slim white plain-top Roland synthesiser pickup (at bridge).
- Three controls (volume, tone, synth volume), five-way selector, two push-buttons and mini-switch, all on pickguard; jack socket in body face; side-mounted multi-pin synth output.

STANDARD SATIN STRATOCASTER 2003–06 Satin body finish, small headstock, white black pickguard, three black single-coils.
Similar to STANDARD STRATOCASTER (see later listing), except:
- Body various colours, satin finish.
- Three black six-polepiece pickups.
- 11-screw black laminated plastic pickguard.

STANDARD STRATOCASTER 1991–current Modern-style 'thick' Fender headstock logo in silver, three white single-coils, six-pivot vibrato.
- Fretted maple neck, or maple neck with rosewood fingerboard; truss-rod adjuster at headstock end; one string-guide.
- Body sunburst or colours.
- Three white six-polepiece pickups (bridge pickup angled).
- Three controls (volume, two tone) and five-way selector, all on pickguard; jack-socket in body face.
- 11-screw white laminated plastic pickguard.
- Six-pivot bridge/vibrato unit.
Originally known as SPECIAL STRATOCASTER in UK.
Modern-style 'thick' Fender headstock logo in black (2010–current).

STANDARD STRATOCASTER FMT 2005–06 Figured-top body, no pickguard, three black single-coils.
- Maple neck with rosewood fingerboard; truss-rod adjuster at headstock end; one string-guide.
- Body with figured top; cherry sunburst or tobacco sunburst.
- Three black six-polepiece pickups (bridge pickup angled).
- Two controls (volume, tone) and five-way selector, all on body; side-mounted jack socket.
- No pickguard.
- Six-pivot bridge/vibrato unit.

STANDARD STRATOCASTER HH 2004–06 Two-pivot vibrato, two black humbuckers, black pickguard, small headstock.
Similar to STANDARD STRATOCASTER (see earlier listing), except:
- Maple neck with rosewood fingerboard only.
- Two black coverless humbuckers.
- 11-screw black laminated plastic pickguard.

STANDARD STRATOCASTER HSS See earlier STANDARD FAT STRAT listing.

STANDARD STRATOCASTER HSS WITH LOCKING TREMOLO *See earlier STANDARD FAT STRAT FLOYD ROSE listing.*

STANDARD 60th ANNIVERSARY STRATOCASTER 2006
Commemorative neckplate, fretted maple neck.
Similar to STANDARD STRATOCASTER (see earlier listing), except:
- Fretted maple neck only; commemorative neckplate.
- Body silver grey only.

STRAT SPECIAL 1994–96 *Black pickups and pickguard.*
Similar to STANDARD STRATOCASTER (see previous listing), except:
- Two black six-polepiece pickups and one black coverless humbucker (at bridge).
- Two controls (volume, tone), five-way selector and coil-switch, all on pickguard.
- 11-screw black laminated plastic pickguard.
- Black-plated hardware
Known as CONTEMPORARY STRATOCASTER in UK.

TEX-MEX STRAT 1996–97 *Vintage-style 'thin' Fender headstock logo in gold, three white single-coils.*
Similar to STANDARD STRATOCASTER (see earlier listing), except:
- Headstock with vintage-style Fender headstock logo in gold.
Fitted with different-specification visually-similar pickups.

TEX-MEX STRAT SPECIAL 1997 *Vintage-style 'thin' Fender headstock logo in gold, two white single-coils and one white humbucker.*
Similar to STANDARD STRATOCASTER (see earlier listing), except:
- Two white six-polepiece pickups and one white coverless humbucker (at bridge).

TOM DELONGE STRATOCASTER 2001–03 *One white humbucker, one control.*
- Maple neck with rosewood fingerboard; truss-rod adjuster at headstock end; one string-guide; large headstock; Tom Delonge engraved neckplate.
- Body various colours.
- One white coverless humbucker (at bridge).
- One control (volume) on pickguard; jack socket in body face.
- 11-screw white or white pearl laminated plastic pickguard.
- Six-saddle small bridge with through-body stringing.

TRADITIONAL FAT STRAT 1996–98 *Modern-style 'thick' Fender headstock logo in black, two white single-coils and one white humbucker.*
Similar to TRADITIONAL STRATOCASTER (see next listing), except:
- Two white six-polepiece pickups and one white coverless humbucker (at bridge).

TRADITIONAL STRATOCASTER 1996–98 *Modern-style 'thick' Fender headstock logo in black, three white single-coils.*

- Fretted maple neck, or maple neck with rosewood fingerboard; truss-rod adjuster at headstock end; one string-guide.
- Body black, red, or white.
- Three white six-polepiece pickups (bridge pickup angled).
- Three controls (volume, two tone) and five-way selector, all on pickguard; jack-socket in body face.
- 11-screw white laminated plastic pickguard.
- Six-pivot bridge/vibrato unit.
Previously known as SQUIER SERIES STANDARD STRATOCASTER, with small Squier Series logo on headstock (1994–96).

50th ANNIVERSARY GOLDEN STRATOCASTER 2004
Gold-finish body.
Similar to CLASSIC 50s STRATOCASTER (see listing in earlier Mexico Replica Stratocasters section), except:
- Body gold only.
- Gold anodised metal pickguard.
- Gold-plated hardware.

JAPAN-MADE STRATOCASTERS

This section lists only the models marketed outside of Japan, all of which have 'Made In Japan' or 'Crafted in Japan' somewhere on the instrument. It does not cover the guitars produced solely for the Japanese market, which include numerous interpretations of Fender's established designs and many combinations of construction, components, and cosmetics.

The periods of availability for models sold in Japan often differ greatly to those of the same models officially sold in export markets. These export models, listed here, often appear to go in and out of availability, usually as demand from a particular distributor fluctuates. For that reason, certain Japanese models are irregularly removed from and then replaced in Fender's catalogues in the USA and Europe – while manufacture of the model in Japan might well remain continuous. These interruptions to availability are confusing from a Western point of view and make it difficult to accurately pin down the true periods of production. We have reflected this in the listing here by simply showing a start date followed by 'onward'.

Japanese Stratocasters are divided into two sections: Japan Replica; and Japan Revised.

JAPAN REPLICA STRATOCASTERS

Listed here in alphabetical order are the Japan-made models for sale outside Japan that replicate various standard-version US-made Stratocasters (see earlier US-made Regular Stratocasters section).

ANTIGUA STRATOCASTER 2004 *Replica of 1977-period US original with white/brown shaded body finish and matching pickguard (see STRATOCASTER CBS SEVENTIES listing in earlier US Regular Stratocasters section).*

STRATOCASTER '68 1988–onward *Replica of 1968-period US original (see STRATOCASTER CBS SIXTIES listing in earlier US-made Regular Stratocasters section).*

STRATOCASTER '72 1985–onward *Replica of 1972-period US original (see STRATOCASTER CBS SEVENTIES listing in earlier US-made Regular Stratocasters section).*

50s STRATOCASTER 1985–onward *Replica of 1957-period US original (see STRATOCASTER PRE-CBS listing in earlier US-made Regular Stratocasters section). Also FIXED-BRIDGE STRATOCASTER with six-saddle bridge and through-body stringing. Previously known in UK as SQUIER SERIES '57 STRATOCASTER, with small Squier Series logo on headstock (1982–83). Sold under the actual Squier brandname (1983–85) and new Fender version introduced in 1985, although Japanese market manufacture continuous since 1982. Foto Flame fake figured wood finish option (1992–94).*

60s STRATOCASTER 1985–onward *Replica of 1962-period US original (see STRATOCASTER PRE-CBS listing in earlier US-made Regular Stratocasters section). Previously known in UK as SQUIER SERIES '62 STRATOCASTER, with small Squier Series logo on headstock (1982–83). Sold under the actual Squier brandname (1983–85) and new Fender version introduced in 1985, although Japanese market manufacture continuous since 1982. Foto Flame fake-figured-wood finish option (1992–94).*

JAPAN REVISED STRATOCASTERS

Listed here in alphabetical order are the Japan-made models for sale outside Japan that we regard as revised and adapted versions of the standard-version US-made Stratocasters (see earlier US-made Regular Stratocasters section).

AERODYNE CLASSIC STRATOCASTER 2006–09
Aerodyne Series on headstock, figured carved body top.
Similar to AERODYNE STRATOCASTER first version (see next listing), except:
● Aerodyne Series on matching colour headstock face.
● Bound body with figured carved top; various colours.
● Three white six-polepiece pickups (bridge pickup angled).
● 11-screw white laminated plastic pickguard.

AERODYNE STRATOCASTER first version 2004
Aerodyne Series on headstock, three black single-coils, black pickguard.
● Maple neck with rosewood fingerboard; 22 frets; truss-rod adjuster at headstock end; one string-guide; Aerodyne Series on black-face headstock.
● Bound body with carved top; black only.
● Three black six-polepiece pickups (bridge pickup angled).
● Three controls (volume, two tone) and five-way selector, all on pickguard; jack socket in body face.
● 11-screw black laminated plastic pickguard.
● Six-pivot bridge/vibrato unit.

AERODYNE STRATOCASTER second version 2005–06
Aerodyne Series on headstock, three black single-coils, no pickguard.
Similar to AERODYNE STRATOCASTER first version (see previous listing), except:
● Three controls (volume, two tone) and five-way selector, all on body; side-mounted jack socket.
● No pickguard.

BLUE FLOWER STRATOCASTER first version 1988–93
Blue floral-pattern body finish, large headstock.
Similar to STRATOCASTER '72 (see listing in earlier Japan Replica Stratocasters section), except:
● Fretted maple neck only.
● Body blue floral-pattern only.
● Eleven-screw blue floral-pattern pickguard.

BLUE FLOWER STRATOCASTER second version 2003
Blue floral-pattern body finish, small headstock.
Similar to BLUE FLOWER STRATOCASTER first version, except:
● Small headstock; truss-rod adjuster at body end,

CONTEMPORARY STRATOCASTER first type 1985–87
One black humbucker, normal logo, black neck.
● Maple neck with rosewood fingerboard; 22 frets; truss-rod adjuster at headstock end; string-clamp; black neck.
● Body various colours.
● One black coverless humbucker (at bridge).
● One control (volume) on body; side-mounted jack socket.
● No pickguard.
● Two -pivot bridge/vibrato unit.
● Black-plated hardware.

CONTEMPORARY STRATOCASTER second type
1985–87 *Two black humbuckers, black neck.*
Similar to CONTEMPORARY STRATOCASTER first type, except:
● Two black coverless humbuckers.
● Two controls (volume, tone) and three-way selector, all on pickguard.
● 11-screw black plastic pickguard.

CONTEMPORARY STRATOCASTER third type 1985–87
Two black single-coils and one black humbucker, black neck.
Similar to CONTEMPORARY STRATOCASTER first type, except:
● Two black six-polepiece pickups and one black coverless humbucker (at bridge).
● Two controls (volume, tone), five-way selector and coil-switch, all on pickguard.
● 11-screw black plastic pickguard.

CONTEMPORARY STRATOCASTER fourth type
1985–87 *Lever-type locking nut, two black single-coils and one black humbucker.*
Similar to CONTEMPORARY STRATOCASTER first type, except:

- Two string-guides; lever-type locking nut; black-face headstock.
- Two black six-polepiece pickups and one black coverless humbucker (at bridge).
- Two controls (volume, tone), five-way selector and coil-switch, all on pickguard.
- 11-screw black plastic pickguard.
- Chrome-plated hardware.

CONTEMPORARY STRATOCASTER DELUXE first type

1985–87 *Two black-cover humbuckers, normal colour neck.*
Similar to CONTEMPORARY STRATOCASTER first type, except:
- Two string-guides; lever-type locking nut; black-face headstock.
- Two black-cover humbuckers.
- Two controls (volume, tone), three-way selector and coil-switch, all on pickguard.
- 11-screw black plastic pickguard.
- Chrome-plated hardware.

CONTEMPORARY STRATOCASTER DELUXE second

type 1985–87 *Two black single-coils and one black-cover humbucker.*
Similar to CONTEMPORARY STRATOCASTER first type, except:
- Two string-guides; lever-type locking nut; black-face headstock.
- Two black six-polepiece pickups and one black cover humbucker (at bridge).
- Two controls (volume, tone), five-way selector and coil-switch, al! on pickguard.
- 11-screw black plastic pickguard.
- Chrome-plated hardware.

FIXED-BRIDGE STRATOCASTER *See later STANDARD STRATOCASTER second version listing, and 50s STRATOCASTER listing in earlier Replica Stratocasters section.*

FLOYD ROSE HRR STRATOCASTER *See later HRR STRATOCASTER listing.*

FLOYD ROSE STANDARD STRATOCASTER 1994–96

Two white single-coils and one white humbucker, normal colour neck, two-pivot locking vibrato system.
- Maple neck with rosewood fingerboard; truss-rod adjuster at headstock end; single-bar string-guide; locking nut.
- Body with Foto Flame fake figured wood finish; sunburst, blue or red.
- Two white six-polepiece pickups and one white coverless humbucker (at bridge).
- Two controls (volume, tone) and five-way selector, all on pickguard; jack socket in body face.
- 11-screw white laminated plastic pickguard.
- Two-pivot locking bridge/vibrato unit.

Also known as SQUIER SERIES FLOYD ROSE STANDARD STRATOCASTER, with small Squier Series logo on headstock (1992–96).

FOTO FLAME STRATOCASTER 1994–96 *Three white single-coils, 21 frets, fake figured wood finish.*

Similar to 60s STRATOCASTER (see listing in earlier Japan Replica Stratocasters section), except:
- Foto Flame fake figured wood finish neck.
- Foto Flame fake figured wood finish body; sunbursts or natural.
- 11-screw white or white pearl laminated plastic pickguard.

HANK MARVIN STRATOCASTER 1996–97 *Signature on headstock.*

Similar to 50s STRATOCASTER (see listing in earlier Japan Replica Stratocasters section), except:
- Hank Marvin signature on headstock.
- Body red only.

HM POWER STRAT first type 1988–89 *One black humbucker, black-face headstock with large flamboyant 'Strat' logo.*

- Maple neck with rosewood fingerboard; 25-inch scale, 24 frets; truss-rod adjuster at headstock end; locking nut; flamboyant 'Strat' logo on black-face headstock.
- Smaller body; various colours.
- One black coverless humbucker (at bridge).
- Two controls (volume, tone) and coil-switch, all on body; side-mounted jack socket.
- No pickguard.
- Two -pivot locking bridge/vibrato unit.
- Black-plated hardware.

Some examples with International Series logo on headstock.

HM POWER STRAT second type 1988–89 *Two black single-coils and one black humbucker, black-face headstock with large flamboyant 'Strat' logo.*

Similar to HM POWER STRAT first type, except:
- Fretted maple neck, or maple neck with rosewood fingerboard.
- Two black six-polepiece pickups and one black coverless humbucker (at bridge).
- Three controls (volume, two tone), five-way selector and coil-switch, all on body.

HM STRAT first type 1991–92 *Black-face headstock with 'stencil'-style 'Strat' logo.*

- Fretted maple neck, or maple neck with rosewood fingerboard; 25.1-inch scale, 24 frets; truss-rod adjuster at headstock end; single-bar string-guide; locking nut; 'stencil'-style Strat logo on black-face headstock.
- Smaller body; various colours.
- Two black six-polepiece pickups and one black coverless humbucker (at bridge).
- Two controls (volume, tone) and five-way selector, all on body; side-mounted jack socket.
- No pickguard.
- Two-pivot locking bridge/vibrato unit.
- Black-plated hardware.

HM STRAT second type 1991–92 *Drooped black-face headstock with long 'streamlined' Fender logo.*
- Fretted maple neck, or maple neck with rosewood fingerboard; 25.1-inch scale, 22 frets; truss-rod adjuster at headstock end; single-bar string-guide; locking nut; long 'streamlined' Fender logo on drooped black-face headstock.
- Smaller body; various colours.
- Two black coverless humbuckers and one black six-polepiece pickup (in centre).
- Two controls (volume, tone) and five-way selector, all on pickguard; side-mounted jack socket
- Eight-screw black laminated plastic pickguard.
- Two-pivot locking bridge/vibrato unit.
- Black-plated hardware.

HRR STRATOCASTER 1990–94 *22 frets, three controls on pickguard with rectangular hole for humbucker, two-pivot locking vibrato system.*
- Fretted maple neck, or maple neck with rosewood fingerboard; 22 frets; truss-rod adjuster at headstock end; single-bar string-guide; locking nut.
- Body sunburst or colours.
- Two white six-polepiece pickups and one coverless humbucker (at bridge).
- Three controls (volume, two tone) and five-way selector, all on pickguard; jack socket in body face.
- 11-screw white plastic or laminated plastic pickguard.
- Two-pivot locking bridge/vibrato unit.

Also known as FLOYD ROSE HRR STRATOCASTER (1992–94). Foto Flame fake-figured-wood finish option (1992–94).

IRON MAIDEN SIGNATURE STRATOCASTER 2001–02 *Iron Maiden on headstock.*
- Fretted maple neck only; 22 frets; truss-rod adjuster at headstock end; single-bar string-guide; locking nut; Iron Maiden on headstock.
- Body black only.
- Two black twin-blade humbuckers and one small black 12-polepiece humbucker (angled at bridge).
- Three controls (volume, two tone) and five-way selector, all on pickguard; jack socket in body face.
- 11-screw mirror plastic pickguard.
- Two-pivot locking bridge/vibrato unit.

JERRY DONAHUE HELLECASTERS STRATOCASTER 1997–98 *Signature on headstock, 'Hellecasters' inlay at 12th fret.*
- Fretted maple neck; truss-rod adjuster at headstock end; one string-guide; roller nut; 'Hellecasters' inlay at 12th fret; Jerry Donahue signature on headstock.
- Body blue only.
- Three white six-polepiece pickups (bridge pickup angled).
- Three controls (volume, tone, two-way rotary switch) and five-way selector, all on pickguard; jack socket in body face.

- 11-screw blue sparkle laminated plastic pickguard.
- Six-pivot bridge/vibrato unit.

JOHN JORGENSON HELLECASTER 1997–98 *Signature and model name on headstock, three split pickups.*
- Maple neck with rosewood fingerboard, gold sparkle dot markers; 22 frets; truss-rod adjuster at headstock end; locking tuners; 'Hellecasters' inlay at 12th fret; John Jorgenson signature on large Stratocaster reverse headstock.
- Body black sparkle only.
- Three black plain-top split pickups (bridge pickup angled).
- Three controls (volume, two tone) and five-way selector, all on pickguard; jack socket in body face.
- 11-screw gold sparkle laminated plastic pickguard.
- Two-pivot bridge/vibrato unit.
- Gold-plated hardware.

MATTHIAS JABS STRATOCASTER 1998 *Ringed planet position markers.*
- Maple neck with rosewood fingerboard, ringed planet position markers; 22 frets; truss-rod adjuster at headstock end; locking tuners; scroll inlay at 12th fret.
- Body red only.
- Two white six-polepiece pickups and one white coverless humbucker (at bridge).
- Three controls (two volume, tone) and five-way selector, all on pickguard; jack socket in body face.
- 11-screw white plastic pickguard.
- Six-pivot bridge/vibrato unit.

PAISLEY STRATOCASTER 1988–onward *Pink paisley-pattern body finish.*
Similar to STRATOCASTER '72 (see listing in earlier Japan Replica Stratocasters section), except:
- Fretted maple neck only.
- Body pink paisley-pattern only.
- 11-screw pink paisley-pattern pickguard.

RICHIE SAMBORA PAISLEY STRATOCASTER 1996 *Signature on headstock, black paisley-pattern body finish.*
- Fretted maple neck, star markers; 22 frets; truss-rod adjuster at headstock end; pearl tuner buttons; single-bar string-guide; locking nut; Richie Sambora signature on headstock.
- Body black paisley-pattern only.
- Two black six-polepiece pickups and one black coverless humbucker (at bridge).
- Three controls (volume, two tone) and five-way selector, all on pickguard; jack socket in body face.
- 11-screw black paisley laminated plastic pickguard.
- Two-pivot locking bridge/vibrato unit.

RITCHIE BLACKMORE STRATOCASTER 1997–98 *Signature on headstock, centre pickup missing – only cover installed.*

- Maple neck with scalloped rosewood fingerboard; 'bullet' truss-rod adjuster at headstock end; two string-guides; Ritchie Blackmore signature on large headstock.
- Body white only.
- Two black six-polepiece pickups (bridge pickup angled); centre pickup missing, cover only installed.
- Three controls (volume, two tone) and three-way selector, all on pickguard; jack socket in body face.
- 11-screw white laminated plastic pickguard.
- Six-pivot bridge/vibrato unit.

SHORT-SCALE STRATOCASTER 1989–95 *Two controls, 22 frets*.
- Fretted maple neck, or maple neck with rosewood fingerboard; 24-inch scale, 22 frets; truss-rod adjuster at headstock end; one string-guide.
- Body sunburst or colours.
- Three white six-polepiece pickups (bridge pickup angled).
- Two controls (volume, tone) and five-way selector, all on pickguard; jack socket in body face.
- Eight-screw white laminated plastic pickguard.
- Two-pivot bridge/vibrato unit.

SPECIAL STRATOCASTER *UK designation for STANDARD STRATOCASTER second version (see later listing).*

SQUIER SERIES FLOYD ROSE STANDARD STRATOCASTER 1992–96 *See earlier FLOYD ROSE STANDARD STRATOCASTER listing.*

SQUIER SERIES '57 STRATOCASTER *See 50s STRATOCASTER listing in earlier Japan Replica Stratocasters section.*

SQUIER SERIES '62 STRATOCASTER *See 60s STRATOCASTER listing in earlier Japan Replica Stratocasters section.*

STANDARD STRATOCASTER first version 1985–89 *22 frets, two-pivot vibrato.*
- Fretted maple neck, or maple neck with rosewood fingerboard; 22 frets; truss-rod adjuster at headstock end; string clamp (locking nut from 1988).
- Body sunburst or colours.
- Three white six-polepiece pickups (bridge pickup angled).
- Three controls (volume, two tone) and five-way selector, all on pickguard; jack socket in body face.
- 11-screw white laminated plastic pickguard.
- Two-pivot bridge/vibrato unit (locking type from 1988).

STANDARD STRATOCASTER second version 1988–91 *21 frets, two string-guides.*
Similar to 50s STRATOCASTER and 60s STRATOCASTER (see listings in earlier Japan Replica Stratocasters section), except:

- Two string-guides.
Also FIXED-BRIDGE STRATOCASTER with six-saddle bridge and through-body stringing.
Previously sold under Squier brandname (1986–88). Production moved to Mexico from 1991 (see STANDARD STRATOCASTER listing in earlier Mexico-made Stratocasters section). Known as SPECIAL STRATOCASTER in UK.

STRAT XII first version 12-string 1988–96 *12-string headstock, offset-cutaway body, 22 frets.*
- Maple neck with rosewood fingerboard; 24.75-inch scale, 22 frets; truss-rod adjuster at body end; one 'bracket' string-guide; six-tuners-per-side headstock.
- Body sunburst or colours.
- Three white six-polepiece pickups (bridge pickup angled).
- Three controls (volume, two tone) and five-way selector, all on pickguard; jack socket in body face.
- 11-screw white laminated plastic pickguard.
- 12-saddle bridge with through-body stringing.

STRAT XII second version 12-string 2005–09 *12-string headstock, offset-cutaway body, 21 frets.*
Similar to STRAT XII first version (see previous listing), except:
- 25.5-inch scale, 21 frets.
- Body sunburst, blue, or red.
- 12-saddle bridge, with through-body stringing for six strings.

THE VENTURES STRATOCASTER 1996 *The Ventures logo on headstock, three white plain-top pickups.*
- Maple neck with bound rosewood fingerboard, block markers; 22 frets; truss-rod adjuster at body end; one string-guide; The Ventures logo on black-face headstock.
- Body black only.
- Three white plain-top Lace Sensor pickups (pickup at bridge is angled).
- Three controls (volume, tone, boost) and five-way selector, all on pickguard; jack socket in body face; active circuit.
- 11-screw white pearl laminated plastic pickguard.
- Six-pivot bridge/vibrato unit.
- Gold-plated hardware.
Optional Ventures logo for body.

YNGWIE MALMSTEEN STANDARD STRATOCASTER 1991–94 *Signature on headstock.*
- Scalloped fretted maple neck; 'bullet' truss-rod adjuster at headstock end; two string-guides; three-screw neckplate.
- Body black, blue, or white.
- Three black six-polepiece pickups (pickup at bridge is angled).
- Three controls (volume, two tones) and five-way selector, all on pickguard; jack socket in body face.
- 11-screw white laminated plastic pickguard.
- Six-pivot bridge/vibrato unit.

KOREA-MADE STRATOCASTERS

Many models made in Korea for Fender bear the Squier brandname and so are outside the scope of this reference section. However, a few have prominently featured the Fender logo, and these are listed here. All have 'Made in Korea' somewhere on the instrument.

KOA STRATOCASTER 2006–08 *Rosewood fingerboard, white pearl pickguard.*
- Maple neck with rosewood fingerboard; 22 frets; truss-rod adjuster at headstock end; two string-guides.
- Body with Koa veneer top; sunburst only.
- Three white six polepiece pickups (bridge pickup angled).
- Three controls (volume, two tone) and five-way selector, all on pickguard; jack socket in body face.
- 11-screw white pearl laminated plastic pickguard.
- Two-pivot bridge/vibrato unit.

LITE ASH STRATOCASTER 2004–08 *Maple neck with maple fingerboard, three Seymour Duncan logo black single-coils, black pickguard.*
- Maple neck with maple fingerboard; 22 frets; truss-rod adjuster at headstock end; two string-guides.
- Body natural, black or white.
- Three Seymour Duncan logo black six-polepiece pickups (bridge pickup angled).
- Three controls (volume, two tone) and five-way selector, all on pickguard; jack socket in body face.
- 11-screw black plastic pickguard.
- Two-pivot bridge/vibrato unit.

SQUIER SERIES STANDARD STRATOCASTER 1992–94 *Small Squier Series logo on headstock.*
- Fretted maple neck, or maple neck with rosewood fingerboard; 21 frets; truss-rod adjuster at headstock end; two string-guides; small Squier Series logo on headstock.
- Body various colours.
- Three white six-polepiece pickups (bridge pickup angled).
- Three controls (volume, two tone) and five-way selector, all on pickguard; jack socket in body face.
- 11-screw white plastic pickguard.
- Six-pivot bridge/vibrato unit.
Replaced by Mexican-made version in 1994 (see TRADITIONAL STRATOCASTER in earlier Mexico-made Stratocasters section).

TIE-DYE STRAT HS 2005 *Multi-coloured body front, matching headstock face.*
- Maple neck with rosewood fingerboard, no front markers; 22 frets; truss-rod adjuster at headstock end; two string-guides; multi-colour headstock face.
- Body black, multi-colour front, two colour combinations only.
- One black six-polepiece pickup (at neck) and one black coverless humbucker (at bridge).
- Two controls (volume, tone) and three-way selector, all on body; side-mounted jack socket.
- No pickguard.
- Two-pivot bridge/vibrato unit.
- Black-plated hardware.

SQUIER

This was a brandname borrowed from the Fender-owned V.C. Squier string company. It first appeared on Japan-made Fender guitars exported into Europe in the early 80s and later elsewhere. Fender's policy was for the Squier line to cater for lower-price instruments, maintaining the company's ever-expanding market coverage – but not by cheapening the Fender name itself.

The Squier logo, supported by a small but important "by Fender" line, appeared on an increasing number of models during the decade. At first these came from Japan, but escalating production costs prompted a move to cheaper manufacturing sources. Korea came on line in 1985, and India made a brief contribution in the late 1980s for early Squier II examples (or Sunn, another borrowed brandname).

Fender's facility in Mexico helped out, too, in the early 90s, and more recently other sources have provided entry-level electrics with the kudos of a Fender connection: China and Indonesia have entered the picture, India has re-entered, and Korea has faded way. Periodic returns to Japanese production have yielded impressive results.

The continuing success story of Squier makes it a very important support brand for Fender, often showing a level of design flair and build quality that exceeds its apparent status as a secondary line.

DATING STRATOCASTERS

Finding a method to date a guitar is important. Not only can it help satisfy our natural curiosity about the origins of a guitar but also, in the case of desirable instruments, the vintage can have a great bearing on the guitar's value. The Fender brand has its fair share of collectables, and as prices of the more sought-after models often reach high levels, any corroboratory clues that indicate the year of production are important.

Changes specific to each Fender model have been indicated in the main listings in the previous pages. Although the respective features for some individual models can provide dating clues, these are comparatively few. We've brought together here some of these few general pointers that are relevant to the period of production of US-made models, but even these should be regarded as fallible.

Neck-plate

The standard method used by Fender to fix a guitar neck to the body is with four screws, often erroneously called 'bolts' in Fenderspeak. This is normally accomplished using a metal neck-plate to reinforce the joint. The rectangular four-screw neck-plate has been used since the inception of the first Fender solidbody electric guitars and provides a simple and secure foundation for the neck.

From 1971 to 1981, a restyled three-screw version (actually two screws and one bolt) was used on the Stratocaster (as well as on three Telecaster models and the Starcaster). After 1981, Fender reverted to using the four-screw type for most instruments (excluding any glued-neck models, of course).

From 1954 to 1976, the neck-plate carried a stamped serial number (some of the earliest Strats had the number on the rear vibrato-cavity back-plate). From 1976 onward, the serial appears on the headstock face, except for various vintage reissues and limited editions.

From 1965 to 1983, the neck-plate (both four- and three-screw types) was stamped with a large, reversed 'F'.

Tuners

It was not easy at first for Fender to find tuners to suit Leo's ideal of a small, neat headstock with straight string-pull. The problem was solved by using products supplied by the Chicago-based Kluson company, although even these had to be cut down by Race & Olmsted to squeeze them into the minimal length available. The Klusons used by Fender each had a safety string post, a slotted shaft with a central vertical hole designed to take the end of the string and thus eliminate the unsightly and dangerous length of protruding string. These tuners were used from 1950 to 1966, and the following variations of the markings on their metal covers can provide an indication of date.

Version 1, used in 1950 and 1951, and thus not relevant to the Strat, has "Kluson Deluxe" and "Pat. Appld" stamped on the cover.

Version 2, used from 1951 to 1957, has no markings on the cover.

Version 3, used from 1957 to 1964, has "Kluson Deluxe" stamped in a single, central, vertical line on the cover.

Version 4, used from 1964 to 1966, has "Kluson" and "Deluxe" stamped in two parallel, vertical lines on the cover.

Due to supply and quality problems with Kluson, Fender wanted to make a tuner of its own, and in 1965 contracted Race & Olmsted to supply a revised, cheaper design. The result was a tuner with an angled baseplate, 'F'-stamped

cover, and a less rounded button. It was used on Fender instruments until 1976, when it was replaced by a more competitively-priced version made by the German Schaller company, until 1983. Although ostensibly very similar in appearance, the Schaller unit has a different construction, and can be distinguished by its closed cover, with no visible axle-end on the side.

Neck / Fingerboard Construction

From 1950 to 1959, Fender used a fretted one-piece maple neck, with no separate fingerboard.

From 1959 to 1962, the top of the maple neck was planed flat and fitted with a rosewood fingerboard, flat on the base and cambered on top. The appearance of the straight join between fingerboard and neck when viewed from the body end of the neck has led to its nickname as a slab board.

From 1962 to 1983, the top of the maple neck itself was cambered and then fitted with a thin-section rosewood fingerboard that followed the same curve. Again, the appearance of the curved join of the neck-end provides its nickname as a laminate board. An even thinner version appeared around 1963. A maple fingerboard was offered as an option, officially from 1967 but often supplied prior to that date. In 1970, the fretted one-piece maple neck was reinstated as an alternative to the rosewood fingerboard.

Since 1983, Fender has reverted to a rosewood fingerboard, and this is the principal version, with the maple equivalent as an option.

Neck Date

During production, Fender dates various components, and one of the most consistent and obvious is the neck. The date is to be found on the body-end, either pencilled or rubber-stamped. There have been times when the neck did not carry this useful information, the longest period being between 1973 and 1981, and for instruments from that period other dating clues must suffice.

Serial Numbers

These should be regarded merely as a guide to dating, and ideally the production year of a guitar should be confirmed by other age-related aspects. As usual with a mass-manufacturer, Fender has not always assign serial numbers in exact chronological order, and number-bearing components such as neckplates have rarely been used in strict rotation. As a result, apparent discrepancies and contradictions of as much as several years can and do occur. Depending on the production period, serial numbers are located either on a Stratocaster's backplate, neckplate, or on the front or back of the headstock.

US number series	Approximate year(s)
Up to 10,000 (4 or 5 digits, inc 0 or - prefix)	1954–56
10,000s (4 or 5 digits, inc 0 or - prefix)	1955–56
10,000s to 20,000s (5 or 6 digits, inc 0 or - prefix)	1957
20,000s to 30,000s (5 or 6 digits, inc 0 or - prefix)	1958
30,000s to 40,000s	1959
40,000s to 50,000s	1960
50,000s to 70,000s	1961
60,000s to 90,000s	1962
80,000s to 90,000s	1963
Up to L10,000 (L + 5 digits)	1963
L10,000s to L20,000s (L + 5 digits)	1963
L20,000s to L50,000s (L + 5 digits)	1964
L50,000s to L90,000s (L + 5 digits)	1965
100,000s	1965
100,000s to 200,000s	1966–67
200,000s	1968
200,000s to 300,000s	1969–70
300,000s	1971–72
300,000s to 500,000s	1973
400,000s to 500,000s	1974–75
500,000s to 700,000s	1976
800,000s to 900,000s	1979–81
76 or S6 + 5 digits	1976
S7 or S8 + 5 digits	1977
S7, S8 or S9 + 5 digits	1978
S9 or E0 + 5 digits	1979
S9, E0 or E1 + 5 digits	1980–81
E1, E2 or E3 + 5 digits	1982
E2 or E3 + 5 digits	1983
E3 or E4 + 5 digits	1984–87
E4 + 5 digits	1987
E4 or E8 + 5 digits	1988
E8 or E9 + 5 digits	1989–90
E9 or N9 + 5 digits	1990–91
N0 + 5 digits	1990–91
N1 + 5/6 digits	1991–92
N2 + 5/6 digits	1992–93
N3 + 5/6 digits	1993–94
N4 + 5/6 digits	1994–95
N5 + 5/6 digits	1995–96
N6 + 5/6 digits	1996–97
N7 + 5/6 digits	1997–98
N8 + 5/6 digits	1998–99
N9 + 5/6 digits	1999–2000
DZ0 + 5/6 digits	2000
Z0 + 5/6 digits	2000–01
DZ1 + 5/6 digits	2001
Z1 + 5/6 digits	2001–02
DZ2 + 5/6 digits	2002
Z2 + 5/6 digits	2002–03
DZ3 + 5/6 digits	2003
Z3+ 5/6 digits	2003–04
DZ4 + 5/6 digits	2004
Z4 + 5/6 digits	2004–05
DZ5 + 5/6 digits	2005

US number series	Approximate year(s)
Z5 + 5/6 digits	2005–06
DZ6 + 5/6 digits	2006
Z6 + 5/6 digits	2006–07
DZ7 + 5/6 digits	2007
Z7 + 5/6 digits	2007–08
DZ8 + 5/6 digits	2008
Z8 + 5/6 digits	2008–09
DZ9 + 5/6 digits	2009
Z9 + 5/6 digits	2009–10
10 + 5/6/7 digits	2009–10
US10 + 7 digits	2010

Mexico number series	Approximate years
MN1 + 5/6 digits	1991–92
MN2 + 5/6 digits	1992–93
MN3 + 5/6 digits	1993–94
MN4 + 5/6 digits	1994–95
MN5 + 5/6 digits	1995–96
MN6 + 5/6 digits	1996–97
MN7 + 5/6 digits	1997–98
MN8 + 5/6 digits	1998–99
MN9 + 5/6 digits	1999–2000
MZO + 5/6 digits	2001–02
MZ2 + 5/6 digits	2002–03
MZ3 + 5/6 digits	2003–04
MZ4 + 5/6 digits	2004–05
MZ5 + 5/6 digits	2005–06
MZ6 + 5/6 digits	2006–07
MZ7 + 5/6 digits	2007–08
MZ8 + 5/6 digits	2008–09
MZ9 + 5/6 digits	2009–10
10 + 5/6/7 digits	2009–10
MX10 + 7 digits	2010

The numbers shown here represent the bulk of Fender's US and Mexican production (although the late-90s Fender California models featured AMXN serial prefixes, reflecting their mix of American and Mexican manufacture).

There have been and continue to be various anomalies, odd series, special prefixes, and the like, but these have no overall dating relevance and are not listed. Also excluded are the series used on Vintage replica reissues, limited editions, signature instruments, and so on, as these are specific to certain models and not directly pertinent to production year.

The listing here and overleaf does not apply to Fenders that originate from countries other than the USA, Mexico, and Japan; these (and Squier-brand instruments) have their own various number series, which unfortunately do sometimes duplicate those in the US system. Prefixes include: Y, CY, and N for China; C, V, and K for Korea; and I for Indonesia. Any confusion has to be resolved by studying other aspects of an instrument to determine its correct origin (often simply determined by a "Made In..." stamp) and production dates.

Starting in 2010, Fender introduced a new serial-numbering system for US and Mexico-made instruments. It

the stratocaster guitar book

consists of a two-letter prefix followed by nine numbers. The two-letter prefix denotes the country of manufacture, with US indicating US-made and MX indicating Mexico-made. The first two digits denote the year of manufacture, as shown in the listings on page 151, while the remaining seven numbers identify the individual instrument.

'MADE IN JAPAN'

number series	Approximate year(s)
JV + 5 digits	1982–84
SQ + 5 digits	1983–84
E + 6 digits	1984–87
A + 6 digits	1985–86, 1997–98
B + 6 digits	1985–86, 1998–99
C + 6 digits	1985–86
F + 6 digits	1986–87
G + 6 digits	1987–88
H + 6 digits	1988–89
I + 6 digits	1989–90
J + 6 digits	1989–90
K + 6 digits	1990–91
L + 6 digits	1991–92
M + 6 digits	1992–93
N + 6 digits	1993–94
O + 6 digits	1993–94
P + 6 digits	1993–94
Q + 6 digits	1993–94
S + 6 digits	1994–95
T + 6 digits	1994–95
U + 6 digits	1995–96
V + 6 digits	1996–97

'Crafted in Japan'

number series	Approximate year(s)
A + 6 digits	1997–98
B + 6 digits	1998–99
N + 5 digits	1995–96
O + 0 [zero] + 5 digits	1997–2000
P + 0 [zero] + 5 digits	1999–2002
Q + 0 [zero] + 5 digits	2002–04
R + 0 [zero] + 5 digits	2004–06
S + 0 [zero] + 5 digits	2006–08
T + 0 [zero] + 5 digits	2007–08

'Made In Japan'

number series	Approximate year(s)
S + 0 [zero] + 5 digits	2007–08
T + 0 [zero] + 5 digits	2008–09

Fender Japan's production started in 1982 and the company has used a series of prefixes to indicate the year of manufacture. The data shown here is approximate and, again, should be used as a general guide only.

Some Japanese series have been used beyond the production spans listed here, in particular the original A-, C- and G-prefix numbers. There was a change from 'MADE IN JAPAN' to 'Crafted In Japan' and then back to 'Made in Japan', somewhere on the guitar, which helps to differentiate between the sets of numbers. Once again these facts underline the need for caution when dating a Fender – and indeed most other guitars – by using only serial numbers.

PART NUMBERS

Since the 70s, many Fender catalogues and pricelists have used part numbers to make the process of ordering and stock-keeping easier for distributors and dealers. Each version and variation of a guitar is allocated a specific number, For instance, at the time of writing, a current (early 2010) sunburst rosewood-board Fender American Standard Stratocaster had the part number 011-0400-700. The digits provide various pieces of information such as model type, fingerboard wood, hardware options, finish colour, and if a case is included in the price. For our purposes it's the first three digits (011 in that American Standard example) that are particularly useful, because they indicate the instrument's country of origin. The list below reveals the manufacturing country that each code indicated at the time of writing. Some codes have been used to indicate different manufacturing countries over the years, and many of the now obsolete sources are indicated here by the word 'formerly'.

010 US factory, US Custom Shop (Fender)
011 US factory (Fender)
012 formerly US factory (Fender)
013 Mexico factory (Fender); formerly Mexico factory (Squier)
014 US factory, Mexico factory (Fender); formerly US factory (Squier)
015 US Custom Shop (Fender)
017 US factory (mostly Fender FSRs or Factory Special Runs)
018 formerly US factory (Fender)
019 US factory, US Custom Shop (Fender)
025 Japan (Fender)
026 Indonesia (Fender); formerly Korea (Fender); formerly Japan, China (Squier)
027 Japan (Fender); formerly Japan, Korea (Squier); formerly Japan (D'Aquisto)
028 China (Squier); China, Korea, Indonesia (Starcaster); formerly Japan (Fender), then India (Squier II, Sunn)
029 formerly India, Korea (Squier II, Sunn)
030 Indonesia, India, China (Squier)
031 China, Indonesia (Squier); formerly Japan (Heartfield)
032 Indonesia, China (Squier); formerly Japan (Squier); formerly Korea (Squier)
033 formerly India (Squier II); formerly Korea (Squier); formerly Japan (Squier); formerly China (Squier); formerly Indonesia (Squier)
034 Korea, China, Indonesia (Squier)
095 formerly US Custom Shop (Fender)
110 formerly US factory (Fender w/ Floyd Rose Tremolo)
111 formerly US factory (Fender w/ Floyd Rose Tremolo)
113 formerly Mexico factory (Fender w/ Floyd Rose Tremolo); formerly Mexico factory (Squier w/ Floyd Rose Tremolo)

114 Mexico factory (Fender w/ Floyd Rose Tremolo)
125 formerly Japan (Fender w/ or w/out Floyd Rose Tremolo);
formerly Japan (Heartfield w/ Floyd Rose Tremolo);
formerly Japan (Squier w/ Floyd Rose Tremolo)
132 formerly China, Indonesia (Squier w/ Floyd Rose Tremolo)
133 formerly Korea (Squier w/ Floyd Rose Tremolo)
150 US Custom Shop (Fender)
152 formerly US Custom Shop (Fender)
155 formerly US Custom Shop (Fender)

156 formerly US Custom Shop (Fender)
157 formerly US Custom Shop (Fender)
632 formerly China (Squier)
633 formerly China (Squier)
921 US Custom Shop (mostly Masterbuilt Fender)
923 US Custom Shop (mostly Custombuilt Fender); formerly
US Custom Shop (mostly Teambuilt Fender)
927 US Custom Shop (Fender)

MODEL CHRONOLOGY 1954–2010

Arranged by year of first appearance.
US production except where marked (J)
for Japan, (K) for Korea, or (M) for Mexico.
Note that *aka* means also known as,
–current indicates a model still in
production at the time of writing, and
–onward indicates a Japan-made model
with fluctuating availability outside Japan.

1954
Stratocaster (pre–CBS) 1954–65

1965
Stratocaster (CBS Sixties) 1965–71

1971
Stratocaster (CBS Seventies) 1971–81

1975
Rhinestone Stratocaster 1975

1977
Antigua Stratocaster 1977–79

1979
25th Anniversary Stratocaster 1979–80

1980
Hendrix Stratocaster 1980
Strat 1980–83

1981
Gold/Gold Stratocaster 1981–83
International Color Stratocaster 1981
Stratocaster Standard (1st version)
1981–83
Walnut Strat 1981–83

1982
Squier Series '57 Stratocaster (J) 1982–83

Squier Series '62 Stratocaster (J)
1982–83

1983
Elite Stratocaster 1983–84
Gold Elite Stratocaster 1983–84
Stratocaster Standard (2nd version)
1983–84
Walnut Elite Stratocaster 1983–84
'57 Stratocaster 1983–85, 86–98
'62 Stratocaster 1983–85, 86–98

1984
Marble Stratocaster (aka Bowling Ball
Stratocaster) 1984

1985
Contemporary Stratocaster (4 types) (J)
1985–87
Contemporary Stratocaster Deluxe (2
types) (J) 1985–87
Standard Stratocaster (1st version) (J)
1985–89
Stratocaster '72 (J) 1985–onward
50s Stratocaster (J) 1985–onward
60s Stratocaster (J) 1985–onward

1986
American Standard Stratocaster (1st
version) 1986–2000

1987
Strat Plus 1987–98

1988
Blue Flower Stratocaster (1st version) (J)
1988–93
Eric Clapton Stratocaster (1st version)
1988–2001
HM Power Strat (2 types) (J) 1988–89
Paisley Stratocaster (J) 1988–onward
Standard Stratocaster (2nd version) (J)
1988–91
Strat XII (1st version) (J) 1988–96

Stratocaster '68 (J) 1988–onward
Yngwie Malmsteen Stratocaster (1st
version) 1988–98

1989
American Standard Deluxe Stratocaster
1989–90
HM Strat (4 types) 1989–90
Short-Scale Stratocaster (J) 1989–95
Strat Plus Deluxe 1989–98
US Contemporary Stratocaster 1989–91

1990
HM Strat Ultra 1990–92
HRR Stratocaster (J) 1990–94
Strat Ultra 1990–98

1991
HM Strat (2 types) (J) 1991–92
Jeff Beck Stratocaster (1st version)
1991–2001
Standard Stratocaster (M) 1991–current
Yngwie Malmsteen Standard
Stratocaster (J) 1991–94

1992
American Classic Stratocaster 1992–99
Floyd Rose Classic Stratocaster
1992–98
Floyd Rose HRR Stratocaster (J)
1992–94
Robert Cray Stratocaster 1992–current
Set Neck Floyd Rose Stratocaster
1992–95
Set Neck Stratocaster (1st version)
1992–95
Squier Series Floyd Rose Standard
Stratocaster (J) 1992–96
Squier Series Standard Stratocaster (K)
1992–94
Stevie Ray Vaughan Stratocaster
1992–current
'54 Stratocaster 1992–98
'60 Stratocaster (1st version) 1992–98

1993

Richie Sambora Stratocaster (1st version) 1993–99
Special Edition 1993 Stratocaster 1993

1994

Aluminum-Body Stratocaster (various models) 1994–95
Dick Dale Stratocaster 1994–current
Floyd Rose Standard Stratocaster (J) 1994–96
Floyd Rose Standard Stratocaster (M) 1994–98
Foto Flame Stratocaster (J) 1994–96
Richie Sambora Standard Stratocaster (M) 1994–2002
Special Edition 1994 Stratocaster 1994
Squier Series Floyd Rose Standard Stratocaster (M) 1994–96
Squier Series Standard Stratocaster (M) 1994–96
Strat Special (M) 1994–96
40th Anniversary 1954 Stratocaster 1994

1995

American Standard Roland GR-Ready Stratocaster 1995–98
Bonnie Raitt Stratocaster 1995–2001
Buddy Guy Stratocaster 1995–2009
Carved Top Strat 1995–98
Contemporary Strat 1995–98
Contemporary Strat FMT 1995–98
Set Neck Stratocaster (2nd version) 1995–98
'54 Stratocaster FMT 1995–98
'60 Stratocaster FMT 1995–98

1996

Hank Marvin Stratocaster (J) 1996–97
Lone Star Strat 1996–2000
Relic 50s Stratocaster 1996–98
Relic 60s Stratocaster 1996–98
Richie Sambora Paisley Stratocaster (J) 1996
Tex-Mex Strat (M) 1996–97
The Ventures Stratocaster (J) 1996
Traditional Fat Strat (M) 1996–98
Traditional Stratocaster (M) 1996–98
'58 Stratocaster 1996–98
'69 Stratocaster (1st version) 1996–98
50th Anniversary Stratocaster 1996

1997

Big Apple Strat 1997–2000
California Fat Strat 1997–98
California Strat 1997–98
Collectors Edition Stratocaster 1997
Deluxe Powerhouse Strat (M) 1997–2007
Deluxe Super Strat (M) 1997–2004
Hank Marvin Stratocaster (M) 1997
Jerry Donahue Hellecasters Stratocaster (J) 1997–98
Jimi Hendrix Stratocaster 1997–2000
Jimmie Vaughan Tex-Mex Stratocaster (M) 1997–current
John Jorgensen Hellecaster (J) 1997–98
Ritchie Blackmore Stratocaster (J) 1997–98
Roadhouse Strat 1997–2000
Tex-Mex Strat Special (M) 1997

1998

American Deluxe Fat Strat 1998–2003
American Deluxe Fat Strat/Locking Trem 1998–2003
American Deluxe Stratocaster (1st version) 1998–2003
American Standard Stratocaster Hard-Tail 1998–2000
American Vintage '57 Stratocaster 1998–current
American Vintage '62 Stratocaster 1998–current
Big Apple Strat Hard-Tail 1998–2000
Carved Top Strat HH 1998
Carved Top Strat HSS 1998
Classic Player Strat 1998–2005
Deluxe Double Fat Strat Floyd Rose (M) 1998–2004
Deluxe Fat Strat Floyd Rose (M) 1998–2005
Floyd Rose Classic Strat HH 1998–2002
Floyd Rose Classic Strat HSS 1998–2002
Matthias Jabs Stratocaster (J) 1998
N.O.S. ('65) Strat 1998
Relic Floyd Rose Stratocaster 1998
Standard Roland Ready Strat (M) 1998–current
Voodoo Stratocaster 1998–2000
Yngwie Malmsteen Stratocaster (2nd version) 1998–2006

1999

Chris Rea Classic Stratocaster (M) 1999
Classic 50s Stratocaster (M) 1999–current
Classic 60s Stratocaster (M) 1999–current
Classic 70s Stratocaster (M) 1999–current
Custom Classic Strat 1999–2008
Deluxe Double Fat Strat (M) 1999–2004
Deluxe Fat Strat (1st version) (M) 1999–2006
Richie Sambora Stratocaster (2nd version) 1999–2002
Ritchie Blackmore Stratocaster 1999–2005
Standard Fat Strat (M) 1999–current
Standard Fat Strat Floyd Rose (M) 1999–current
'56 Stratocaster (N.O.S./Closet Classic/Relic) 1999–current
'60 Stratocaster (2nd version) (N.O.S./Closet Classic/Relic) 1999–current
'69 Stratocaster (2nd version) (N.O.S./Closet Classic/Relic) 1999–current

2000

American Double Fat Strat 2000–03
American Double Fat Strat Hard-Tail 2000–03
American Fat Strat Texas Special 2000–03
American Strat Texas Special 2000–03
American Stratocaster 2000–07
American Stratocaster Hard-Tail 2000–06
Hank Marvin Classic Stratocaster (M) 2000
Sub-Sonic Stratocaster HH baritone 2000–01
Sub-Sonic Stratocaster HSS baritone (1st version) 2000–01

2001

Eric Clapton Stratocaster (2nd version) 2001–current
Iron Maiden Signature Stratocaster (J) 2001–02
Jeff Beck Stratocaster (2nd version) 2001–current
Sub-Sonic Stratocaster HSS baritone (2nd version) 2001
Tom Delonge Stratocaster (M) 2001–03

2002

Buddy Guy Polka Dot Strat (M) 2002–current
Deluxe Double Fat Strat HH (M) 2002–03
Deluxe Double Fat Strat HH With Locking Tremolo (M) 2002–03
Deluxe Fat Strat HSS (M) 2002–03
Deluxe Fat Strat HSS With Locking Tremolo (M) 2002–03
Highway One Stratocaster (1st version) 2002–06

Standard Fat Strat With Locking Tremolo
(M) 2002–03
Strat Special With Locking Tremolo HH
2002
Strat Special With Locking Tremolo HSS
2002
'68 Reverse Strat Special 2002

2003
American Stratocaster HH 2003–06
American Stratocaster HH Hard–Tail
2003–05
American Stratocaster HSS 2003–07
Blue Flower Stratocaster (2nd version)
(J) 2003
Highway One Stratocaster HSS (1st
version) 2003–06
Mark Knopfler Stratocaster 2003–current
Robert Cray Stratocaster (M)
2003–current
Splatter Stratocaster (M) 2003
Standard Satin Stratocaster (M) 2003–06
Strat-O-Sonic DVI 2003–04
Strat-O-Sonic DVII 2003–06
'65 Stratocaster (N.O.S./Closet
Classic/Relic) 2003–06, 2010–current

2004
Aerodyne Stratocaster (1st version) (J)
2004
American Deluxe Ash Stratocaster
2004–current
American Deluxe Stratocaster (2nd
version) 2004–current
American Deluxe Stratocaster FMT HSS
2004–09
American Deluxe Stratocaster HSS
2004–current
American Deluxe Stratocaster HSS LT
2004–06
American Deluxe Stratocaster QMT HSS
2004–09
American Deluxe Stratocaster V Neck
2004–current
American Deluxe 50th Anniversary
Stratocaster 2004
American 50th Anniversary Stratocaster
2004
Antigua Stratocaster (J) 2004
Deluxe Players Strat (M) 2004–current
Deluxe Strat HH (M) 2004
Deluxe Strat HH With Locking Tremolo
(M) 2004
Deluxe Strat HSS (M) 2004–06
Deluxe Strat HSS With Locking Tremolo
(M) 2004–05

Eric Clapton Signature Stratocaster
2004–current
Jeff Beck Signature Stratocaster
2004–current
Lite Ash Stratocaster (K) 2004–08
Rory Gallagher Stratocaster
2004–current
Standard Stratocaster HH (M) 2004–06
Standard Stratocaster HSS (M)
2004–current
Standard Stratocaster HSS With Locking
Tremolo (M) 2004–current
50th Anniversary Golden Stratocaster
(M) 2004
'66 Stratocaster (N.O.S./Closet
Classic/Relic) 2004–08

2005
Aerodyne Stratocaster (2nd version) (J)
2005–06
Deluxe Big Block Stratocaster (M) 2005–06
Eric Johnson Stratocaster Maple
2005–current
John Mayer Stratocaster 2005–current
Robin Trower Stratocaster 2005–current
Standard Stratocaster FMT (M) 2005–06
Strat-O-Sonic HH 2005–06
Strat XII (2nd version) (J) 2005–09
Tie-Dye Strat HS (K) 2005

2006
Aerodyne Classic Stratocaster (J)
2006–09
American Vintage 70s Stratocaster
2006–current
American 60th Anniversary Stratocaster
2006
Classic Player 50s Stratocaster (M)
2006–current
Classic Player 60s Stratocaster (M)
2006–current
Deluxe Power Stratocaster (M)
2006–current
Highway One Stratocaster (2nd version)
2006–current
Highway One Stratocaster HSS (2nd
version) 2006–current
Koa Stratocaster (K) 2006–08
Standard 60th Anniversary Stratocaster
(M) 2006
Strat Pro 2006–08

2007
American VG Stratocaster 2007–09
American Vintage 1957 Commemorative
Stratocaster 2007

Gold Sister Stratocaster (M) 2007
Silver Sister Stratocaster (M) 2007
Vintage Hot Rod '57 Strat 2007–current
Vintage Hot Rod '62 Strat 2007–current
Yngwie Malmsteen Stratocaster (3rd
version) 2007–current
'57 Commemorative Stratocaster 2007
'57 Stratocaster Heavy Relic 2007
'62 Stratocaster Heavy Relic 2007
60s Closet Classic Competition Stripe
Stratocaster 2007

2008
American Standard Stratocaster (2nd
version) 2008–current
American Standard Stratocaster HSS
2008–current
David Gilmour Stratocaster N.O.S. &
Relic 2008–current
Deluxe Fat Strat (2nd version) (M)
2008–09
Deluxe Lone Star Stratocaster (M)
2008–current
Deluxe Roadhouse Stratocaster (M)
2008–current

2009
Billy Corgan Stratocaster 2009–current
Classic HBS-1 Stratocaster 2009–current
Custom Deluxe Stratocaster
2009–current
Dave Murray Stratocaster 2009–current
Eric Johnson Stratocaster Rosewood
2009–current
Ritchie Blackmore Stratocaster (M)
2009–current
Road Worn 50s Stratocaster (M)
2009–current
Road Worn 60s Stratocaster (M)
2009–current
Stratocaster Pro Relic 2009–current

2010
American Special Stratocaster
2010–current
American Special Stratocaster HSS
2010–current
Jim Root Stratocaster 2010–current
Kenny Wayne Shepherd Stratocaster (M)
2010–current
'59 Stratocaster Heavy Relic
2010–current
'63 Stratocaster (N.O.S./Relic)
2010–current
*Some further 2010 models appeared too
late for inclusion in the Listing.*

INDEX

A page number in *italic type* indicates an illustration, usually a guitar, musician, catalogue, or ad. A page number in the range 125–149 indicates an entry in the Reference Listing. Signature models (and some brandnames, where relevant) are listed by the first word of the name, not the surname; for example, the Billy Corgan Stratocaster model is found under B, not C, and the Seymour Duncan brand is under S, not D.

ACKNOWLEDGEMENTS

INSTRUMENT PICTURES
Guitars photographed came from the collections of the following individuals and organisations, and we are most grateful for their help. The owners are listed here in the alphabetical order of the code used to identify their instruments in the Key below. **AG** Arbiter Group; **AN** owner wishes to remain anonymous; **BM** Barry Moorhouse; **BW** Bruce Welch; **CC** Chinery Collection; **CH** courtesy of Christie's; **DGI** David Gilmour; **DGR** Dave Gregory; **EMP** courtesy of Experience Music Project, Seattle, WA; **FJ** Fender Japan; **FM** Fender Musical Instruments Corporation; **GC** Guitar Center; **GG** Gruhn Guitars; **GH** George Harrison; **GW** Gary Winterflood; **JB** Jeff Beck; **JE** John Entwistle; **MS** Mike Slubowski Collection; **PD** Paul Day; **PM** Paul Midgley; **RG** Rory Gallagher; **SA** Scot Arch; **SC** Simon Carlton; **SH** Steve Howe.

The following **Key** is designed to identify who owned which guitars at the time they were photographed. After the relevant bold-type page number(s) we list a model identifier followed by the owner's initials (see 'Guitars photographed' above). **22** Champ SH. **22–23** Precision JE; Telecaster GG. **26–27** Les Paul MS. **27** Duo Jet JB. **30–31** '54 Strat DGI. **35** Gilmour 0001 Strat DGI. **39** '56 Strat CC. **42** Mary Kaye Strat AN. **43** '58 Strat SA. **46–47** Shadows Strat BW. **47** '59 Strat MS; '61 Strat SA. **54–55** '64 Strat SA. **55** '66 Strat PM; '62 Strat SA; '66 Strat DGR. **58** Harrison Rocky Strat GH. **59** Hendrix Woodstock Strat EMP; '64 Strat AN. **62–63** Clapton Blackie Strat GC. **63** Clapton Brownie Strat CH. **66–67** Beck '54 Strat JB. **67** Gallagher '61 Strat RG. **70–71** Rhinestone Strat PD. **71** '73 blue Strat GW; '73 natural Strat SC. **74–75** '79 Strat SC. **75** '78 Strat PM. **78** '81 Taupe Strat PD; '81 yellow Strat SC; '80 Strat PM. **78–79** '81 orange Strat SC. **79** '82 Strat PM. **82–83** '88 Strat SC; '83 Strat PM. **83** '82 Strat BM. **86** '83 Strat PM. **86–87** Vaughan Lenny Strat GC. **94–95** '91 Strat PM. **95** '90 red Strat PM; '90 yellow Strat PM. **98–99** '97 Strat AG. **99** '90 Strat XII AG; '96 Strat MS. **102–103** '92 Strat AG. **103** '92 blue Strat FJ. **106–107** '97 Strat MS; '98 Strat MS. **107** '97 Monterey Strat AG. **110** '04 gold Strat FM. **110–111** '04 sunburst Strat MS. **114–115** '05 Strat FM. **115** '07 Strat FM. **118–119** '10 Strat FM. **119** '09 Strat FM.

Guitar photography was by Garth Blore, Nigel Bradley, Matthew Chattle, Miki Slingsby, and William Taylor. A few additional pictures were supplied, as indicated, by Fender and its international agencies.

ARTIST PICTURES
Images were supplied principally by Redferns at Getty Images, London. Getty photographers/collectors are indicated by the following key. **AE** Amanda Edwards; **EC** Echoes/Redferns; **ER** Ebet Roberts/Redferns; **GH** Gljsbert Hanekroot/Redferns; **GP** Gilles Petard/Redferns; **ID** Ian Dickson/Redferns; **JH** Jo Hale; **KK** K&K Ulf Kruger OHG/Redferns; **MO** Michael Ochs Archive; **MT** Marty Temme/WireImage; **PB** Paul Bergen/Redferns; **PO** P. Ouderkirk/WireImage; **RB** RB/Redferns; **RK** Robert Knight Archive/Redferns; **TM** Tim Mosenfelder/ImageDirect. Other sources are indicated by the following key. **BI** Balafon Image Bank; **DM** David Magnus/Rex Features; **RS** Richard Smith.

Pictures and photographers are identified by bold-type page number, subject, and, other than a few exceptions, by the Getty photographer/collection key. **26** Tavares group RS. **27** Gallion RS. **30** Carson BI. **34** Vincent MO. **35** Turner GP; Watson MO. **38** Holly MO; Merrill BI. **42** Kaye BI. **43** Guy MO. **46** Shadows RB. **47** Dale MO. **54** Dylan MO. **58** Harrison DM. **59** Hendrix KK. **62** Clapton GH. **63** Winwood KK. **66** Gallagher MO. **67** Beck GH. **70** Blackmore ID. **71** Isley EC. **75** Knopfler ER. **79** Raitt PB. **87** Vaughan RK. **94** Edge PO. **98** Corgan MT. **107** Delonge TM. **111** Gilmour JH. **118** Sayce AE.

MEMORABILIA
Items illustrated in this book, including advertisements, brochures, catalogues, colour charts, patents, and photographs (in fact anything that isn't a guitar), comes from the collections of Scot Arch, Tony Bacon, Paul Day, Fender Musical Instruments Corporation, Martin Kelly, *The Music Trades*, The National Jazz Archive (Loughton), Don Randall, Alan Rogan,

ACKNOWLEDGEMENTS

Richard Smith, and Steve Soest (Soest Guitar Repair). These alluring pieces were transformed for your visual enjoyment by Tony Bacon and Miki Slingsby.

INTERVIEWS

Original interviews used in this book were conducted by Tony Bacon as follows: Jeff Beck (January 1984, April 2005); Adrian Belew (January 1984); George Blanda (May 2010); Bill Carson (September 1991); Mike Eldred (March 2007, June 2010); Phyllis Fender (February 1992); George Fullerton (February 1992); Dale Hyatt (February 1992); Bobby Jones (November 2007); Justin Norvell (March 2007, June 2010); Karl Olmsted (February 1992); John Page (February 1992, December 1997); Don Randall (February 1992); Dan Smith (February 1985, February 1992, December 1997, June 2005, March 2007); Terry Tavares (May 2010); and Forrest White (February 1992). The sources of previously published quotations are footnoted where they occur in the text.

THANKS

Thanks to the following for help on this book and my earlier Fender books: Julie Bowie; Larry Acunto (20th Century Guitar); Tony Arambarri (NAMM); Ivor Arbiter (Arbiter); Laura E. Armstrong (Christie's); Laun Braithwaite (Dave's Guitar Shop); Dave Burrluck (Guitarist); Joe Carducci (Fender US); Michael Caroff (Fender Frontline); Bill Carson & Susan Carson; Walter Carter (Gruhn Guitars); Gayle A. Castro (Fender Custom Shop); Doug Chandler; Cheryl Clark (G&L); Paul Cooper; Merelyn Davis; Jane, Sarah & Simon Day; Nicky Donnelly (Arbiter); Mike Doyle (Guitar Center); André Duchossoir; Mike Eldred (Fender Custom Shop); Phyllis Fender; Brian Fischer; George Fullerton & Lucille Fullerton; Dave Glover (Arbiter); Jon Gold (Fender US); Scott Grant (Fender Custom Shop); Alan Greenwood (Vintage Guitar); Dave Gregory; Clay Harrell; Bob Heinrich (Fender US); Bob Henrit; Iain Hersey; Doug Hinman; Christopher Hjort; Lee Holtry (Fender US); Dave Hunter; Dale Hyatt & Eileen Hyatt; Nina Jackson (September Sound); Tom James; Mike Kaskell; Kerry Keane (Christie's); Martin Kelly; Mel Lambert; Mike Lewis (Fender US); Miriam Linna (Norton Records); Seth Lover & Lavone Lover; Brian Majeski (The Music Trades); Neville Marten (Guitarist); Charles Measures; Howard Meek; Bill Mendello (Fender US); John Morrish; Jun Nakabayashi (Fender Japan); Justin Norvell (Fender US); Karl Olmsted & Katherine Olmsted; John Page; Gary Peal (Fender Great Britain & Ireland); John Peden; Steve Preston (Arbiter); Don Randall; Simon Raymonde (September Sound); Julian Ridgway (Redferns); Jim Roberts; Dave Rogers (Dave's Guitar Shop); John Ryall; Johnny Saitoh (Fender Japan); Sam Sekihara (Fender Japan); John Seman (Experience Music Project); Rich Siegle (Fender US); Richard Slater (Hal Leonard); Chris Sleet (Getty Images); Mike Slubowski; Dan Smith (Fender US); Richard Smith; Steve Soest & Amy Soest (Soest Guitar Repair); Sally Stockwell; Fred Stuart (Fender Custom Shop); Terry Tavares; Mick Taylor (Guitarist); Phil Taylor (David Gilmour Music); Guy Wallace (Music Man); Jim Werner; Tom Wheeler; Neil Whitcher (Fender Great Britain & Ireland); Forrest White; Larry White; Bob Willocks (Fender US); Spike Wrigley (Arbiter). SPECIAL THANKS to Paul Day for the remarkable Stratocaster Reference Listing herein, and to Jason Farrell at Fender USA for constant help and guidance.

BOOKS

Andy Babiuk The Story Of Paul Bigsby: Father Of The Modern Electric Solidbody Guitar (FG 2008).
Tony Bacon The Fender Electric Guitar Book (Backbeat 2007), Six Decades Of The Fender Telecaster (Backbeat 2005), 60 Years Of Fender (Backbeat 2010).
Tony Bacon (ed) Electric Guitars: The Illustrated Encyclopedia (Thunder Bay 2000).
Tony Bacon & Paul Day The Ultimate Guitar Book (DK/Knopf 1991).

Paul Balmer The Fender Stratocaster Handbook (Voyageur 2007).
Bill Carson My Life And Times With Fender Musical Instruments (Hal Leonard 1999).
Walter Carter & George Gruhn Gruhn's Guide To Vintage Guitars (Backbeat 2010).
Scott Chinery & Tony Bacon The Chinery Collection – 150 Years Of American Guitars (Balafon 1996).
Christie's Crossroads Guitar Auction: Eric Clapton & Friends for The Crossroads Centre, Thursday 24 June 2004 (Christie's 2004).
Eric Clapton with Chrisopher Simon Sykes The Autobiography (Century 2007).
A.R. Duchossoir The Fender Stratocaster (Hal Leonard 1994), Guitar Identification (Hal Leonard 1990).
Fender Custom Shop Guitar Gallery (Fender/Hal Leonard 1996).
George Fullerton Guitar Legends: The Evolution Of The Guitar From Fender to G&L (Centerstream 1993).
John G. Goldrosen Buddy Holly: His Life And Music (Panther 1979).
Guitar Magazine Mooks The Fender 1: Stratocaster (Rittor 1987).
Guitar Trader Vintage Guitar Bulletin Vol.2 (Bold Strummer 1992).
Christopher Hjort Eric Clapton & The British Blues Boom: The Day-By-Day Story 1965-1970 (Jawbone 2007).
Christopher Hjort & Doug Hinman Jeff's Book (Rock'n'Roll Research Press 2000).
Martin Kelly, Terry Foster, Paul Kelly The Golden Age Of Fender 1946–1970 (Cassell 2010)
Ray Minhinnett & Bob Young The Story Of The Fender Stratocaster (IMP 1995).
Sam Orr Fender Stratocaster (Crowood 2009).
Keith Shadwick Jimi Hendrix: Musician (Backbeat 2003).
Richard R. Smith Fender: The Sound Heard 'Round The World (Hal Leonard 2009).
Sotheby's Rock'n'Roll And Film Memorabilia, London, Wednesday 25 April 1990 (Sotheby's 1990).
Phil Taylor The Black Strat: A History Of David Gilmour's Black Fender Stratocaster (Hal Leonard 2008).
Tom Wheeler American Guitars (HarperPerennial 1990); The Stratocaster Chronicles (Hal Leonard 2004).
Forrest White Fender: The Inside Story (Miller Freeman 1994)
YMM Player We Love Fender Guitars (Player Corporation 1982); History Of Electric Guitars (Player Corporation 1988).
We also consulted various back issues of the following magazines: Fender Bridge, Fender Facts, Fender Frontline, The Guitar Magazine, Guitar & Bass, Guitar Player, Guitar World, Guitarist, Making Music, MI Pro, Music Business, Music Industry, The Music Trades, One Two Testing, Vintage Guitar, 20th Century Guitar.

TRADEMARKS

UPDATES?

The author and publisher welcome any new information for future editions. Write to: Stratocaster, Backbeat, 2A Union Court, 20-22 Union Road, London SW4 6JP, England. Or you can email: strat@jawbonepress.com.

"You don't get kids saying: 'What's that old guitar; ain't you got a new one?' It still looks futuristic." *Jeff Beck*